AMERICAN
POPULISM

AMERICAN POPULISM

A SOCIAL HISTORY 1877–1898

Robert C. McMath, Jr.

Eric Foner, Consulting Editor

HILL AND WANG
A division of Farrar, Straus & Giroux
New York

Published simultaneously in Canada by HarperCollins*CanadaLtd*
Printed in the United States of America
Designed by Tere Lo Prete
Published simultaneously in paperback by
Hill and Wang/The Noonday Press,
a division of Farrar, Straus and Giroux
First edition, 1993
Library of Congress Cataloging-in-Publication Data
McMath, Robert C.
American populism : a social history, 1877–1898 / Robert C.
McMath, Jr. — 1st ed.
p. cm. — (American century series)
Includes bibliographical references and index.
1. Populism—United States—History—19th century. 2. United
States—Politics and government—1865–1933. I. Series.
E661.M43 1992 973.8—dc20 92-14769 CIP

Acknowledgments

A book like this necessarily draws upon the work of others. *American Populism* rests upon a foundation of books, articles, and graduate theses written by scholars over the past half century and more on the history of populism and of rural America. My debt to those authors whose ideas have most directly influenced this study are acknowledged in the Bibliographical Essay. To them and to all our fellow travelers go my thanks and admiration.

My own exploration of the agrarian movement began twenty-five years ago, thanks to inspired teachers like J. B. Smallwood and Robert A. Calvert. They, along with my graduate advisor, George B. Tindall, opened up a world which was both an intriguing chapter of history and an unexplored part of my own past. In the course of that early work I discovered that my own great-grandfather had been a local leader in the Farmers' Alliance and the People's party.

For the chance to sum up a quarter century of research and reflection in one volume, I am deeply grateful to Arthur Wang and Eric Foner, who first suggested that I set the dramatic story of populism within the context of rural social history, about which scholars have taught us so much in recent years. Neither they nor I knew that before the work was half finished the dreaded curse of academic administration would claim much of my time, and that completion of this slender volume would stretch beyond the agreed-upon deadline. Only because of their patience and encouragement has this book seen the light of day. Their editorial suggestions have helped me to sharpen my own thinking about many aspects of the movement and vastly improved my telling of the story.

William F. Holmes, Steven P. Vallas, and David H. Ray read portions of the manuscript and provided valuable suggestions from their store of knowledge about populism, social theory, and comparative politics. Thanks also to the editors of *Locus* for permission to incorporate a portion of my article "Populist Base Communities: The Evangelical Roots of Farm Protest in Texas," *Locus* 1 (1988). My administrative colleague Fred A. Tarpley, Jr., not only tempered my enthusiasm for the movement with his own no-nonsense brand of economics but also selflessly shouldered more than his share of our joint responsibilities to allow me to finish the book. And to the many Georgia Tech students who heard and commented on parts of this story I will be forever grateful, both for their rejuvenation of an aging professor and for their penetrating questions.

Linda, David, and Angie have sensed that this book, more than the others, was special to me, and have, within the family circle, encouraged me to see it through.

Finally, it gives me great pleasure to dedicate this book to my parents, Roberta and Carroll McMath. I will reserve for a more private conversation an acknowledgment of the specific ways in which they empowered me to write it. For now let me say that they represent, in their own persons and in their lineage, the highest values to which the populists aspired.

For my parents,
Roberta and Carroll McMath

Contents

AMERICAN
POPULISM

Introduction

In the long sweep of American history, the year 1877 marks important endings and beginnings. In April, newly inaugurated President Rutherford B. Hayes signaled his intention no longer to use federal troops in protecting the civil rights of African-Americans in the South. The United States' halfway revolution in race relations was seemingly at an end. Scarcely three months later President Hayes rushed other troops to Martinsburg, West Virginia, in a futile effort to quell a railroad strike that threatened to spread nationwide. At the very moment when tensions between northern and southern whites were easing (at the expense of African-Americans), the Great Strike of 1877 ushered in an era that would divide Americans along lines of wealth and occupation for the next two decades.

Spawned by the nation's worst depression to date, this bloody strike revealed the sharp edge of class conflict in industrializing America. Much of the nation's rail network was paralyzed, and in cities from Baltimore to San Francisco, from Chicago to Galveston, railroad men were joined by other workers in angry confrontation with company representatives and local militia units. In Pittsburgh militiamen sent to protect private property joined the mob in attacking the hated Pennsylvania Railroad. In St. Louis workers called a general strike and briefly established what they called the nation's only *"genuine commune."*

The very word terrified men of property and standing, who feared that the United States was about to replay on a grand scale the uprising of the Paris Commune of 1871. That bloody revolt, brutally suppressed by French authorities, had already become a byword for the evils of socialism and a spur to vigilance against just such outbursts as had begun at Martinsburg. For Americans on either side of the conflict, the events of 1877 seared into memory images that would last a generation: on one side, images of the arrogant power of giant corporations backed by the military might of the state; on the other, horrifying images of America's own brand of Commune-ism.

The end of Reconstruction and the Railroad Strike of 1877 are the stuff of history books: large, dramatic public events about which much is known and much has been written. Let us turn from them to reflect on two small events of that same year. In 1877 these two stories attracted little attention outside the communities where they occurred. They are so poorly documented that the "facts" about them were in dispute barely a decade later. Both might have vanished from historical memory altogether had they not been revived and fitted out as a usable past—stories of creation, we might call them—by a great social movement that swept rural America in the 1880s and 1890s. They are creation stories of the movement known as Populism.

The first story takes place in the Genesee Valley of western New York, which within living memory had been part of America's first great agricultural frontier. Spurred by the opening of the Erie Canal in the 1820s, the region's commercial hub, Rochester, had become the nation's first inland boomtown. Also, under the tutelage of the famed evangelist Charles Grandison Finney, Rochester had become a focal point of the institutionalized revivalism that in the 1830s mobilized American women and men into voluntary associations intent on spreading the gospel and remaking society.

But by 1877 the farmers and merchants of western New York were hurting. They believed themselves to be the victims of discrimination in freight rates at the hands of the trunk-line railroads that were then connecting the East Coast and the new grain belt of the Midwest. In March 1877, F. P. Root, a prominent Monroe County farmer and a leader of the Patrons of Husbandry (the Grange), convened a meeting of wheat farmers and cattlemen at the Rochester courthouse for the purpose of establishing a Farmers' Alliance. Its aim was to join representatives of existing agricultural organizations (the Grange, the Western New York Farmers Club, and the State Agricultural Society) in a loose alliance to lobby the state legislature for redress of grievances. In a formulation that harked back to the tactics of the antebellum labor and nativist movements and anticipated the approach of farmers' and laborers' organizations of the 1880s, the founders of the Alliance vowed that it would be "political but non-partisan."

This New York Farmers' Alliance was short-lived. Dominated as it was by large landowners and focusing on relief from high property taxes and freight rates, the Alliance never won a mass following. Farmers and laborers who were impatient with its nonpartisan approach and its concentration on the transportation issue found a more congenial home in the Greenback Party (1878) and in the new Antimonopoly League (1881).

By the latter year the Farmers' Alliance had virtually disappeared, but before its demise the germ of organization was transferred to the Midwest. In 1880, Milton George, an Illinois farmer and editor of the Chicago *Western Rural*, established a Farmers' Alliance in Cook County, apparently basing it on the New York model. When later that year George organized a "national" Alliance in Chicago, the secretary of the New York Alliance became its first president.

The second story of beginnings takes place half a continent away from the Genesee Valley, on the Texas frontier. In 1877 this land was barely free of Indian raids, and the Texas Rangers were still being called upon to resolve bloody feuds. But the tier of counties west of Fort Worth was already filling up with settlers. Here converged two great migratory streams of southern farmer-stockmen: one had flowed through Georgia and the pine barrens of the lower South into the plains of South Texas, the other through Kentucky, Tennessee, and Missouri (and even Indiana and Illinois) into northeastern Texas.

The point where these human streams met along the 98th meridian marked the agricultural convergence of South and West. It was already the point of origin of the Great Plains cattle industry. It would become the western boundary of the cotton kingdom stretching from the Carolinas to the southern terminus of the wheat belt that extended to the Dakotas and Manitoba.

In September 1877 a group of farmer-stockmen met at the farm of John R. Allen in Lampasas County and formed a club that they first named the Knights of Reliance and later called the Farmers' Alliance. Like the men who gathered in the Rochester courthouse, these Texans were landowners, though not so well-to-do. They combined general farming with stock raising. Following the old customs of the seaboard South, they allowed their cattle to roam free on the unfenced prairies in search of food and water and rounded them up once a year to separate them by owner. Unlike the New York Alliance, theirs was a secret oath-bound society, complete with passwords, grips, and ceremonial regalia patterned after the Grange. The order's purposes were economic and political as well as social. Appropriately for a community where open-range cattle raising still prevailed, the Alliance adopted a cooperative system for locating lost stock and for the apprehension of rustlers. Like the New York Alliance, the Lampasas order confronted the dilemma of political advocacy, but with a different outcome.

The same Greenback Party that drew potential support away from the New York group made its presence felt on the Texas frontier in 1877. Some members of the infant Alliance believed that their group should stick to "education" in antimonopoly principles, but in 1878, after intense debate, the Lampasas Alliance voted to endorse the Greenback Party and its candidates. That move split the organization, and it soon all but disappeared. But, as with the New York Alliance, a remnant remained.

William T. Baggett, a schoolteacher in neighboring Coryell County, had organized one of the subordinate chapters of the Lampasas Alliance. In 1879, Baggett packed his schoolbooks and moved north along the frontier to the new settlement of Poolville in Parker County. There he organized first a school and then a Farmers' Alliance. From that new beginning would emerge the National Farmers' Alliance and Industrial Union, known as the "Southern" Farmers' Alliance.

Two dimly remembered stories of beginnings from that momentous year of 1877. What are we to make of them? While both may be mildly interesting as entries in the genealogy of a farm protest movement (Lampasas begat Poolville, Poolville begat Cleburne, and so on), it is not their primacy or uniqueness that gives them significance. On the contrary, it is precisely their ordinariness, their similarity to organizations and movements stirring elsewhere in America at that moment, that invests them with meaning.

The founders who gathered at the Rochester courthouse and at John Allen's farm did not invent Populism. Neither the form nor the content of their movements were brand-new. Both drew upon techniques for mobilizing people and for channeling their enthusiasm that were understood in communities across the land. (Lampasas, like Rochester, had its fair share of churches, Granges, temperance organizations, and Masonic lodges.) Both were informed by a loosely defined but powerful ideology of antimonopolism, "producerism," and (at least in the Lampasas case) radical republicanism, which was part of the cultural heritage of antebellum farmers and artisans. Both struggled with a political dilemma that had bedeviled workingmen's organizations since the 1830s: in a nation where a two-party system prevailed and where individual citizens took partisan identity *very* seriously, how could an interest group express its grievances politically without being destroyed by partisan controversy, and what happens when both major parties ignore its petitions?

Finally, these two short-lived organizations, like scores and even hundreds of other community-based movements, were called into being by the transformation of American capitalism amidst the economic and social trauma of the 1870s. Neither could ignore this wrenching experience, for both were within the orbit of important inland centers of commerce and transportation (Rochester, as we have seen, but also Fort Worth and Dallas). Participants in both organizations understood, if only dimly, that old rules and old values were crumbling, and that powerful new economic institutions, buttressed by the state, threatened their independence. In another moment of crisis for the new industrial and financial order a decade later, groups like these two, scattered throughout the island communities of the American heartland, would coalesce and grow into a grand crusade. For a brief moment millions of Americans would invest in the People's Party their hopes for the preservation of individual liberty, the establishment of a just polity, and the creation of a new cooperative commonwealth.

In June 1891, when the Farmers' Alliance had reached the peak of its popularity and the People's Party was about to be launched, a crowd of about one hundred people gathered at John Allen's farm eight miles north of Lampasas. They thronged in and around a cabin that had housed schools, churches, and other community organizations, including the first Farmers' Alliance. After this reunion the old house was to be taken down and displayed, first in Lampasas and then, it was hoped, at the World's Fair in Chicago. Fourteen charter members of that alliance (five women and nine men) posed for the camera in full regalia on the porch of their old meeting place and patiently answered questions put to them by newspaper reporters.

One inquisitive journalist from the Galveston *Daily News* raised a question that has plagued students of Populism ever since:

> Thus I plied John R. Allen and his alliance brethren with questions with a view of accounting for the origin of the Farmers' Alliance. But the more facts elicited the greater became the enigma. Such a social and political product at the time and place, among such a people and under such circumstances, is inexplicable.

J. J. Hill's investigative journalism, which might be called the first sociological analysis of American Populism, identifies for us the question that has preoccupied scholars who have studied the movement: who joins, and why, and, conversely, why do others similarly situated not join?

Let us now examine briefly the ways in which scholars have replied to that reporter's query, and then consider what else we may want to know about the movement that began, in part, among John Allen and his neighbors.

Historians and social scientists have been studying Populism for over fifty years. One might expect that by now we could agree on what happened and why, but that is not the case. It is not just that students of Populism are particularly cranky and contrary, although that may also be true. Scholars continue to discover and compile new information about the Populists and especially about the rural world that they inhabited. Furthermore, since Populism was a major force in three very different regions of the country (the South, the Great Plains, and the Mountain West), the answer to the question "Who were the Populists?" depends on where you look. And finally, those who think and write about the Populist experience continue to read into that historical moment the social concerns of their own time and the social theories most commonly used to explain contemporary events. Selection of evidence, regional focus, and the inevitable intrusion of the present into our study of the past have worked against one unified view of the movement.

It is not surprising that the first classic works on Populism were written during the Great Depression of the 1930s. Americans then could readily understand the anger of the Populists and could easily imagine their reform agenda to be the forerunner of farm programs of the 1920s and 1930s. John D. Hicks's general treatment of the movement, *The Populist Revolt: A History of the Farmers' Alliance and the People's Party* (1931), located the source of Populism in the economic distress of farmers on the Great Plains frontier and in the depressed kingdoms of cotton and tobacco. In the 1880s and 1890s southern and western farmers, already locked into an agricultural market economy over which they exercised little control, were hit hard by a series of financial shocks: falling commodity prices, high freight rates, and expensive credit, compounded by capricious acts of nature, especially crippling droughts that parched the West from Texas to Canada in the mid-1880s.

Hard times made people Populists, Hicks concludes. Immediate economic difficulties pushed them to rebel. Farmers put the blame for their distress neither on themselves nor on "acts of God" (whom they believed to be very much on their side), but rather on the nation's institutions of credit, transportation, and commerce—abetted, they were convinced, by federal and state governments. Farmers turned for relief to a multiplicity of voluntary associations, the Alliances among them, and to direct political action through the People's Party. In acting politically they drew upon well-defined traditions of protest in order to press for reform of the nation's financial and transportation systems. And their demands, even when not immediately translated into law, prefigured the farm legislation of the twentieth century.

If *The Populist Revolt* made the case that Populism was one movement with branches in the South and West, C. Vann Woodward's biography of a leading southern Populist confirmed that view. Begun as a doctoral dissertation in the depths of the depression and published in 1938, *Tom Watson, Agrarian Rebel* made the case that southern farmers, like their western counterparts, were driven to Populism by legitimate economic grievances. Economic self-interest could bring farmers from the late Confederacy into political alignment with farmers who had made war on the South. It was even possible, despite the racial "settlement" symbolized by President Hayes's withdrawal of the troops, that white Southerners would make common cause with former slaves. To both, Watson preached: "You are kept apart that you may be separately fleeced of your earnings. You are made to hate each other because upon that hatred is rested the keystone of the arch of financial despotism which enslaves you both." Who would join the Populist crusade in the South? Potentially, said Woodward, a biracial coalition of the poor.

The economics of late-nineteenth-century agriculture has been intensely scrutinized since Hicks and Woodward first outlined their explanation for the Populist revolt, and the preponderance of evidence supports them and the Populists themselves: the farmers' complaints were real enough, and at critical points the institutions of credit, marketing, and transportation worked to their disadvantage. Having acknowledged this to be the case, we are still left to wonder why one hard-pressed farmer would join the revolt while his equally impoverished neighbor or relative would not. (My own great-grandfather did; his first cousin did not.)

The question of whether shared economic distress could overcome the legacy of racism is another matter. Historical evidence uncovered since Woodward wrote his biography of Watson has called into question the likelihood of a color-blind Populist coalition and forced us to deal with an uglier side of the movement. While the mutual interests of those who were kept separate so that they might be "separately fleeced" sometimes led black and white farmers to cooperate under the Populist banner, such cooperation had its limits. Populists, we must acknowledge, were not immune to the racism that saturated American culture.

The dark side of Populism attracted both scholarly and popular attention in the 1950s. This was a time when many American intellectuals were becoming disenchanted with mass movements and with what they considered to be the "excesses" of democracy. To social scientists like Victor Ferkiss and Peter Viereck, populism was an unpredictable movement of the folk which exhibited alarming similarities to fascism and McCarthyism. Where Hicks and Woodward saw a rational reform-minded protest movement, Viereck detected something more sinister: "Beneath the sane economic demands of the Populists of 1880–1900 seethed a mania of xenophobia, Jew-baiting, intellectual-baiting, and thought-controlling lynch-spirit."

Rural people, worried about their declining social status in an urbanizing society, were drawn to an irrational crusade that fanned their prejudices and led to scapegoating and even violence rather than to legislative remedies for economic grievances. Cut adrift from the moorings of familiar associations in a frighteningly disorganized "mass society," provincial Americans were subject to the enticements of demagogues and charlatans of all stripes.

The scholar most prominently associated with this view of populism (though not, in all fairness, with the extreme version of it just stated) was the distinguished intellectual historian Richard Hofstadter. In his essay on modern American politics, *The Age of Reform: From Bryan to FDR* (1955), Hofstadter sketched a portrait of the Populists substantially at odds with that found in *The Populist Revolt*. While acknowledging that American farmers of the late nineteenth century faced a real economic crisis, he downplayed economic factors in explaining why they flocked to the Populist banner:

> Rank in society! That was close to the heart of the matter, for the farmer was beginning to realize acutely not merely that the best of the world's goods were to be had in the city . . . but also that he was losing in status and self-respect as compared with [urbanites].

Farmers had willingly entered the modern world of commerce in pursuit of the main chance, but when the terms of trade went against them they sought comfort in the agrarian myth of an earlier and simpler time when those who toiled in the earth were thought to be closest to God. It is in this irrational retreat from the consequences of their own actions that Hofstadter finds the Populist movement "to foreshadow some aspects of the cranky pseudo-conservatism of our time." *Status anxiety made people Populists*, Hofstadter concluded.

Hofstadter's characterization of the Populists was attacked on both factual and theoretical grounds. The intensity of the attacks suggested that some of the critics were aiming not so much at Hofstadter as at the social scientists and journalists who had played fast and loose with the historical evidence and had equated Populism with fascism.

Hofstadter's own analysis has been subject to four challenges. First, critics have charged that the study of Populist rhetoric from which he drew his negative conclusions was restricted to a handful of texts that were not proven to be representative of the movement. Other studies have shown that Populists, while sometimes exhibiting xenophobia and racism, were no more inclined in that direction than Americans in general. Second, most social historians now agree that rural America was not a disorganized, atomistic "mass society" ripe for the demagoguery of an American Hitler, but was in fact blanketed by a thick network of community and familial associations. Third, while the Populists' cultural traditions did look backward to an earlier rural America, they were not "dysfunctional." Their values and beliefs were part and parcel of the radical republicanism that was, even in the late nineteenth century, a vital force among working people in America. And fourth, the theoretical perspective upon which Hofstadter's work rested (a perspective tracing its roots to Emile Durkheim) assumes that the natural state of society is one of harmony among its constituent parts. Conflict and protest occur when there are temporary strains in the social structure caused by rapid social change. The source of protest is thus located in the protesters themselves: protest is an irrational response to change. The critics called this blaming the victim. Both Hicks and Hofstadter located the answer to J. J. Hill's question in the environment of rural Americans: hard times or status anxiety pushed people to revolt. These two answers (Hicks's in particular) still find support among scholars seeking to expand our knowledge of the movement.

However, in recent years some historians and social scientists have insisted that while economic distress constituted a *necessary* condition for the emergence of Populism, it did not offer a *sufficient* explanation of why people flocked to its banner. These scholars have focused much of their attention on the formation of "movement organizations," the mobilization of resources (both material and cultural) by the movement, and the movement's interaction with the larger social structure and its dominant institutions.

The scholars who have adopted this perspective of "resource mobilization" approach the subject from a variety of disciplinary and ideological viewpoints. However, like Hicks, Woodward, and Hofstadter before them, they bring to the study of Populism the great social issues of their own day. Specifically, they find a powerful analogy to Populism in the civil rights movement and community organizing efforts of the 1960s and 1970s. Sociologists first applied resource mobilization theory to civil rights and community organizations and then, retrospectively, to Populism. Lawrence Goodwyn, the historian whose work most closely fits this theoretical perspective, covered the civil rights movement as a reporter for *The Texas Observer* before turning his attention to Populism.

These scholars, regardless of orientation, take very seriously the organizations that rural people formed among themselves and the *historical* careers of those organizations. In introducing her study of farm protest in Texas, sociologist Donna Barnes put it this way:

> Protest movement development must be viewed in a dialectical manner: protest organizations continually mobilize resources, utilize those resources in a chosen strategy, and then experience the consequences of that strategy in a manner that affects subsequent rounds of strategy selection and strategy outcome.

This notion of how protest movements work is theoretically consistent with the interpretation of Populism advanced in the first general history of the movement published since Hicks. In *Democratic Promise: The Populist Moment in America* (1976), Lawrence Goodwyn gives this succinct explanation of why people became Populists:

> To describe the origins of Populism in one sentence, the cooperative movement recruited American farmers, and their subsequent experience within the cooperatives radically altered their political consciousness. The agrarian revolt cannot be understood outside the framework of the economic crusade that not only was its source but also created the culture of the movement itself.

Through its network of traveling lecturers who spread the gospel of economic cooperation across the South and West, the Farmers' Alliance recruited millions of rural Americans into an organization where they developed a new sense of their own capability and a new political culture that led them to form the People's (Populist) Party. *The cooperatives recruited farmers to the Alliance, and the Alliance made people Populists*, Goodwyn concludes.

Goodwyn's sharply drawn interpretation of Populism has attracted critical attention on several counts. Critics argue that he overstates the extent and significance of the Alliance's marketing and purchasing cooperatives and that he arbitrarily excludes from Populism those expressions of agrarian protest (the free-silver movement in particular) which do not fit the historical progression of Populism in Texas, which he takes to be normative for the movement as a whole. Finally, his notion of the "movement culture" of Populism so emphasizes the separate and unique cultural setting of the movement that it causes us to overlook the ways in which Populism was grounded in and interacted with the dominant political culture of nineteenth-century America.

Goodwyn's claims for the cooperatives may be overblown, but

his critics have most certainly underestimated the extent to which the cooperatives and the *expectation* of relief through cooperation mobilized rural men and women in communities across the South and West. The critics are on firmer ground with their other points. The Populist experience took different forms in different parts of the country, and the "movement culture" that he attributes solely to the radicalizing experience of the Alliance has other identifiable antecedents. But, like Hicks, Woodward, and Hofstadter before him, Goodwyn writes about the Populists with grace and conviction, and his view of the movement, like theirs, has had an impact far beyond the little band of scholars who concern themselves with such matters of history.

Let us now imagine that the Alliance veterans gathered on John Allen's porch could evaluate for us these academic interpretations of their own movement, just as they answered questions put to them by that young reporter from Galveston in 1891. What would they make of Hicks, and Hofstadter, and Goodwyn—of economic interest, and status anxiety, and resource mobilization? I think the first and third of these would have made sense to them. And while they would not recognize themselves in the shriller diatribes of Viereck et al., and would consider themselves to be at least as rational as university professors, they would acknowledge that almost from the beginning their movement had to defend itself against charges of vigilantism.

Having put words in the mouths of these long-dead Texans, let me say that I think such an assessment would be a truthful rendering of Populism. My own telling of their story pays close attention to the economic distress of farmers and workers in the South, the Great Plains, and the Mountain West, and especially to those sharp and unexpected jolts that struck the farming regions in the decade between 1886 and 1896, leading people to believe that the great economic and political institutions of the United States and Europe were aligned against them. This telling of the story also follows closely the careers of the grass-roots organizations through which rural men and women interpreted those personal and collective crises and out of which they fashioned a movement of protest. By chronicling these organizations, their battles with the dominant institutions of an industrializing nation, and their own internal struggles, we can move beyond the sometimes static question of who joined to explore the dynamics of the movement. And though my sympathies are with the Populists, I do not ignore the dark and irrational side of their movement.

Finally, the telling of the Populists' story needs to be connected to the social history of rural America. Since Hicks's time we have learned a great deal about the social, cultural, and economic life of rural families and communities, yet little of this knowledge illuminates the general histories of Populism.

Populism developed among people who were deeply rooted in the social and economic networks of rural communities, not, as some would have it, among isolated and disoriented individuals. It is now possible to connect the story of Populism more fully than before with the rhythms of family and community life in the countryside, with the face-to-face networks of rural trade and the rounds of "swap work" among neighboring farmers, with the tilling of crops and relations of production on the land (including relations between landowners and laborers), with the bonds and divisions between rural people and townsmen, and with what Joel Williamson has called "the etiquette of race relations" in the countryside.

It is also possible to examine farmers' organizations in relation to other social institutions that dotted the countryside and crossroads towns: churches, schools, fraternal and veterans' organizations, trade unions and workingmen's associations, and even vigilante groups. And we can probe the multiple sources of the "movement culture" through which these organizations transmitted to their members a sense of agency, of people making their own history.

Where to begin? The porch on John Allen's farm is as good a place as any, for from there you can survey Populist country. To the east, across Texas and the Gulf states and curving up into the Carolinas, lay the kingdoms of cotton and tobacco. There, at that moment, the sharecropping system was fixing itself upon the land and the long decline of world cotton prices was reducing the farmers' chances of success. To the north, running in a line from Lampasas straight up to Canada and broadening out into the Rocky Mountain West, families were edging out onto what had been called the Great American Desert and risking their fortunes on cattle, corn, and wheat in an unforgiving environment and an uncertain market. The story of Populism begins on this land.

1

Populist Country Before Populism:

Rural Life in the New West and the New South

Rural America changed dramatically in the decade following the formation of the Knights of Reliance on John Allen's farm. Out of that cycle of hope and despair would come the Populist revolt, rooted in the soil of the West and the South. Differing climates, crops, and connections to the world of commerce would give the transformation of agriculture a different look in the two regions, but underneath there were profound similarities.

Before embarking on our tour of the countryside, two points need to be understood. First, we are not presently concerned with *all* of rural America but with those regions where Populism came to life and had its greatest strength: the Great Plains and its extension westward into the Rocky Mountain states, and portions of the South—particularly the kingdoms of cotton and tobacco. (Later we will visit other parts of the rural Midwest that *looked* like fertile ground for Populism, but weren't.) Second, the farmers whom we will observe were not the isolated, self-sufficient yeomen of agrarian legend. They were all more or less involved in the modern world of commerce, finance, and transportation which produced both enormous economic growth and tremendous human suffering in the late nineteenth century. But for all their involvement in the market, these rural men and women understood farming to be more than a way of making money; it was still a way of life. Alongside the unpredictable world of the market lay familiar rhythms of work and community life, deeply rooted ideas about what held society together, and the hope of passing on to their children a secure inheritance of land.

Now to our tour, which begins in the New West. In April 1877, John Wesley Powell, soon to become the chief of the U.S. Geological Survey, issued a warning to those considering taking up farming on the Great Plains. In a speech before the National Academy of Sciences, Powell drew a line on a map from central Texas through central Kansas to western Minnesota. Land west of the line, Powell announced, was too dry to support traditional agriculture. Among the Westerners who rushed to dispute Powell's findings was James B. Power, land agent for the Northern Pacific Railroad, who claimed the "arid" region was already being settled by "practical men who form their opinion of the fertility of the country and its adaptability for settlement by the practical test of cultivation rather than the statements in issues by a school of such scientists as Major Powell."

As the exchange between Power and Powell suggests, the Great Arid Lands Debate would be resolved, not in scholarly meetings or in the quiet sanctuary of the laboratory, but amid the frenzy of railroad expansion and a land boom. This was no mere academic dispute, for on the outcome hung the livelihood of would-be settlers and the viability of the great American dream of family security on the land.

The plain fact was that only in unusually wet years could the land west of the 100th meridian support the cultivation of crops by traditional means. In the 1870s, agricultural experiments in western Kansas and Nebraska (supported largely by the railroads) produced minimal returns in grain, vegetables, and fruit, but a bumper crop of pamphlets and reports that purported to show that "rain follows the plow." Richard Smith Elliott of western Kansas was the most prominent advocate of the theory that acting as if these lands were suitable for farming would make them so:

bringing the plains under cultivation would improve nature. These claims were dismissed by most scientists (including Powell), but the fact that rainfall did increase in parts of the Great Plains in the 1870s and early 1880s gave them credence among those who, for whatever reason, devoutly hoped they were true.

In 1880 a withering drought in western Kansas discredited Elliott's theory, but another panacea popped up to take its place. In 1882 the Garden City (Kansas) *Irrigator* boasted that just as irrigation "has transformed that once bleak desert, Utah, from its former natural barrenness and unproductiveness to the garden spot of the entire country," the same man-made diversion of water would soon "place Garden City and Sequoyah County upon the highest plane of agricultural development of which it is possible to conceive."

Irrigation *did* work in parts of the West. In Kansas, however, ditch irrigation based upon diversion from the Arkansas River and other streams proved to be of little more use than Elliott's fantasies, but not before tens of thousands had invested in the dream.

One more piece of "evidence" from the 1870s helped fuel the western land boom of the 1880s, and that was the success of the great bonanza farms of the Red River valley of northern Dakota Territory and northwestern Minnesota. In the early 1880s giant "corporate farms," heavily capitalized and highly mechanized, produced stunning profits and turned the Red River valley into North America's leading wheat-producing region. Although most of the bonanza farms lasted barely a decade, glowing reports of their success helped trigger a land rush that eclipsed the gold rush of the nearby Black Hills.

The Great Plains land boom of the 1880s was a decisive event in the history of the American West. So quickly did the plains fill up with hopeful settlers that at the end of the decade the Census Office declared the frontier to be closed. The boom moved unevenly across the Plains, surging forward first in Dakota Territory (with a parallel Canadian movement into Manitoba), then in Kansas and Nebraska, then westward almost to the slopes of the Rockies, responding to vagaries of the weather (ample rain fell on much of the Plains during some years of the decade) as well as to public and private land distribution schemes. The evidence, scientific or otherwise, that settlers could live securely and profitably on the Plains was persuasive enough to make the land boom thinkable. More tangible and thoroughly modern agencies made it a reality.

In order to understand this unique episode we must dispense with a familiar stereotype of frontier settlement, that of families in covered wagons trekking across the prairies and fording streams to stake out isolated claims miles from "civilization." The boom of the 1880s happened differently. Its immediate stimuli were railroads, the towns spawned by the railroads, and eastern investment capital, funneled into the real estate market by loan agents who set up shop in those same railroad towns. An aging Walt Whitman, who as a young man had seen a very different rural America, looked at the prairie states in 1880 and called them

A newer garden of creation, no primal solitude
Dense, joyous, modern, populous millions, cities and farms
With iron interlaced, composite, tied, many in one . . .

The "interlacing" of the Great Plains with branch railroads—and even the completion of some of the trunk lines—had been stopped cold by the depression that began in 1873. By 1879, however, construction was booming and the Plains states were soon "interlaced" by networks of rail. Railroads that had received government land grants moved aggressively to sell land to settlers or to speculators for resale, and even those lines without such a windfall promoted settlement to boost their freight business.

While they were laying down track, the railroads laid out towns along their rights-of-way. Towns that predated the railroads lived or died according to whether the tracks came their way. Creation of the towns typically *preceded* extensive rural settlement, and each one flourished or failed depending on the ability of its boosters to win in the highly competitive game of real estate. The sale of farms and town lots, along with competition for county seats and federal land offices, was the towns' main business. The town boosters' stock-in-trade, it seemed, was hot air. As eastern investors grumbled about boosters in Dakota, "every townsite was a city, every creek a river, every crop a bonanza, every breeze a zephyr, and every man a damned liar." (That according to the distinguished agricultural historian and South Dakota native Gilbert Fite.)

Hot air and high hopes alone could not fuel the land boom; capital was required, and lots of it. The return of prosperity that triggered railroad expansion at the end of the 1870s also attracted eastern lenders looking for good investments. During the boom of the 1880s, mortgages on western farms were highly sought after, so much so that loan agents could not satisfy the demands of Easterners who wanted to invest! Historian Craig Miner tells of one New Yorker who wrote to his brother from Pratt, Kansas, in 1888, "A man is a fool to loan any money in the East when he can come here and get any such rates and security."

The leading scholar of farm credit concludes that the rates of interest on western mortgages were not excessive (they averaged 12 percent in western Kansas), given the risk involved. But some were far higher, and most were augmented by the fees of local agents. *All* rested on a premise like that held by investors in the stock market in the 1920s, that the boom in land, wheat, and corn would continue forever.

The Great Plains land boom began in earnest in the southern part of Dakota Territory, and there it reached its greatest intensity. During the 1880s the federal government distributed more acres under the public land laws than were contained in the whole state of Iowa, and sale of land by the railroads boosted the total even higher. (Under the Homestead Act of 1862 settlers could secure a 160-acre farm in return for a $10 filing fee and proof that they had actually settled and developed the land.) For the year ending June 30, 1883, over 22,000 homestead claims were filed in Dakota. Hamlin Garland, whose father homesteaded near the James River in 1881, later captured the flavor of the boom in *A Son of the Middle Border*:

> The epoch of the canvas-covered wagon had passed. The era of the locomotive, the day of the charter car, had arrived. Free land was receding at railroad speed, the borderline could be overtaken only by steam, and every man was in haste to arrive.

Settlers and their possessions arrived in long trains of railroad cars (up to eighteen trains a day reached Huron in 1882), and at every railroad station one could see lines of would-be settlers, their household goods piled up along the right-of-way, waiting to be taken to farm sites as quickly as they could be surveyed and mapped. The phrase "doing a land office business" took on new meaning as settlers lined up to wait their turn for filing. At the Huron land office alone (one of several in the territory) the federal government gave away over 1.8 million acres of land in 1883, more than was distributed in any other *state* except Nebraska.

The Dakota boom peaked in the mid-1880s, but the land rush merely shifted to Kansas and Nebraska, where the killing drought of 1880 was forgotten or explained away. There, in 1886 and 1887, the scenes from Dakota were replayed. At the land office at Garden City, Kansas, just getting in the door to file your claim might take a day of waiting in line! In the year ending in June 1886, the Garden City office recorded 18,958 claims covering over 2 million acres.

To be sure, many of the claims had been staked by speculators and were never "proved up" by actual settlers, but still the population of western Kansas and Nebraska grew by one-third between 1885 and 1887, and by then the boom had spread into the cruelly misnamed "rain belt" of eastern Colorado. The country-side filled up, the towns boomed, and who was to deny that this little town or that one was about to become the new Chicago, or that this stretch of prairie or that one was about to reach "the highest level of agricultural development of which it is possible to conceive"?

As the spread of Great Plains farming into Colorado indicates, the agricultural frontier of the 1880s stretched into the front range of the Rocky Mountains from Montana down to New Mexico Territory. Here again, we need to discard a familiar stereotype, that of the lone prospector in search of gold or silver. To be sure, mining was crucial to the economy of the Rocky Mountain states, but so were farming and stock raising, first as a source of food for the mining settlements and later as an integral part of national markets in grain and livestock.

The eastern sections of the front-range states belonged to the semi-arid Great Plains. The same combination of rail service and insatiable land hunger that had fueled the rapid settlement of the states just to the east stimulated agricultural development on the western Plains and in the river and mountain valleys of the front-range states. And the same cattle industry that had spread from the Texas hill country to the northern Plains now pushed into the pasturelands of the Rockies.

Except for the momentary illusion of the damp mid-1880s, there was never any doubt about the number one problem of farming in the front-range states: water, or the lack of it. The solution was irrigation. In present-day New Mexico, Indians and then Hispanic settlers had introduced irrigation long before Anglo intrusion into the area. In Utah and elsewhere in the Great Basin, Mormon pioneers had begun to build massive irrigation systems before the Civil War.

In Colorado, irrigation by American settlers began in the 1850s and became more extensive in the 1870s and 1880s, redeeming the promise of boosters in western Kansas and Nebraska to make the desert bloom. In northern Colorado a communitarian settlement inspired by Horace Greeley launched a cooperative irrigation project on the Cache la Poudre River (thus the town, Greeley), while farther to the south foreign-owned corporations developed irrigation systems along the same Arkansas River that those Kansas boosters had hoped to tap.

Irrigating the western lands took capital and cooperation: not the traditional cooperation of corn shucking and log rolling practiced by eastern farmers, but a system of water distribution centrally planned and controlled by the leaders of a religious or utopian community or by large corporations. For farmers and stock raisers who were heirs of the Jeffersonian traditions of independence and neighborhood self-sufficiency, operating in these centrally controlled "hydraulic societies" (as Donald Worster has aptly named them) was a new and not altogether satisfactory experience.

Between 1870 and 1890 the combined populations of Nebraska, Kansas, and Dakota jumped from just under a half million to almost three million, and similar growth could be found elsewhere in the Great Plains. The land boom of the 1880s, though differing in detail from place to place, was remarkably consistent in several respects. Rural settlement was dependent upon institutions of the modern capitalist world—railroads, boomtowns, and lending agencies. Settlements were relatively compact: land was laid out in the customary grid of townships and family-size farms, and those grids tended to fill up evenly. Thus, the typical settler was never far from neighbors. Many of the settlers came in groups, seeking to replicate familiar and familial communities from Illinois, Iowa, Michigan, and other midwestern states, and even from the Old World. While some of these settlements were religious and communal, most merely reflected national and neighborhood ties, reinforced by the inducement of cheap group rates from the railroads. Finally, the typical unit of agricultural production on the Plains was the "family farm" producing grain and possibly livestock for a commercial market. This last point requires a bit of elaboration before we leave the Great Plains.

Federal homestead programs and the railroads' land sales were designed to fill up the countryside with households (families, possibly augmented by nonfamily laborers) situated on farms of 160 acres or more. Both private and public distribution schemes anticipated that a family could support itself and secure clear title to the land, farm buildings, and equipment by raising crops for sale. The family farm was both a kinship network and a producer of commodities, with twin goals of family security and profit making, of reproduction as well as production.

In the forest lands of the East, frontier settlers had started out with subsistence or "safety first" agriculture—food crops supplemented by hunting and fishing, and maybe a small cash crop as surplus—even if their ultimate aim was to produce income through sale of commodities. In the unforgiving environment of the Plains, agricultural subsistence was often impossible. Here everything had its price; everything was a commodity.

In the first year or two of settlement—and later if the year's cash crop failed—the survival of the family farm and of the family itself could depend upon finding work away from home (on the railroad, in town, or on someone else's farm) or upon charity or government relief. The governments of all the Plains states, plus many private organizations, dispensed aid to beleaguered farmers at some point during the 1880s.

If the Plains farmers were commercial operators, what commodities did they grow and with what tools? Settlers lured to the Dakota prairies by the success of the bonanza farms naturally turned to wheat (spring wheat, which could mature within the short northern growing season). In the beginning they also grew some corn, which could be planted by chopping a hole in the prairie sod before the land had been broken for wheat.

Nebraska and Kansas settlers also planted wheat (winter wheat there and in the Texas terminus of the Great Plains), but not exclusively so. In both Kansas and Nebraska, farmers actually grew more corn than wheat during the 1880s, although they were not yet integrated into the corn-hog market that was beginning to give farmers in Iowa and other midwestern states some safe-guards in an uncertain economy. (If the price of corn is high, you sell it; if the price of corn is low, you feed it to the hogs and sell them.) Most Plains farmers owned only a few head of cattle and swine, and probably a few chickens.

The technology that they employed was undergoing rapid change which would make the family farm more viable on the Plains. Horse-drawn machinery for the production of grains and for the harvesting of wheat was now commonplace. For wheat farmers, the self-binding reaper and header (labor-saving refine-ments on the original mechanical reaper) were coming into com-mon use. In 1884 alone one South Dakota merchant sold 108 carloads of self-binders to farmers in a two-county area. Even the steam-powered thresher made its presence felt in the wheat belt during the boom of the 1880s, leading one man from Great Bend, Kansas, to remark:

> . . . in every direction may be seen the ascending columns of coal smoke until our vast farming region has more the appearance of an enormous manufacturing center than a quiet, unobtrusive, unparalleled grain raising community.

To acknowledge that the family farm was the basic unit of production and that new machinery augmented the labor of the family is not to say that the farms of the Great Plains were mech-anized islands unto themselves. Plains farmers socialized with their neighbors as much as their eastern counterparts. Further-more, the culture of farming that they brought with them in-cluded traditions of "swap work" and other cooperative activities directly related to the production of crops.

In the midwestern wheat belt from which many of these Plains boomers had come, the spread of horse-drawn and steam-powered machinery did not obliterate the old cooperative ways; in some instances, it reinforced them. For example, when the first generation of reapers appeared in the Midwest in the 1850s and 1860s, neighbors often banded together to purchase them cooperatively or to contract for their use on a custom basis.

The advent of the self-binder and steam-powered threshing machines in the 1870s actually brought to its highest stage of development a cooperative arrangement known as threshing rings. These were neighborhood associations of families who cooperated each year to thresh each other's wheat. The threshing rings were highly structured and even ritualized associations that confirmed a sense of group identity and tradition while carrying out an essential task of production. In the new environment of the Great Plains, the threshing ring gave way to entrepreneurial custom threshing, but the memory of the ring, along with other habits of mutuality, was part of the cultural baggage that settlers brought to this new frontier.

Having gazed from John Allen's porch toward the New West, let us turn our attention to the New South, and specifically the kingdoms of cotton and tobacco. There too, old habits of mutuality, old relations between people on the land, were being transformed into new and more distinctly capitalistic relations. But despite the changes in Dixie, old times there were not forgotten.

In 1880 the cotton belt covered a swath of land that arched down from the Carolinas, cut diagonally through Georgia and across central Alabama, then broadened out into the alluvial plain of the Mississippi River before ending in central Texas. The core of this cotton South was the historic plantation region, but by 1880 commercial production had spread beyond the antebellum plantation belt into the upland home of the yeoman farmer, into the newly settled wire-grass and pine barrens of the coastal plain, and as far west as the Cross Timbers of Texas.

The story of the cotton kingdom in the New South is really two stories. One takes place on the plantation and the other on the small farming regions beyond. In the antebellum plantation belt, masters and slaves and cotton had defined the Old South

by creating an agricultural system that was at once brutally an-
achronistic (slavery was dying out elsewhere) and intimately
linked to the modern world of markets and manufactures. The
world that masters and slaves had made was gone, but their sons
and daughters would define its successor, with help from the
yeoman farmers who scratched out a living on the less desirable
lands of the plantation districts and the hills and pine barrens.

In 1881, Henry Grady, editor of the Atlanta *Constitution* and
booster of a New South based on commerce, manufacturing, and
"scientific" farming, proclaimed that the planters were "still lords
of acres, though not of slaves." Grady had it just about right.
Although some individuals lost their land in the upheavals of war
and Reconstruction, planters as a class succeeded in holding on
to much of the land. However, their economic options were now
limited by two profound changes: they had no slaves and precious
little money or credit. As for the former slaves, with few exceptions they had neither land nor credit, but where they had recently *been* a commodity, they now *owned* one—their own labor.

The dreams of former masters and former slaves were tied to
the land—often the very same plot of land they had shared before
the war—but how different were those dreams! Planters wished
for things to go on much as they had before emancipation, for
the freedmen to keep on working the land in gangs under their
supervision and observing the etiquette of racial subservience.
Former slaves longed for economic freedom through ownership
of their own small plot of land: not the freedom to risk all on a
crop of wheat or cotton like a Dakota boomer or a Mississippi
planter, but the freedom to grow enough food to feed a family,
to sell enough cotton to pay the taxes and have a little money
left over. To be free meant to be secure and independent on
their own land, surrounded by neighbors and bound to them by
ties of kinship and production and the association of church and
school. It was a dream that Thomas Jefferson would have understood, the dream shared by generations of white yeomen farmers.

A few of the former slaves achieved their dream of landownership, but most of the freedmen, and all of the planters, did not get exactly what they wanted. The system of land tenure that came to dominate the plantation district by the end of Reconstruction was sharecropping, a rough and unequal compromise between the desire of the planter for control and of the freedman for independence. Title to most of the land remained in the hands of whites (planters, substantial farmers, and merchants), but under the sharecropping system the land was subdivided into small plots to be worked by families, most of them black, who were paid with a share of the marketable crop (usually one-third or one-half) rather than in cash.

When this compromise arrangement first began to appear across the cotton belt in the late 1860s, it seemed to offer some hope of advancement for the freedmen. Sharecroppers were still subject to the supervision of the landowner or his agent, but less so than under the hated gang system, and the new arrangement offered a degree of autonomy to the rural black family. Furthermore, with the exceptionally high price of cotton in the late 1860s and early 1870s, a share of the crop just might produce enough income for a family to move up the agricultural ladder to the status of cash renter or even farm owner.

Events conspired to shatter the dream. The end of Reconstruction (which actually occurred in some states as early as 1870–71) meant that planters and their allies could, with little fear of federal reprisal, create and enforce laws to protect their interests vis-à-vis those of the sharecroppers. The decline in world cotton prices and the stagnation of world demand, which began in the early 1870s and continued for over two decades, meant that there was precious little profit to be made by anyone.

Along with the sharecropping system, the interlocking institutions of farm credit, cotton marketing, and retail trade worked to the disadvantage of the freedmen through an instrument of credit known as the crop lien. Under this system, a planter or merchant extended a line of credit (often at rates in excess of 50 percent per year), taking as collateral the year's cotton crop. The sharecropper—or even a renter or small landowner who had given a lien—could then draw food and farm supplies during the growing season from the store of the planter or merchant. The high rate of interest on the lien was compounded by the "two price" system typically found at the country store: one price for cash, and another, higher price for credit purchases. When the crop was harvested, the *holder* of the lien sold it for the producer and then settled the account. Not surprisingly, the producers often found themselves unable to "pay out" at the end of the year.

Later we will explore the ways in which rural people living under this system tried to gain control over their own lives. For the moment, there are three crucial points to be understood about sharecropping and the relationships it created among owners of land, labor, and credit. First, while the ties between planters and sharecroppers resembled the old bond between masters and slaves, this new relationship was distinctly capitalistic. Sharecropping did retain vestiges of the paternalism and reciprocity of slavery, but these could also be found in the relationship between managers and workers in the cotton mills of the New South. Planters were no longer masters. Habits of command would sometimes suffice as in the old days, but more often planters had to learn new arts of persuasion.

Second, while the sharecropping system was exploitive, the croppers themselves were not totally without control over their own lives. Their labor was now a commodity, and the mere prospect of their withholding it left planters in fear of a labor shortage at crucial times in the growing cycle. Scholars are still debating the fairness of the sharecropping system. Much of that debate goes on at a rather abstract or theoretical level. Sharecropping, however, was not one giant abstraction, but millions of face-to-face relationships in thousands of southern rural neighborhoods. Planters and merchants tried to keep sharecroppers in a state of slavelike dependency, but at every turn the croppers resisted. They might work indifferently, appeal to local customs

about what constituted reasonable labo
at the end of the year. All in all, they d
and from the community-based religiou:
organizations that had appeared with l
emancipation.

Third, while sharecropping began as
former masters and former slaves, by th
many whites were joining the ranks of sha

drawn from among the landless population in the plantation districts (where tenure arrangements resembling sharecropping had
existed before the Civil War), but by 1880 both sharecropping
and cotton culture were spreading beyond the plantation belt
into predominantly white farming areas.

Having a white skin did not make sharecropping a better deal
for the producer. The effective wage for cropping was set by the
world price of cotton, a distinctly color-blind market force. The
South was becoming, in Gavin Wright's phrase, a "low-wage
region in a high-wage country," and the agricultural wage was
no respecter of race. Black and white sharecroppers were finding
themselves in the same ditch. The only question was whether,
once in the ditch, they would insist on separate accommodations.

Prior to the 1870s, most of the white Southerners who farmed
beyond the boundaries of the old plantation belt had maintained
their independence on the land, though never in complete isolation from market forces. In the upper piedmont of the Carolinas,
Georgia, Alabama, and Mississippi, and even in the thinly settled
wire-grass regions of the Georgia-Alabama coastal plain, a kind
of rural self-sufficiency prevailed, in which farm families grew
food crops, let their cattle and hogs forage on the open range,
hunted and fished, and raised small amounts of cash crops for
sale in local markets—cotton for most, tobacco for some.

Unlike the wheat farmers of the Plains and the cotton planters
of the South, these farm families had been weakly connected to
national and international markets. But even before the Civil
War they had been integrated into local networks of exchange in

...d labor. Within the local markets of the nonplantation
..., payment for goods might well include a mixture of pro-
...ce, labor, and cash. The labor of household members was
augmented at critical points in the crop season with cooperative
labor among neighbors. In this world beyond the plantation,
private ownership of land coexisted with communal relations in
which the "social" could hardly be separated from the "economic." As Jess Hudgins recalled of Cherokee County, Georgia:
"Farmers swapped work so that families could work together and
enjoy the company."

The Civil War itself began to break down the isolation of the
nonplantation South, and the combination of military destruction
and the economic policies of the Confederacy plunged many small
farmers into debt and increased the temptation to gamble on
commercial agriculture.

Wartime disruption opened the door for three interrelated
developments that in the 1870s broke through the relative isolation of the up-country and changed forever the rhythms of
traditional rural life: first, railroads spread into many parts of the
upper piedmont, linking the region directly to the cotton markets
of New York and Liverpool by means of cotton buyers who spread
out into the interior; second, merchants set up shop in the towns
and crossroads communities of the up-country, providing points
of connection between farmers and those larger markets; and
third, the railroad and the country store brought phosphate fertilizers to the up-country, making commercial cotton production
more viable but also increasing the cost, and thus the risk.

The same three developments would bring the frontierlike
wire-grass regions of the coastal plain into the realm of King
Cotton, but somewhat more slowly. In 1870, the agriculture practiced in the sparsely populated wire grass was an extreme version
of what was to be found in the up-country—subsistence farming
combined with herding. By the end of the 1880s, the country
was beginning to fill up (with much of the increase coming from
the overflowing population of the up-country), and commercial

cultivation of cotton was on the rise, with effects similar to those in the up-country.

North of the cotton belt along the Virginia–North Carolina border, yet another agricultural transformation was taking place in the 1870s and 1880s, one which in some respects resembled the wheat frenzy of the Dakotas as much as it did the southern yeoman's shift toward cotton. In this case the miracle crop was bright flue-cured tobacco, a new strain ideally suited to the siliceous soil of the area and much sought after by the booming cigarette industry.

Farmers there had long grown small patches of darker, heavier tobaccos, but extensive production of bright leaf meant far greater involvement in commercial agriculture. Granville County, North Carolina, emerged as the center of this booming industry, and the names of successful producers became household words. The lure of this new crop is easily explained by looking at testimonials such as this one from a North Carolina farmer who

> in 1875 bought ten acres adjoining the corporate limits of Henderson, paying for the same about $20 per acre. In 1884 he rented out said land for one-half the crop, and his part realized him $300 per acre—a rental fifteen times more than the land cost him; and the crop from these ten acres sold for $6000.

The spread of bright leaf tobacco was as much a market-driven phenomenon as the Dakota wheat boom. New manufacturing plants in Durham and Winston fueled the demand, fertilizer companies disseminated tips on how to grow the new crop, and civic boosters in the small cities of the region promoted it with as much enthusiasm as any Dakota land agent. Farmers responded by adopting new techniques of growing and curing and by plunging into debt to buy the commercial fertilizer without which bright leaf could not be successfully grown.

As farm profits from the high-priced weed created one success story after another in the 1880s, bright leaf production spread from its point of origin around Granville County into eastern North Carolina, where commercial farmers viewed it as the solution to the problem of falling cotton prices. An instruction booklet for eastern farmers entitled *Tobacco: How to Grow It! And Better Still—Make It Pay* included this bit of doggerel:

> Cotton was once king
> And produced Carolina's cracker;
> But now we have a better thing—
> The glorious Bright Tobacco.

In the course of the 1890s, farmers in eastern North Carolina shifted from cotton to tobacco, much as their neighbors to the west had shifted away from general farming toward bright leaf tobacco. The new king would prove to be every bit as tyrannical as the old.

In the booming tobacco belt, as in the cotton-growing fringes of the old plantation district, the change in the southern countryside was dramatic, but it was not the drama of independent yeomen being dragged against their will into the world of commercial agriculture. They thought they could eat their cake and have it too: secure independence on the land and commercial success. The typical small farmer had not meant to play the high-stakes game of get-rich-quick; he believed he could make his independence on the land more secure by growing some cotton or tobacco and selling it at a high price. Some well-established farmers with substantial landholdings and cash reserves achieved that goal. But for many owners of the little one-horse farms in the piedmont, things didn't work out that way.

For up-country farmers as a whole, the balance shifted during the 1870s from self-sufficiency in foodstuffs to cotton or tobacco for sale, and the price of sale was now set by distant and capricious cotton markets or by equally unfathomable tobacco warehousemen, rather than by local custom and face-to-face exchange. The country or small-town merchant was no longer just a neighbor. He was the last link in a chain of commercial relationships reaching to the wholesale centers of the South and beyond them to the capitals of commerce and industry. While marketing the crop and selling supplies the local merchant also introduced the crop lien with its entanglement in the web of expensive credit and served as a conduit for an important new technology, phosphate fertilizer.

From a mechanical standpoint, the technology of cotton and tobacco production lagged far behind that being applied to the production of small grains in the West in the Populist era. However, the rapid diffusion of commercial fertilizer across the Southeast had almost as great an impact on cotton production as the advent of the self-binding reaper did on wheat. It was absolutely essential for growing bright leaf tobacco. The new phosphate fertilizer increased yields and shortened the growing season (the former was essential in the poor siliceous soils of the tobacco belt and sandy wire grass; the latter was welcome in the up-country, where an early frost could wipe out a year's effort).

But this chemical technology, like the mechanical technologies of the Great Plains, locked the up-country farmer ever more tightly into a cycle of indebtedness. Almost all small producers of cotton and tobacco bought their fertilizer on credit. Sometimes when the roll of the dice left a farmer unable to pay out, the result was the loss of land, and the independent farmer became a dependent sharecropper or left the land altogether.

The extent of land loss due to foreclosure is still disputed. There was actually a net increase in owner-operated farms in the upper piedmont during the late nineteenth century. Sharecropping spread, in part, because of the pressure of a growing population in a finite space. But the fear of land loss due to indebtedness became the constant companion of farmers in the up-country, just as it did on the Great Plains. By the 1880s, it seemed as if the worlds of the white yeoman and the freedman were beginning to converge.

The prospect of joining black sharecroppers in the ditch of dependency was doubly galling to some yeomen because of their historic struggle with planters for control of land. As one northern Georgia farmer had told an English traveler at the close of the war: "We should tuk the land . . . and split it, and gin part to the niggers and part to me and t'other Union fellers." Years later, at the depth of the cotton depression that threatened to render landless a generation of up-country farmers, one South Carolina congressman and champion of the Farmers' Alliance expressed both the intensity of feeling that could unite black and white farmers in opposition to the planter-merchants and the difficulty of really acting as one class:

> It is not now a question of the freedom of the few million blacks from chattel slavery. It is a question of the eman- cipation of our race from financial shackles that are infinitely more galling to Anglo-Saxon manhood.

One way of avoiding the "financial shackles" of sharecropping was moving to Texas. In the 1870s thousands of farmers from the southern up-country were doing just that, following paths well marked since the 1830s and then pushing on to the frontier west of Fort Worth. (We are back now to John Allen's neck of the woods, to the Cross Timbers and prairies stretching north from Lampasas.) Settlement of the land west of Fort Worth had begun in the 1850s, only to be disrupted by weather, Indians, and the internal civil war that raged there throughout the 1860s. Now, with something like order restored, this country looked to many like the last good place to fulfill the dream of independence on the land.

As in the booming Great Plains, many of the people who filled this Texas frontier arrived by rail and were carted on to little towns that harbored ambitions of becoming the next Fort Worth or St. Louis. There they discovered that much of the best farm- land had to be bought from foreign-owned land syndicates or from the railroads themselves, if clear title could be had at all. But that did not slow the flood of settlers.

To immigrants from the upland South, this land looked a little bit like home. The trees were smaller, but there were trees, as well as streams (most of the time), and sandy soil not unlike the land they had worked in Mississippi or Georgia. In years when the rains fell, this was good poor man's land. Here a southern dirt farmer could put in his old bull-tongued plow and raise a crop of corn and cotton in the bottomlands of the Trinity and Brazos rivers and, when that was taken, on the upland slopes. Here he could let his hogs root for acorns in the timber and his cattle graze on the unfenced prairie as his forebears had done in Carolina and Alabama.

At first, the settlers grew a little cotton along with corn and small grains in the old pattern of self-sufficiency. Some wheat had been raised there since first settlement in the 1850s. By 1883 the Texas & Pacific and the Fort Worth & Denver railroads bisected the Cross Timbers. The railroads, which brought families to this edge of the South and West, also brought access to world markets in cotton and wheat. In the creek bottoms and prairie openings of the Cross Timbers, southern yeomen began again the historic shift from self-sufficiency to cotton specialization. Soon cotton buyers crowded the streets of Decatur and Weatherford at harvesttime, as they did in the small towns of the southern piedmont. And on the richer prairies just to the east, looming grain elevators in Rhome and Denton signaled the shift from the pioneer beginnings of wheat culture to commercial production in what was becoming the southern terminus of the winter wheat belt.

Here on the Texas frontier the South met the Great Plains, and from that point of intersection would spread one particularly important carrier of the Populist revolt, the Farmers' Alliance. Recruiters for that organization would claim that, for all their differences, farmers in the South and West were brothers and sisters.

Those agrarian organizers spoke to western and southern farmers of shared grievances over the balance of economic power in the United States, and did so in terms familiar to both. Assume for now that those agitators had the economics of it straight, and consider the radical implications of the fact that in a moment of deep distress farmers in the South and West had similar understandings of what it meant to live in community.

We have seen that though situated on individual farmsteads, rural families in the South and Great Plains lived in relatively compact settlements. We have also seen how families and neighbors worked together in the production of crops. "Habits of mutuality" remained strong in the countryside, even in the face of modern technology and the intrusion of the market. Whether measured in spatial or social terms, farmers lived in communities.

In our own time, the term "community" is applied not only to a particular space but also to human networks that extend beyond a single locale (thus the "scientific community" or the "business community"). In sorting out the social origins of Populism, it helps to think of rural communities both as *places* on a map and as *networks* that link groups of people. Let us envision the communities inhabited by people like John Allen and his neighbors as "two-dimensional" sets of social networks, with one dimension being those bonds of kinship and association within a particular neighborhood and the other being those networks that linked the neighborhood to the world beyond.

On the local plane of community life, the family was the first and most cohesive network in rural America, regardless of region. Even among the southern freedmen, where we might expect the long nightmare of slavery to have obliterated family ties, recent studies have demonstrated the resilience and power of both nuclear and extended family groups. The family was an important economic unit, both for production of crops and, particularly in the South, for the securing of credit (family stability helped ensure the "good name" upon which credit was often based), but it was more than an economic unit. Agricultural production existed to sustain the family, not the other way around.

Among the many threads that wove individual farm families into a social fabric was the almost forgotten custom of visiting. Modern suburbanites who hardly know the names of their neighbors may be surprised to learn how much time nineteenth-century farmers spent visiting one another. Consider the case of Elam Bartholomew, who kept a careful record of the visitors to his northwestern Kansas home in 1880. A total of 1,081 people visited the Bartholomew home that year, and Rachel Bartholomew served meals to 783 persons, not counting children under three years of age. As Gilbert Fite notes: "Bartholomew's wife may have been weary, but she was surely not lonesome."

Visiting was equally important in southern rural culture. More is known about this custom before the Civil War than after, but it certainly continued into the Populist era and beyond. William Daniel, a Virginian whose record keeping was as precise as Bartholomew's, noted that on two-thirds of the days in 1852 he or his wife, Julia, either visited someone or had callers at their farm. Some trips were to the home of a neighbor, others to church services or other public gatherings. Some were business calls, others social. Many combined the two.

What does all this have to do with the spread of protest organizations? Organizers for groups like the Farmers' Alliance did not operate in a social vacuum. In the first place, many of the Texas organizers who fanned out across the South and West headed straight for their home communities. Some began by recruiting members of their own extended families. All made full use of rural visiting networks in soliciting new members.

The same farm families who engaged in endless visitation with their neighbors also took part in a wide array of community activities, including church services and camp meetings, the public "exercises" of neighborhood schools, fraternal organizations (including the Masons, Odd Fellows, Knights of Pythias, and their respective "Ladies' Auxiliaries"), singing conventions and other musical entertainments, literary and debating societies, agricultural societies, political rallies, community barbecues, and gatherings of Civil War veterans—either Union or Confederate, depending on the region.

All these social networks could be found in rural communities throughout the South and West. Indeed, for the better part of a century they had been fundamental ingredients of community life everywhere in rural and small-town America. Note that many of these activities took place within membership organizations— voluntary associations such as churches, fraternal organizations, and agricultural societies.

Voluntary associations not only broke the monotony of day-to-day life; they also served to maintain ties of community through participation in familiar rituals and the reaffirmation of shared values. They were, or claimed to be, nonsectarian and nonpartisan (though they were never totally free from the class and ethnic divisions of rural communities). They created new roles outside the home for women as well as men and served as schools to teach important skills of organizing and public speaking. Since most of the associations required some test of character for admission, membership could boost the reputation of the initiate and, through the privilege of transferring membership from one local lodge or church to another, could offer a portable certificate of respectability.

In the 1880s and 1890s the Alliances and other farmer-labor groups would develop new variations on this old and familiar way of organizing people in community. When the traveling lecturer-organizer for one of these groups appeared in a rural community anywhere in America, the form, if not the message, was already well known.

Social networks *within* particular communities were themselves linked to the wider world. In a society in motion like America of the nineteenth century, even the basic "local" institution, the family, could be dispersed over several states. In addition, many of the voluntary associations that knit together the local community were members of national organizations.

But increasingly the ties that defined the countryside's relationship with the wider world were economic. That was true in the South as well as in the Great Plains and the Mountain West, for by the eve of the Populist revolt farmers in the three regions were well within the orbit of the market economy, and all in their own way were dependent upon expensive new technologies for success: horse-powered machinery on the Great Plains, irrigation in the Mountain West, and phosphate fertilizers in the cotton and tobacco belts. Each of these technologies magnified both the rewards and the risks of commercial farming.

The sinews that knit farming communities to the wider world of commerce were lines of transportation, communication, trade, and credit: railroads, telegraphs, formalized markets, and mortgage companies. As we have seen, in the regions where the Populist movement would take root the completion of a dense network of railroads in the decade after 1877 stimulated population growth and the production of staple crops for market. We should also note (in anticipation of further discussion) that the railroads brought farmers into their most direct contact with labor radicalism in the 1880s. Railroads were systems of people as well as iron, and the organization of railroad workers went wherever the rails went. Paralleling the transportation revolution was a transformation of the way in which grain, livestock, and cotton were marketed. The railroads' introduction of through bills of lading in the 1870s meant that commodities could be shipped directly from interior points to mills or foreign markets. Through institutions like the Chicago Board of Trade and cotton exchanges from Liverpool to Galveston, the era also witnessed the further standardization of commodity markets, including "futures" markets in which commodities were bought or sold for future delivery or acceptance. By means of the telegraph, buyers and sellers thousands of miles from the central markets could know instantly of the slightest change in world prices.

Nowhere was the transformation of marketing more dramatic than in the cotton belt. Prior to the Civil War, planters had shipped their cotton on consignment to factors (merchants) in port cities. But by 1885 southern correspondents for *Bradstreet's* magazine were reporting that "cash buyers were in every neighborhood, crops were being bought up promptly and shipped direct to the mills and export." Buyers employed by cotton trading firms and textile mills—or speculating on their own account—spread out along the rail lines to purchase cotton directly in the villages and plantations of the South. Telegraphic communications gave them current price information from exchanges in the United States and Britain, as well as reports on the needs of mills in New England and Europe.

These very changes in the market system, changes that signaled a further shift of economic power away from the countryside, helped farmers to imagine that they could establish their own cooperative means of selling the crop and thus of maintaining their independence. The new system had already cut out one southern middleman (the factor); why not another (the local furnishing merchant)? Farmers could read the telegraphic reports as well as cotton buyers; why not bargain collectively with the purchasing agents or bypass them altogether? The farmers' hope of salvation through economic cooperation, grounded in ancient habits of mutuality, seemed achievable because of market institutions that came into being after the Civil War.

In the West and in the South, farmers were of two minds about the networks of transportation and trade that linked them to the outside world. Railroads and markets were as essential to their way of life as the land itself, and they knew it. Those agents of modernity held great promise, but farmers increasingly viewed them as engines of oppression. When in 1893 the nation slid into a depression even worse than the one that had racked the country in the 1870s, farmers would heap even greater abuse upon the masters of transportation, markets, and credit.

Railroads provided essential service but at high and seemingly capricious rates, which were set by unseen and therefore "foreign" hands. To farmers hard pressed to pay the freight, it seemed that railroad barons made a profit, not because they added value to the economy, but because of their political influence and the strategic control over the lanes of commerce.

The standardization of commodity markets and their penetration into the countryside made it easier to sell the crop, but sales seemed to benefit mainly speculators, symbolized by those who rolled the dice in the futures market. In the natural order of things, farmers believed, rewards should go to the producers of goods, whose independence was thereby secured. But instead, profits were accruing, not to the person who produced the crop, but to the one with capital or credit enough to hold it for speculation.

In the modern world of fluctuating prices, this ability to hold the crop and bargain for the best price was for many farmers as sure a test of independence as ownership of the land itself. The knowledge that they could not pass the test—could not hold the crops they had produced by the sweat of their brow—was a primary source of their anger.

The farmers' divided mind on transportation and trade was matched by similar feelings about the towns and interior cities that were the nodal points connecting their communities and the global market. In both the South and the West, the commercial energy that transformed the countryside was focused in the new and revitalized towns that dotted the interior. It was in urban places ranging in size from St. Louis and Atlanta down to whistle stops of a few dozen souls and twice that many dogs that land and credit were offered for sale, crops were purchased, and retail and wholesale trade carried out.

On some issues the interests of townsmen and farmers coincided (railroad freight rates, for example—the issue that had brought Rochester merchants and Genesee farmers together in

1877). And when farmers launched their own alternative systems of cooperative purchasing and marketing, they did so in those same hubs of transportation and wholesale trade—Kansas City, Dallas, Memphis, and Atlanta—often with the blessings of the local chamber of commerce.

But on other issues—from control of free-ranging livestock to the need to maintain the booster façade in the face of economic disaster—farmers and townsmen were fundamentally at odds. The economic and political battles of the Populist era ended up pitting townsmen and rural people against each other in sharp and sometimes violent confrontation.

But I am getting ahead of the story. We shall have ample opportunity to consider the Populists' grievances, the remedies they proposed, and the ways in which familiar patterns of community shaped their protest. But by way of ending this reconnaissance of Populist country, let us note a series of economic jolts that shook the countryside *before* the onset of the great depression of the 1890s and that triggered the movement that swept the rural South and West with such force that one witness called it a "Pentecost of Politics."

In 1889 and 1890 a withering drought—coupled with declining prices for wheat and corn—ended the western land boom, destroyed the hope of profit and security on prairie farms, and left tens of thousands of families facing bankruptcy and even starvation. On land that had recently produced twenty bushels of wheat to the acre, farmers were now lucky to grow four. By the end of the 1880s the price that one bushel would bring had dropped from $1.19 to $0.49. It soon became clear that the boosters had been terribly wrong. In the frenzy of speculation farm prices had been overinflated, loans overextended, and towns overbuilt. Farm mortgages that had seemed like reasonable risks while the price of wheat and land escalated were now burdensome in the extreme. Sixty percent of the farm acreage in Kansas was mortgaged, and in the hard-hit central portion of the state, up to 75 percent. In the western half of the Plains states many of those who could simply walked away from a failed farmstead.

In the South, the decline into rural poverty and privation was equally severe, if less precipitous. Farmers there had, with momentary exceptions, known little else but poverty since the Civil War. The region's farmers had never experienced the massive infusion of outside capital that had spurred the growth of agriculture in the Plains states, and in the immediate aftermath of the Civil War the threat of starvation had been every bit as real in parts of the rural South as it was in western Kansas at the end of the 1880s.

By the mid-1870s the world price of cotton had begun its long retreat from the postwar high that had drawn many small farmers into producing the fleecy staple. By 1890 tobacco prices were also falling, although, as was not true with cotton, a major source of the decline was the growing concentration of ownership in manufacturing, symbolized by the creation of the hated American Tobacco Company in 1889.

Although economists and historians still argue about whether cotton was "profitable" in the late nineteenth century, most would agree that by the late 1880s the farm-gate price of cotton barely covered the cost of production. It would drop well below the break-even point after 1890, and even before then any sudden surge in costs spelled disaster for the great majority of farmers, who had to borrow money for current operations. Like their western counterparts, southern farmers experienced several such surges, which to them could only be explained by the workings of distant and malevolent "trusts."

In 1888 the price of jute bagging used to wrap cotton bales doubled after a domestic cartel cornered the market for jute. Similarly, consolidation of railroad ownership in the late 1880s and 1890s caused freight rates to skyrocket—as, for example, when the Richmond Terminal Company monopolized rail service in the Augusta region in 1890. On average, railroad freight rates and other farm costs declined in late-nineteenth-century America, but averages can be deceiving. The cotton South experienced sharp increases in published freight rates beginning in the late 1880s, and the same happened in the West beginning around 1890.

Declining commodity prices, coupled with unpredictable and sometimes increasing costs and the constant burden of debt, pushed countless southern farmers to the brink of disaster. While the gyrations of commodity markets and freight rates might be attributable to distant and unseen forces, farmers could associate a face and a name—that of the local furnishing merchant or planter—with the ever-present crop lien and the potential decline into sharecropping.

White yeomen came to understand as well as black sharecroppers that these institutions of credit and land tenure that lay heavy upon the South were instruments of exploitation. The strain this created on the fabric of community can be seen in this exchange, recorded years later, between a white cropper and his wife: "The landlords is fair, most of 'em. They's good ones and bad ones," recalled Steve Lee. But his wife, Josie, interjected, "You've been robbed! They robbed you of thousands of dollars, and you know it!"

The common reaction of farmers in the West and South was that something was terribly wrong. They had been tricked by the smooth-handed fellows who promised that rain would follow the plow or that buying fertilizer and planting cotton would be the way to get ahead. In despair they turned to those whom they believed could help: to governments (which had provided relief to farmers in earlier times of drought and destitution), to churches (which told them they were the chosen people of God), to townsmen (who had encouraged them to take up new land and plant wheat or tobacco).

This time their pleas fell on deaf ears. President Cleveland vetoed an appropriation of $50,000 to provide seed grain to drought-stricken farmers. Civic boosters denounced the "calamity howlers," whom they feared would frighten away prospective settlers. Even the churches seemed strangely silent when confronted with this rural disaster. Faced with the hostility or unresponsiveness of the nation's dominant institutions, farmers banded together to seek redress.

2

Cultures of Protest, 1867–86

We are back to the question the city reporter asked John Allen and his neighbors at the high point of the Farmers' Alliance: why such a movement "at the time and place, among such a people and under such circumstances"? No doubt J. J. Hill sensed that it had something to do with the circumstances of families on the land, with the condition of agriculture in that meeting place of South and West, and with the particular crises which the forces of nature and the engines of commerce had loosed upon rural people.

Having surveyed the countryside on the eve of the Populist revolt, we know that at the end of the 1880s a crisis loomed for southern and western farmers. But the movement that was to sweep across the land like a prairie fire did not emerge among people who had been ground down by nature or commerce into disconnected atoms. It did not spread among people so ensnared by habits of deference and enthralled by the pageantry of politics that they could not imagine freeing themselves, cooperatively, from the powers and principalities of the age. Rather, it began among people who possessed, as part of their birthright, cultures of protest—patterns of thought and action growing out of their own history on the land.

To understand the character of this Populist uprising and why it spread so rapidly, we must understand something of the culture of protest that was at its core. The "stuff" of such a culture includes the practices, beliefs, and values that grew out of people's historical rhythms of work and patterns of community life. Its elements derived from both their experiences on the land and their position within the larger network of "producers" in industrializing America.

Pause for a minute over that word "producer." It is one of several names that Populists applied to themselves. Those terms once named a set of values that, unfortunately for us, no longer have any particular meaning or, even more confusing, now stand for something altogether different. Take, for example, the words "radicalism," "republicanism," and "equality," which now have political and sociological meanings quite different from those which Populists attached to them. Those words, along with "producerism" and "antimonopolism," are central to the Populists' understanding of how society ought to work, their "moral economy."

The Populists' vision of a well-ordered society derived in large measure from a body of thought dating back to the founding fathers, but more directly accessible to them through the beliefs and values of antebellum artisans and farmers. In its antebellum form this set of ideas is known variously as "artisanal republicanism," "radical republicanism," or, as the Populists would most often call it, "producerism." It was based on the simple idea that the producer deserves the fruits of his or her work. Put another way, labor creates value. Or expressed biblically (and believers in producerism *often* expressed it biblically), "the laborer is worthy of his hire."

From that basic moral premise, certain conclusions about the good society followed. As Richard Oestreicher put it:

A republican society guaranteed the equal opportunity to labor, guaranteed to each the fruits of his or her toil, ensured that no arbitrary social distinctions offered special privileges to some, and gave equal rights to all.

What could threaten this blissful state? "Special privileges," the modern name for which was "monopoly." What must the ever-vigilant citizen do? Stand firm against privileged monopolies wherever they occur: in banks that through their "nonproductive" use of capital gain a monopoly over credit, in land syndicates that monopolize the acres that should go to settlers, among manufacturers who substitute for the traditional relations of shop and mill a new kind of "wage slavery."

The antidote to "special privilege" was thus "equal rights." Andrew Jackson himself had identified "equality among the people in the rights conferred by government" as "the great radical principle of freedom." The proper role of government was, in the present-day vernacular, to provide a level playing field, both economically and politically. The Jacksonian slogan of "equal rights to all, special privilege to none" would appear on the mastheads of Populist newspapers all over the country. It was a central element of the intellectual birthright bequeathed by one generation of reformers to another.

These were the central concerns of antebellum radical republicanism, and like the message of the twentieth-century civil rights movement, they were given additional urgency by the medium through which they were often conveyed, the language of evangelicalism.

For farmers and artisans of the 1830s and 1840s it was still possible to imagine a real world that approximated the republican ideal. The workingmen's campaigns to outlaw private banks and have the government issue paper money, to substitute cooperative manufacturing and distribution for wage labor, and to distribute public lands to homesteaders: these were all serious attempts to usher in a "cooperative commonwealth." They did not oppose private ownership of property, only the unearned use of capital and the abuse of ownership through monopolistic power.

In the 1870s and 1880s radicalism or producerism still provided the basic vocabulary of the North American labor movement. Antimonopolism, the rights of workers to enjoy the fruits of their labor and of settlers to occupy the land, the right of the people to a money supply not controlled by private banks: these were still powerful themes. Industrialization did not loosen their grip upon workers; rather it stimulated additions to the list: demands for the eight-hour day, for government ownership of railroads and telegraph, and for fiat money (greenbacks).

To say that the culture of Populism drew heavily on this tradition is not to say that Populists were blinded by nostalgia for some golden age of agrarianism. As Bruce Laurie has demonstrated, radical republicanism—producerism—remained the most powerful organizing principle of working-class consciousness in America throughout most of the nineteenth century. Post-Civil War labor and farm organizations took this tradition and modified it in the face of new realities.

In searching for the origins of a specifically rural culture of protest, it helps to remember that the term "culture" had first to do with the tilling of crops. And even while American farmers were busily expanding commercial production of wheat, cotton, and tobacco, they kept alive age-old cooperative labor practices that affirmed the principles of community and equality, and their communities were knit together by a remarkable array of social institutions. The culture of protest begins with social relationships on the land.

The basic elements of such a culture can be detected among rural people of the West and South before the Alliance movement began attracting national attention in the late 1880s. Mingled with labor radicalism, this culture shaped the responses of the Farmers' Alliance and the People's Party to new circumstances, and in the process helped to define a movement that was grounded in the values of an older day but fully in touch with contemporary issues and methods.

Before we explore the elements of that culture, a word of caution: rural folk were not all one happy family. We must be alert for signs of division among them—divisions of race, class, culture, and region—and between them and their sometime allies, the tradesmen and workers with whom they shared the category of "producers." On some issues the interests of these groups were as one, but on others they were not. These internal contradictions are as crucial to the story of Populism as the moments when "the people" converge.

Rural communities were not without conflict, and not all neighborhood organizations exhibited the decorum of a literary or debating society. Even before the American Revolution, backcountry farmers formed vigilante groups that took the law into their own hands to maintain the security and independence of the farm household. Throughout the nineteenth century, vigilantes used threats, destruction of property, and even lynchings to protect the rights of settlers against land syndicates and claim jumpers and to defend against cattle rustlers and horse thieves. In the 1880s, young Theodore Roosevelt attempted to join one such group while he was trying his hand at ranching in western Dakota Territory, but the real cattlemen refused to take him along on their murderous foray into Montana in which thirty-five suspected rustlers were killed. In the 1880s the enclosure of large tracts of land within barbed-wire fences triggered a wave of vigilantism in the rural South and West. The issue revolved around the practice, sanctioned by long-standing custom if not by law, of allowing livestock to roam at will in search of forage and water. Under the traditional open-range system, farmer-stockmen fenced growing crops to keep livestock out, rather than pastures to keep them in.

The tradition of the open range had prevailed in the South and West from the inception of livestock raising in the Carolina cradle in the eighteenth century through its spread to Texas and up into the Great Plains in the nineteenth. In the Southeast, the practice had allowed even the poorest farmer access to food for his stock. In the Southwest, it allowed the movement of great herds to pasture or market and ensured access to limited supplies of water. In both regions, it had achieved the status of a common right and a symbol of republican equality. As one Georgia farmer put it: "The citizens of this county have and always have had the legal, moral, and Bible right to let their stock . . . run at large."

The invention of barbed wire in the 1870s made it possible to alter the traditional system. In the rural Southeast, well-to-do advocates of "scientific" farming began a campaign for enclosure in order to upgrade herds and protect crops. They were joined by railroad officials who were tired of being ordered by hostile country juries to compensate farmers for livestock that had wandered into the path of an oncoming train. In the Southwest, land syndicates and other large landowners enclosed vast acreages (some of it actually in the public domain), blocking access to water and even towns.

In both regions, small landowners and tenants understood very well that the issue was one of control as well as tradition. The yeoman or sharecropper who could not let his hogs forage in the woods was even more at the mercy of the furnishing merchant than he had been before, and the settler whose cattle could not get to pasture or to the only source of water was not likely to survive long enough to prove up his claim.

Victims of the enclosure movement reckoned it to be part of a much larger struggle between people like themselves and monopolists. When the Texas Farmers' Alliance published its first political manifesto, it included fencing in the catalogue of "the onerous and shameful abuses that the industrial classes are now suffering at the hands of arrogant capitalists and powerful corporations." As the Alliance's legislative demand demonstrates, American farmers addressed the enclosure issue with their votes as well as with their wire cutters. A headline in the Atlanta *Constitution* in 1883 announced that the hottest issues of local

politics in Georgia were "Whiskey, Fences, and Dogs." More
Georgians were turning out for local-option elections on prohibition and the fence issue than for most presidential elections,
and the issue of taxing dogs (intended, some said, to get rid of
the poor man's hound) was a close third.

Fence elections divided voters along town-rural lines, and
within the rural districts they separated relatively well-off "progressive" farmers from their poorer neighbors. A provision of the
Texas state constitution, drafted by large landowners, made it
unconstitutional to carry wire cutters in your pocket! The lines
of demarcation over fencing foreshadowed the division within the
rural South and Southwest during the Populist era. Long after
the agrarian crusade, one old-time Democrat told the historian
of Texas Populism: "Where you found the hogs running loose,
there were lots of Populists; where you found them penned up,
the Democrats were in a majority."

Just as the fencing controversy evoked both political protest
and vigilantism, so too did farmers' anger against the overweening
power of the railroads. We will have occasion to examine the
farmers' efforts to bring the railroads under governmental control.
But for now, observe their vicarious and sometimes active support
for the "social bandits" who roamed the Southwest in the 1870s
and 1880s.

The most famous of these robbers were Frank and Jesse James
of Clay County, Missouri. The James brothers had developed
their craft through an apprenticeship in the principal training
ground of western desperadoes, Quantrill's Raiders, an outfit that
operated as Confederate guerrillas during Missouri's own internal
Civil War. Like guerrilla bands in other wars, Quantrill's men
conducted lightning raids against enemy outposts and transportation lines, and they avoided capture by winning the support or
acquiescence of the rural population, operating according to their
own code of honor and claiming to be the defenders of home and
tradition.

Quantrill's men were excluded from the general amnesty after the Civil War; consequently many of them applied their guerrilla training to other pursuits. The postwar career of the James gang began in 1872 with a daring holdup in Kansas City, where they made off with the ticket receipts of a fair organized by civic boosters to promote the growth of the city. Over the next two years they perfected the dangerous technique of stopping trains and robbing the railroad express agent and wealthy passengers.

So long as they stayed in Missouri, the James gang avoided capture with the aid of local residents, many of whom took delight in their daring attacks on "foreign" railroads. Far more significant than the actual support given the James boys was the growth of their popular reputation (cultivated by themselves, of course) as heirs of legendary European social bandits like Robin Hood, Dick Turpin, and Claude Duval. Jesse James claimed Robin Hood as his hero and explained to the Kansas City *Times*: "We rob the rich and give to the poor." Rural Missouri was full of stories of their daring and generosity. If all the widows allegedly saved from eviction by the famous highwaymen had actually received the gold dollars supposedly handed over to them after one train robbery or another, there would have been no more poverty in the Missouri countryside.

Sensational newspaper accounts and popular legends no doubt exaggerated the *social* banditry of the train robbers. Their exploits were mainly limited to regions where the disruption of the Civil War had been most severe and were facilitated more by that disruption than by any kind of protorevolutionary sentiment. Nevertheless, vigilantism, represented by the legendary bandits of the Southwest and by the western fence wars, drew upon the social organization of rural communities and upon a set of shared values about the sanctity of community and family. It reveals a violent strain within the cultures of rural protest, etching in sharp relief the conflict between modernity and tradition, between monopolists and their victims.

The zenith of Jesse James's career coincided with the high point of a farmers' organization that drew its strength from a very different strain of rural culture, the Patrons of Husbandry, commonly known as the Grange. The state that produced and harbored Jesse James also led the nation in Grange membership. (In 1875, Missouri had over 80,000 Grangers, followed by Indiana, Ohio, Kentucky, Iowa, Kansas, Tennessee, Texas, Michigan, and Mississippi.)

Although rural vigilantism and social banditry were connected to the culture of protest through their own distinctive forms of social organization, the primary social medium in which Populist culture developed was the voluntary association, of which the Grange was a typical example. This social form was so commonplace in nineteenth-century America as to seem part of the way society naturally arranged itself. Just as the language of producerism and evangelicalism provided a common vocabulary for nineteenth-century Americans of many divergent backgrounds, so too the voluntary association gave them a common understanding of how communities worked.

Like most voluntary associations, the Grange began with a written constitution that set the requirements for membership, rules governing behavior of members, and duties of the various officers of the association—not the least of whom was the lecturer-organizer whose job it was to recruit new members. Also in typical fashion, the Grange featured a hierarchy of local, county, state, and national bodies, connected to each other through a corresponding hierarchy of officers and through official publications. Women were admitted to full membership in the Grange, although the intent was less to ensure equality for individual women than to promote the harmony of the farm family. Like many nineteenth-century organizations, the Grange was to be a secret oath-bound society with rituals and "degrees" (levels of membership) modeled on the Masonic order, and its meetings were to be clothed in the language and hymns of evangelicalism.

The Grange was the brainchild of Boston-born Oliver Hudson Kelley, whose wanderings had taken him by stages across the Midwest to a Minnesota homestead, then in 1864 to a clerkship in the new U.S. Department of Agriculture. At the close of the Civil War, Kelley conducted a presidential survey of agricultural conditions in the South. In the course of his tour Kelley consulted with prominent southern agriculturalists—many of whom were both Masons and veterans of antebellum agricultural societies— about the creation of a new order, national in scope, which would combine the educational work of the agricultural societies with the social features of Masonry.

Once back in Washington, Kelley and several associates crafted a plan of organization for just such a fraternity. In 1867, armed with a constitution and ritual and with forms for enrolling members, Kelley embarked on a recruiting tour. At first, farmers were leery of the new order. As Kelley put it years later: "The education and social features of our Order offer inducements to some to join, but the majority desire pecuniary benefits—advantages in purchase of machinery, and sales of produce."

The prospect of "pecuniary benefits" within a fraternal order —cooperative purchasing and marketing—attracted hundreds of thousands of farmers in the 1870s. Borrowing from urban and British cooperative models, the Grange developed by far the largest network of cooperative enterprises up to that time. At first, local Granges simply concentrated the trade of their members with merchants who promised the best rates. These local arrangements often broke down quickly, and by 1873 Grangers in several states had created business agencies that filled Grange members' orders with goods purchased directly from wholesale houses and manufacturers. This system also faltered under competition from commercial wholesalers catering to Grangers, most notably the Chicago mail-order firm of Montgomery Ward.

The business agency system, though unstable in the long run, temporarily brought sizable savings and thereby drew in many new recruits. These early successes, followed by frustration with the "Harvester Ring" and other combinations that seemed to control production of farm implements, led Grangers to consider manufacturing their own farm machinery. The Nebraska and Iowa

Granges actually manufactured headers and other harvesting machinery in 1873 and 1874, and the momentary success of the Iowa project spurred interest in other states. However, the Grange's infant cooperative factories lacked the required technical and managerial leadership, and they quickly failed.

Only in this one experiment did the Grange's cooperative work mirror the grand vision of early labor organizations in which cooperation was to transform society by supplanting the wage system. By 1875 the failure of Grange manufacturing and the weaknesses of the business agency system pushed the National Grange in a more conservative direction.

In that year a Grange commission visited England to study cooperative enterprises there. The commissioners came back urging local and state Granges to adopt a plan developed in the 1840s by British weavers organized as the Rochdale Equitable Pioneers. The Rochdale plan called for the establishment of cooperative associations, with capital raised by sale of stock to members. Goods were sold to members *at retail rates for cash*, and profits distributed to purchasers on a quarterly basis.

The Grange opened many Rochdale cooperatives for purchasing and for marketing crops and livestock. Several were quite successful, including the Texas Co-operative Association, which survived two depressions and paid handsome dividends to its stockholders for almost two decades. But the very features that made the Rochdale system financially sound rendered it useless to farmers who, however much they might wish to do so, could not pay cash. The Grange was not for them.

The National Grange's Declaration of Purposes asserted, "No Grange, if true to its obligations, can discuss political or religious questions, nor call political conventions, nor nominate candidates, nor even discuss their merits in its meetings." Like most voluntary associations, the Grange tried to hold itself above partisan politics, but its members could no more avoid the political debates of their day than they could avoid breathing. Grange leaders appeared as candidates for public office, and in state after state Grange pressure led to the establishment of agricultural colleges and departments of agriculture.

The movement even gave its name to the "Granger laws" of Iowa, Illinois, Minnesota, and Wisconsin. These were state laws that established stringent regulation of railroads and grain elevators. In the campaigns to enact them, local and state Granges worked in harmony with other segments of the community, and thus political activism did not threaten the good fellowship of the order. As the modern historian of the Grange has demonstrated, in each of those midwestern states the Grange's political advocacy took place within a broad coalition of community groups, and the Patrons of Husbandry played a distinctly secondary role. The press lumped members of the order together with other rural advocates as "Grangers," while local commercial interests took the lead in pushing the regulatory bills through the various state legislatures.

In the South, leaders of the order had an additional objective which *did* put them at odds with some segments of rural society, the overthrow of Reconstruction and the "redemption" of Dixie through the politics of the ballot or the politics of the gun. With a handful of exceptions, the Grange was for whites only. While most rank-and-file Grangers were yeomen, the leadership came largely from among the planters, who at that moment were struggling to regain control of the South, politically and economically. Grange leaders in Mississippi and Georgia doubled as leaders of the Ku Klux Klan. In South Carolina, national committeeman D. Wyatt Aiken gave new meaning to the term "cooperative" when he proclaimed that "co-operation among farmers [could] redeem the entire South from political thralldom, because it is our [black] employees, and they alone, who impede the return [to Democratic rule]."

The southern Grange's entanglement in the struggle for planter control illustrates the ambiguous position of the Grange in rural society. When Grangers championed regulation of railroads, grain elevators, and warehouses, they spoke for the entire rural community—all would benefit from fair treatment by the lords of transport and commerce. But when they promoted the Rochdale plan they spoke for only the more affluent, and when they pressed their advantage as employers of labor and heirs of the planter tradition, they put themselves at odds with sharecroppers, farm laborers, and even the independent yeomen. The lower orders of rural society would have to look elsewhere for *their* salvation. The organizations that sprang up to meet their needs would sometimes put them directly at odds with the brothers and sisters of the Patrons of Husbandry.

One such oath-bound secret society was spreading like wildfire among southern blacks in the very year of the Grange's founding. In 1867 itinerant lecturers of the Union League fanned out across the South, attaching the League to the dense network of black churches, clubs, and other community organizations. Local chapters functioned much like other voluntary associations, but under the circumstances, the mere acts of assembly, ritual, and discussion had radical implications. As one North Carolina veteran of the League recalled: "We just went there, and we talked a little; made speeches on one question and another."

Here was the beginning of a movement culture. In the presence of their peers and in the security of the League's meeting place—a church or a school, or even the open air—members swore to uphold the principle of equal rights and to "stick to one another." That oath translated into collective bargaining among farm laborers and croppers and, more frequently, into working for the Republican Party, which seemed, for a moment, to be the vehicle through which freedmen and poor whites could achieve independence and security on the land.

The Union League did not survive the reign of terror that ended Reconstruction, but in succeeding years other organizations found their way into the recesses of the rural South to revive the culture of protest among poor blacks and whites, groups with names like the Cotton Pickers' League, the Agricultural Wheel, and the Knights of Labor. Wherever they sprang up, they posed a threat to gentlemen of property and standing, even if those gentlemen also belonged to "agrarian" organizations.

Neither the extralegal activities of a fence cutter nor the fraternal and cooperative work of the Grange fully explains the movement culture of Populism. The appeal of the Union League and the Knights of Labor among the South's rural underclass points to another source of that culture of protest, the tradition of labor radicalism, as modified after the Civil War by the experience of the National Labor Union and the Knights of Labor.

In the critical moment of Populist insurgency farmers and laborers failed, in most parts of the country, to establish a common political front, and as a result scholars have minimized labor's contribution to this predominantly rural movement. But as Chester McArthur Destler noted many years ago, ignoring the labor side of Populism blinds us to Populism's profound debt to urban and eastern labor radicalism of the 1830s and 1840s. It also blinds us to the ways in which the labor movement of the period 1867–86 anticipated the organizational problems, cooperative agenda, and political demands of the Farmers' Alliance and the People's Party.

In organizational structure, core values, and program of action, the Knights of Labor was the complement of the Farmers' Alliance. The history of the Knights is well described elsewhere, and a brief sketch will suffice here. Like the Grange and the Alliance, the Knights of Labor was a fraternal order (so secret at first that even its name was not given to the public) organized along the usual lines of voluntary associations. It was founded in 1869 as a craft union of garment cutters in Philadelphia. But the founder, Uriah Stephens (a Mason who had trained for the ministry), envisioned a broad association of workers held together by principles of fraternalism and religion, not just craft loyalty.

By 1885 the Knights had succeeded in building a grand labor army of over 100,000, an umbrella organization open to all producers, with local assemblies in virtually every good-sized town in America. The following year membership increased sevenfold, as the Knights became, almost unwittingly, the nerve center of a wave of railroad and industrial strikes, including a general strike in support of the eight-hour day.

We shall return to the dramatic events of 1886, but it is important to note that the Knights of Labor was also the repository of the antebellum tradition of labor radicalism. Uriah Stephens' successor as Grand Master Workman, Terence Vincent Powderly, a Pennsylvania machinist, was very much a product of that small-town America where radical republicanism was the reigning philosophy.

In 1878, Powderly helped to fix the aims of producerism onto the Knights' agenda through passage of a preamble to the order's constitution, adopted at its meeting in Reading, Pennsylvania. The Reading document borrowed extensively, sometimes verbatim, from manifestos of the National Labor Union (1867) and the Industrial Brotherhood (1874). Another point transmitted intact from those earlier documents was a commitment to "the establishment of co-operative institutions, productive and distributive." Cooperation remained one lever by which monopoly was to be overturned.

The other lever was greenbackism and, as with cooperatives, it seemed to be a lever that the Knights and organized farmers could operate together. Spurred in part by the writings of Alexander Campbell, an Illinois protégé of antebellum currency reformer Edward Kellogg, greenbackism spread rapidly among farmers and laborers after the Panic of 1873. Taking its name from the legal-tender treasury notes issued by the federal government during the Civil War, greenbackism embodied the idea that the federal government should, on a continuing basis, adjust the currency supply to meet the fluctuating but generally expanding demands of the economy.

In its early form the monetary crusade was, as Chester Destler put it:

at once a western inflationist proposal and an eastern radical philosophy by means of which its urban working-class adherents sought to substitute a cooperative economy for the mercantile and industrial capitalism of the day.

Between 1876 and 1884 greenbackism gave its name and philosophy to a third party which struggled, with limited success, to bring farmers and laborers together under the banner of antimonopolism. For labor organizations like the Knights, and for the earliest Farmers' Alliances, this third-party movement posed a particularly thorny organizational problem: should they endorse directly a movement of political insurgency that espoused an agenda virtually identical to its own? Most such groups, including the Knights, kept partisan politics outside their meeting rooms for fear they would split the brotherhood, even though many of their members participated under other auspices. Terence Powderly was a vehement foe of direct Knights involvement in insurgency: "Let politics alone" was his rule. Yet Powderly himself was elected mayor of Scranton on the Greenback-Labor ticket in 1878 and was serving as mayor when he became Grand Master Workman.

Even with the sharpening of industrial conflict in the depression of the 1870s, radicalism or producerism never acquired the hard edge of proletarian class consciousness, but it did enable farmers and workers to imagine, collectively, an alternative to the domination of labor by capital, to the "wage slavery" of the industrial revolution and the tyranny of money loaned at interest. As late as the 1880s and 1890s, radicalism remained plastic enough to express the shared values and aspirations of the various classes of Americans living in the "island communities" of the nation's heartland. That is to say, radicalism was a bulwark for the protection of neighborhood and family, the familiar and the familial, against the powerful intrusion of far-off monopolies.

Protest movements are not static. They grow and respond to the changing conditions of the people whose common history created them. The "genetic materials" of Populism's movement culture were present in the embryonic movements of the 1870s, but that culture itself was to be shaped over the next two decades by events, in particular the economic jolts that farmers and workers experienced in the decade beginning in 1885 and the response of the dominant culture to their cries for help.

Both branches of the Farmers' Alliance which trace their roots to 1877 drew their identity from the various strands of this movement culture, but in different ways. The northern variant, transplanted in 1880 from western New York to Chicago by farm editor Milton George, drew on only some of the traditions of protest that we have examined. According to George, this Alliance was based on the idea that "an open organization among farmers would be a grand aid to the Grange in bringing farmers together for mutual protection," by which he meant nonpartisan political advocacy, especially railroad regulation.

George financed the new order out of his own pocket. He advertised it through his paper, the *Western Rural*, and issued charters to individuals or farm clubs interested in affiliating with his organization. Through the liberal distribution of memberships (no dues were required), George was able by 1881 to claim 24,500 members for the National Farmers' Alliance, most of them concentrated in Kansas and Nebraska and in other midwestern states. Interest in the organization declined as rapidly as it had risen, and no meetings of the national body were held between 1883 and 1886. By the latter year, a revived and growing National Farmers' Alliance was helping to channel the burgeoning farmers' revolt in the northern Plains.

By 1886 the Texas-based Alliance which traced its roots to John Allen's farm had broken out of its frontier enclave. Just as the geography and agriculture of South and West converged in the territory beyond Fort Worth, so too did the strands of the movement culture that we have observed. Those who joined the Farmers' Alliance in its infancy were touched by all of them.

The Lampasas Alliance survived only for a couple of years, but in 1879 one of its members, a Georgia-born rural schoolteacher, William Baggett, took its constitution with him when he moved one hundred miles north to the village of Poolville, in Parker County. There he started a school and a Farmers' Alliance, recruiting into the latter small farmers and stockmen very much like John Allen's neighbors.

In 1879, Parker County and neighboring Wise County contained all the elements of the movement culture, including a violent strain of vigilantism. During the Civil War the western Cross Timbers, like parts of rural Missouri, had been contested by Union and Confederate sympathizers. In Wise County, five Unionists were hanged in 1863 amidst a wave of lynching that swept across northern Texas. After the war, vigilantism took many forms. In 1872 the widow of a murdered Unionist was killed by vigilantes, along with her five daughters. Their home was thought to be a center of prostitution and a meeting place for horse thieves.

Violence broke out over disputed land titles, with settlers banding together to protect their claims against land syndicates. In 1883 and 1884 the fencing controversy reached the Cross Timbers with violent consequences. A message left on a pile of uprooted fence posts in Parker County tells the story:

> We understand you have plenty of money to spend to build fences. Please put them up again for us to cut them down again. We want the fence guarded with good men so their mettle can be tested.

This country even had its own version of Jesse James, an Indiana-born farmhand named Sam Bass, who raced fine horses on the streets of Denton and robbed the Texas & Pacific Railroad for a living. He was known as the Robin Hood of the Cross Timbers, and his exploits created the same legends of social banditry as his more famous Missouri counterpart. According to Bass's biographer, supposed hideouts of his gang became "almost as numerous as George Washington beds in Virginia," and there were countless stories of farm families (often headed by a poor widow) who hid Sam Bass and were repaid with stolen $20 gold pieces.

Texas was also home to 40,000 Patrons of Husbandry at the height of the Grange movement and boasted one of the strongest Grange business agencies, the Texas Co-operative Association. Although Grange membership was concentrated in the richer cotton lands of northeastern and central Texas, the Patrons of Husbandry also reached the frontier. Lampasas County had two subordinate Granges, and several early Alliancemen belonged to the order, including William Baggett.

By the early 1880s, the Knights of Labor had arrived in the Cross Timbers and was aggressively organizing farmers, artisans, railroad workers, and coal miners (from the mines at Gordon and Thurber which supplied the Texas & Pacific.) By 1885 and 1886 the majority of members in some local assemblies were farmers who also belonged to the Alliance. During that crucial period, the two organizations remained separate, but with such overlapping membership that the differences were almost moot.

The birthplaces of the Texas Alliance were also strongholds of the Greenback Party. A Greenback club was organized in Lampasas in 1878, and in that year the infant Alliance decided, by split vote, to endorse the new party. In 1880 the Greenback slate for county offices included two Alliance leaders. Similarly, the Alliance's home in Parker and Wise counties was a center of Greenbackism, although issues related to landownership seemed to interest them as much as financial reform. A visitor reported in July 1880 that there were "Greenbackers by the 'wholesale' around here." Some of those Greenbackers were Alliance lead-

ers, including William Forster, editor of a Greenback newspaper which was the first paper to champion the Alliance, and
S. O. Daws, about whom more later.

Finally, the community around Poolville experienced its own
particular alienation from the larger community. It had been a
stronghold of the Union League during Reconstruction, and during the land boom of the mid-1870s the community filled up with
poor farmers from the South and Midwest who were treated with
contempt by more prosperous farmers in southern Parker County
and by bankers, merchants, and editors in the county seat of
Weatherford, who branded them as shiftless, lawless, and bad
credit risks.

The infant Alliance came under attack from those who viewed
it as a dangerous secret society. Its members were accused of
being "Molly Maguires, Anarchists, and Communists." The order
defended itself against charges of lawlessness, but there may have
been some truth to them, for it almost certainly used force, or
the threat of force, in battling land company agents, fencers, and
rustlers. Even the resolution adopted by Alliancemen and townsmen at a mass meeting in Weatherford in 1881—a meeting called
to resolve the charges of Alliance vigilantism—did not exactly
exonerate the order: "While we acknowledge that there may be
a few unprincipled men who are members of the Farmers' Alliance . . . we most emphatically deny that the Alliance, as a
body, recognizes mob law or anything that is not in strict ac-
cordance with the laws of our state."

If the census enumerator could have been called as a character
witness for the Alliance members, he would have testified (as the
census returns for 1880 indicate) that they were fairly representative of the settlers struggling to make a go of it in the Cross
Timbers and broken prairies west of Fort Worth. General farming
and stock raising were the rule for them, with cotton patches
only beginning to whiten the bottomlands. Furthermore, by accepting a constitution typical of fraternal orders and voluntary

associations, members of the Alliance were trying to cover themselves with the mantle of respectability that membership in such groups typically provided.

The plan of organization that William Baggett brought with him from Lampasas encompassed a network of neighborhood lodges, called subordinate Alliances, where members gathered behind closed doors to repeat the rituals of the order, discuss the affairs of the day, and lay plans for action. The Alliance's "secret work" was modified from the rituals of the Grange and would have been generally familiar to members of any fraternal order. Some of the original secret signs and passwords were directly related to the initial activity of the organization, locating strays and apprehending rustlers.

The Alliance sought to restrict its membership to people of good character who were part of the "producing class." The earliest constitution limited membership to men and women who believed in a supreme being and were of industrious habits, and who were either a "farmer, farm laborer, a country mechanic, a country merchant, a country school teacher, a country physician, or a minister of the gospel." Beginning in 1882, the constitution limited membership to whites, although there is no evidence of blacks having belonged to the order before then. Racial exclusivity was a common feature of fraternal and even labor organizations of the time, and the addition of such a clause to the Alliance's constitution seems to have reflected a filling in of the gaps in that document rather than a change of policy.

In its earliest days the Alliance fit into the existing network of family and community organizations in rural Parker and Wise counties. Many of the earliest members were related by blood or marriage. Early expansion of the movement followed familiar paths of trade and immigration. (The first subordinate lodges outside the Poolville-Springtown communities were established in neighboring Jack County among people who had just moved there from Poolville.) Most of the early recruiters were, like

Baggett, men of proven experience in organizing and leading community organizations. Some were teachers, one was a physician who had organized a neighborhood Sunday school, others were preachers.

Rural ministers understood the plight of their parishioners because most of them were farmers too. When the Alliance entered Wise County, Mississippi-born S. O. Daws, for example, had been operating a small farm there for a decade, as well as serving as a lay preacher. Almost immediately, he was sought out by his neighbor Dr. O. G. Peterson (the physician–Sunday school superintendent) to serve as an organizer for the Alliance.

In the 1880s many farm organizations popped up in the South and West, but their life expectancy was short. The Alliance that William Baggett brought to Parker and Wise counties very nearly died as quickly as its Lampasas antecedent. By the summer of 1883, only 30 of the 140 suballiances were functioning, and the "state" organization had ceased to meet. However, three years later the Alliance not only had been rejuvenated in the frontier counties but had swept across northern and central Texas, enrolling over 90,000 members, and was poised to expand across the South and the Great Plains.

In part, the resurgence was due to the efforts of individuals like S. O. Daws, and we shall want to look closely at their work. But first, note the context of the Alliance's revitalization. In 1883 two railroads cut across the Cross Timbers, drawing farmers much more deeply into commercial cotton production. In 1883 and 1884 the fence wars reached their peak. In several frontier counties "antimonopoly" parties emerged, using the issues of fencing, land, and greenbacks to challenge Democrats for local office. By 1885 the Knights of Labor was intertwined with the Alliance both in membership and in agenda. Finally, Texas farmers were aware that this moment of Alliance resurgence coincided with the birth of similar groups in the lower Mississippi Valley and a reawakening of farmer organization in the Great Plains under the aegis of the Chicago-based Farmers' Alliance. Farther north, the Manitoba Farmers' Union was mobilizing Canadian wheat growers under the antimonopoly banner.

In January 1884, William Garvin, president of the Texas Alliance, appointed his neighbor S. O. Daws to the new position of "traveling lecturer," with authority to revive old suballiances, create new ones, and deputize additional organizers. Within three months, Daws and his assistants had stirred up the Alliance in its home territory and were spreading the Alliance message to farmers all across northern Texas.

Daws and his cadre of assistants visited one farming community after another, always with the same twofold message. Daws reiterated both his points at the state Alliance meeting in February 1884, barely a month after he had begun his work. First, he introduced a motion declaring that the state body would "encourage the formation of joint stock companies in Sub and County Alliances." Second, he delivered a rousing speech (probably a formal version of his standard talk to suballiances) on "the condition of American farmers as a class and their duties as American citizens." Daws reminded the members of "their obligation to stand as a great conservative body against the encroachments of monopolies and in opposition to the growing corruption of wealth and power."

Daws's first act set the Alliance on a course of cooperative enterprise. His second act defined the order's campaign of political education, placing it squarely within the tradition of producerism.

We should not be misled by the appeal to patriotism and Daws's depiction of the Alliance as a "conservative body." As Norman Pollack has noted, one powerful source of Populist ideology

lay in its literalist approach to America. . . . Populists espoused an unashamed patriotism . . . in which America became the source of a permanent standard. The love of country was fashioned into an argument for the democratic control of economic affairs.

Similarly, the "conservative" label, which Alliancemen and Populists repeatedly applied to themselves, locates them in the same spot on the social spectrum as the Knights of Labor, who occupied, according to Bruce Laurie, "a middle ground between the individualistic libertarianism of bourgeois America and the collectivism of working-class socialists."

Before the Populist movement had run its course little more than a decade later, it would include people with a broad range of views, from committed socialists to opportunistic office seekers with only the slightest opposition to the emerging industrial order. But Daws's classical formulation of antimonopolism and producerism identifies the core of Populist thought. This was the "class" appeal of the Alliance: not the class consciousness of the proletariat, but the shared experience of producers.

If Daws's exegesis of antimonopolism enabled Alliancemen to name their enemy, his motion to establish "joint stock companies" gave them something concrete to do about their problem. Within a year members of suballiances and county Alliances had tried most of the standard forms of cooperation, including trade agreements with local merchants, establishment of joint-stock stores (which sold goods to members at an immediate discount), and formation of Rochdale-style purchasing and marketing cooperatives. The most ambitious of the Rochdale ventures was the Alliance store at Rhome, a combination cotton yard, grain elevator, lumberyard, and general store. By 1886 the Alliance had also launched several cooperative flour mills in the wheat-growing areas of northern Texas, the first of which was a joint-stock venture in Denton.

The most dramatic cooperative undertaking in those early years was the campaign to market cotton in bulk. By 1884 the system of buying cotton at interior points on the rail lines (described in Chapter 1) had reached the little towns of the Cross Timbers.

Alliance members achieved some successes by sticking together in dealing with the buyers. On one October day in 1884, 2,000 Alliance members from Wise and surrounding counties descended on Decatur with 3,000 bales of cotton to sell through the Alliance yard. Taking the buyers by surprise, they were able to command a slightly higher price than the going rate.

In 1885 the Alliance announced an even more ambitious marketing plan, to sell directly to textile manufacturers from the Alliance cotton yards. This time they were not so successful. Negotiations with manufacturers broke down, and local buyers dug in and presented a united front against the Alliance. Simultaneously, Alliance business agents were reporting that wholesalers and manufacturers were refusing to do business with the cooperatives, particularly when it involved extending credit. Without credit, many of the farmers simply could not participate.

These setbacks did not slow the growth of the Alliance; indeed, the pace of expansion quickened. However, the sense of confrontation with the united forces of capital gave new meaning to Daws's lessons on "the encroachment of monopolies" and "the growing corruption of wealth and power." That same lesson was driven home in 1885 and 1886 by the machinations of a real live monopolist, the railroad magnate Jay Gould.

By 1885 Gould's Southwestern system dominated rail service in Texas. It included the Texas & Pacific, which traversed the state east to west, passing through the frontier home of the Alliance and the East Texas cotton lands that were becoming Alliance country. Texas farmers and merchants cheered when machinists in Sedalia, Missouri, struck the hated Gould system in March 1885 and, with widespread community support in Missouri, forced the restitution of wage cuts and reinstatement of longtime employees who had been summarily dismissed.

The workers' victory boosted membership of the Knights of Labor throughout the Gould system, and nowhere more so than in Texas. The Knights had not initiated the 1885 strike, but under the leadership of machinist Martin Irons they stepped in to form "a broad and comprehensive union for labor on a basis that would counterbalance the power of aggregated and incorporated wealth." All along the line of the T&P, the Knights recruited new members by the thousands, paralleling the astounding growth of the Alliance in the same territory.

In the summer of 1885, local assemblies of the Knights and the Alliance jointly sponsored mass meetings, picnics, and barbecues. They even explored plans for joint operation of cooperative stores. Fraternal greetings were exchanged at the state meetings of the two orders, and the state Alliance adopted a resolution anticipating that "a perfect unity of action may at an early day be effected between the K. of L. and the Farmers' Alliance." This resolution was put to the test the following January, when pro-Knights Alliancemen, led by business agent William R. Lamb, supported a Knights boycott of the Mallory Steamship Line in Galveston and the Dallas dry-goods firm of Sanger Brothers. Having failed to win the support of manufacturers and wholesalers for Alliance cooperatives, Lamb saw it this way:

Knowing that the day is not far distant when the Farmers' Alliance will have to use Boycotts on manufacturers in order to get goods direct, we think it is a good time to help the Knights of Labor in order to secure their help in the near future.

More cautious Alliance leaders, including the state president, Andy Dunlap, bitterly opposed involving the Alliance in these labor disputes, but even while the two sides were arguing the point through the columns of Alliance newspapers, the young farmers' movement was caught up in a far greater and more violent labor dispute. A second strike against the Gould system broke out on March 10, 1886.

This strike, which began in Marshall, Texas, was not as well supported by Missouri unionists and their sympathizers as the one in 1885. Sensing the lack of unity, Gould's agents moved to crush both the strike and the Knights. Less able to rely on mass community support than the year before, striking workers disrupted freight service by disabling engines and threatening nonstrikers. Rural support for the strike was strongest in Texas. Along the route of the Gould lines Alliancemen showed their solidarity by donating food and money to the strikers and by holding joint rallies with them.

Nevertheless, the strike failed, in part for lack of specific and well-articulated grievances among the workers. Eugene Debs of the Brotherhood of Locomotive Firemen said Irons' strike call was "hasty and rash." On May 3, Terence Powderly officially called off the strike, but it had in fact already been lost.

May 3 was a momentous day in American labor history on another count. In Chicago, policemen fired on striking workers who were taking part in a nationwide work stoppage in support of the eight-hour day. Four strikers were killed. The following day a bomb exploded in Haymarket Square at the conclusion of a peaceful rally called to protest police brutality. Eight policemen were killed. Although the identity of the bomber was never discovered, four anarchists were executed for the act, and the labor movement in general was blamed for it. The Knights of Labor was among the principal casualties.

In the long view of things, the prospects of a farmer-labor coalition in America were drastically diminished by the events of May 1886, both in Chicago and in the Southwest. One need only imagine how much stronger that coalition would have been by the summer of 1886 if the eight-hour movement had prevailed in the nation's industrial centers, if there had been no explosion in Haymarket Square, and if the second strike against Gould's Southwestern system had been won. But at the moment, the dimensions of their lost opportunity were not clear to the participants, and they pressed ahead with their plans.

During the Gould strike, many local Alliances had issued proclamations like this one from Red River County: "[We] sympathize deeply in the misfortunes of the Knights of Labor in their struggle to feed and clothe their families, and ask them to meet us at the ballot box and help overthrow all monopolies." In 1886, farmers and workers were both engaged in a "struggle to feed and clothe their families." Their aspirations for a cooperative commonwealth and "a broad and comprehensive union for labor" led many of them toward a movement of political insurgency based on antimonopolism.

Farmers and workers fielded independent tickets in at least twenty counties across northern Texas in 1886. Their platforms, such as the one agreed to by the Laboring Men's Convention of Wise County, put them squarely within the tradition of the National Labor Union, the Reading platform of the Knights of Labor, and the Greenback Party. They demanded such things as state laws to prevent large-scale engrossment of land, abolition of convict labor, federal control over the money supply, and creation of an Interstate Commerce Commission to regulate railroads.

Political alignment with the Knights of Labor, based on antimonopoly greenbackism and aimed at electing independent local slates, was a reasonable outgrowth of the Alliance's formative experience, but it posed a familiar organizational threat. Partisan politics had killed the Lampasas Alliance. In rural communities where Democrats outnumbered Greenbackers, the Alliance, like other voluntary associations, risked fatal divisions by direct endorsement of insurgency. To avoid this trap, the Alliance employed a device that trade unionists had used since the 1840s. As S. O. Daws explained it three weeks after the collapse of the Gould strike, the Alliance itself should remain a nonpartisan agency for political education, but in each neighborhood Alliancemen should help establish "antimonopoly leagues" to nominate candidates for office.

Many local Alliances followed Daws's plan, sometimes to the confusion of local Democrats. The editor of the Palo Pinto *Star* praised Alliance lecturer W. F. Westellison for saying that it was "contrary to the principles of the Farmers' Alliance to go into politics and if we ever prosper we must stand aloof of all political bearing *as an organization*" (italics added). Meanwhile, Westellison was busy organizing an insurgent coalition among farmers, artisans, coal miners, and railroad workers who belonged to the Alliance and the Knights of Labor.

The spring and summer of 1886 was a time of intense activity and incredible strain within the Alliance. While Alliancemen in their neighborhood, county, and state assemblies dealt with the strike and political insurgency, they were also chartering new Alliances at a rapid rate, establishing new cooperative ventures, and carrying out an ambitious program of drought relief. A crippling drought hit West Texas but spared farmers to the east. The Dallas *Mercury*, a labor and Alliance paper, arranged for the shipment of wheat and cornmeal from suballiances in East Texas to Alliance families west of Fort Worth.

All these matters came under consideration when the state Alliance convened for its annual meeting in August. Delegates from eighty-four counties descended on the little town of Cleburne, bringing with them the hopes and fears of rural Texans. For the first time the Alliance's deliberations were covered by reporters from metropolitan newspapers. The issue that would dominate the convention and split the Alliance was politics. Many Alliance members steadfastly opposed political alignment with the Knights in the form of running joint candidates in local elections, even when the order's nonpartisan status was safeguarded by the Daws formula.

On the other hand, the dynamics of the movement was pushing the Alliance toward political positions that could hardly be accommodated within the two-party system. At Cleburne a special committee of the state Alliance called for adoption of political demands that had a distinctly radical ring to them. The Cleburne platform, drafted by the insurgents who had cobbled together political platforms for the local "antimonopoly leagues," emphasized the application of equal rights principles to issues of land, labor, transportation, and finance. Particular schemes for eliminating special privilege in these areas were expressed as legislative demands. After hours of intense debate and parliamentary maneuvering, the demands were adopted by a vote of 92 to 75.

The Cleburne demands stand as a direct antecedent of the great Populist platforms of the 1890s. They reflected the searing experience of men and women mobilized into the Alliance in the preceding two years. The document did not, however, spring full-blown from the meeting houses of the Farmers' Alliance at the forks of the creek. If it was, as Lawrence Goodwyn contends, "the first major document of the agrarian revolt," it was also a reaffirmation of the antimonopoly creed passed down through generations of labor radicals. Its main points were even then being reiterated in other gatherings of farmers and laborers in the South and the Great Plains.

All but four of the fifteen substantive demands made at Cleburne were essentially the same as points addressed in the 1878 Reading preamble of the Knights of Labor, which was itself a recapitulation of earlier antimonopoly platforms. Both the Cleburne and Reading documents affirm the importance of cooperatives; both affirm greenback monetary policies (although this point was somewhat muted in the Cleburne document for the sake of Alliance harmony); both upheld, in a variety of ways, the principle of equal protection for the rights of labor and capital; both were devoted to the principle that land should be reserved for actual settlers, not speculators; both call for the establishment of a National Bureau of Labor Statistics and for the protection of laborers' rights to their wages through payment in legal tender and through mechanics' and laborers' liens; both oppose the use of prison contract labor.

Of the four Cleburne demands not addressed in the Reading preamble, two dealt with agricultural matters of recent interest (one to outlaw dealing in futures in agricultural commodities and the other to remove illegally placed fences), a third called for the establishment of an Interstate Commerce Commission to regulate the railroads, and the fourth for "minting of silver and gold to full capacity and offering both without discrimination."

Through the Cleburne demands the Alliance would introduce itself, politically, to farmers and laborers of the South and West. The familiar antimonopolism of the Cleburne demands would ease the entrée of the Texas order into communities of like-minded folk elsewhere. Furthermore, while the document evoked traditional themes of producerism, it also anticipated a greatly expanded role for the state in protecting the rights of farmers and laborers. Finally, the Cleburne program for political education was embedded in an *organization* that combined fraternal and evangelical appeals and a promising cooperative system.

Of course, the Cleburne minority and the wing of the Alliance they represented would not have been impressed by these points. After the final vote on the political demands, a group of them met to establish a rival "Grand State Farmers' Alliance." What was worse, the treasurer went with them, and with him the funds of the state Alliance. It looked as if the Alliance was about to meet the fate of its Lampasas predecessor.

But for all that divided the two wings of the Alliance, they still had a great deal in common. An inventory of the shared assets of the order (not including funds in the hands of the decamped treasurer), would show there was hope for its survival.

The two warring camps believed, with equal fervor, in the efficacy and moral correctness of the cooperatives. And for all their differences about politics, both accepted the broad tenets of antimonopolism. As one astute participant in the Cleburne meeting observed many years later, the minority objected to the Cleburne demands "not because of opposition to their substance, but because many felt it was a [partisan] political move."

That participant observer was himself one of the Alliance's principal assets in the aftermath of Cleburne. Charles William Macune, a thirty-five-year-old Milam County physician and onetime farmhand, cowboy, circus clown, newspaper editor, and lay Methodist preacher, stepped forward to assume the role of mediator once played by S. O. Daws. He was elected chairman of the state executive committee at Cleburne and then became acting president when the conservative Andy Dunlap resigned.

A less likely candidate to save the Alliance would be hard to imagine. Macune had been a member of the Alliance for only four months before being chosen as a delegate to the Cleburne convention. One of the thousands of Texans swept up into the Alliance during the Gould strike, Macune had in that same month lost part of his landholdings in Milam County to foreclosure.

Wisconsin-born and Illinois-raised, Macune seemed more like the quintessential town booster and frontier promoter than the leader of a militant farmers' organization. He "read" medicine and later law prior to practicing those professions in the little towns of central Texas. As editor of a tiny newspaper in the frontier town of Burnet, he praised the Democrats, cussed the carpetbaggers, and purveyed commonplace booster rhetoric about railroads, town building, and the weather. (Sitting on the edge of the semi-arid West, he advised farmers to plant trees to increase rainfall.)

But look a little closer. A well-read, self-taught man, master of several languages (German and Czech were both useful in those central Texas towns), a Mason and joiner of civic enterprises, handsome and gregarious, Macune, like Oliver Kelley and Terence Powderly, was typical of the men who could be counted on to organize and lead whatever new association came to their town and whose sense of the moral economy tended toward producerism.

Macune's political memories stretched back to a childhood introduction to Lincoln and Douglas just before their debate in his hometown of Freeport, Illinois. He was a Democrat, but like many small-town boosters of his era he was deeply influenced by greenbackism. He read deeply in monetary theory, understood the nuances of greenback dogma, and would himself contribute to its development. To remain a Democrat and a greenbacker would require some fancy footwork. In electoral politics and the internal politics of the Alliance, Macune was a clever tactician— sometimes *too* clever.

But that is getting ahead of the story. In the months following the Cleburne schism, Macune managed to mediate between the warring factions (he had not been around long enough to be identified with either one) and to lead the Alliance to adopt an ambitious program of statewide economic cooperatives and expansion of the Alliance beyond Texas. Macune's vision for the Alliance was large, but no larger than those of the farmers who still had faith that the cooperative commonwealth could destroy monopoly power and those of the boosters who believed that their little town could become the next St. Louis. The good doctor's vision contained a little bit of both, as we shall see.

3

The Farmers' Alliance in Search of the Cooperative Commonwealth, 1887–89

At the beginning of 1887, ten years after the Great Strike and the founding of the Farmers' Alliances, the agrarian movement in America consisted of many separate islands of protest scattered across the South and West. Farmers' Alliances in Texas and the Plains states, the Farmers' Mutual Benefit Association in the Midwest, the Agricultural Wheel in the lower Mississippi Valley, and rural assemblies of the Knights of Labor were giving voice to the anger and the hope of rural Americans.

Simultaneously, in almost two hundred cities across the land local workingmen's parties had translated the antimonopoly tradition into third-party politics, most notably in New York City, where in 1886 Henry George ran second in the mayoral race as the United Labor Party candidate. (George ran well ahead of the Republican candidate, young Theodore Roosevelt.)

By 1887 it was possible to imagine the consolidation of urban and rural protest groups into a permanent cooperative movement and labor party. By the end of 1889 it looked as if these disparate groups would merge into one grand army of producers, confident of its ability to usher in the cooperative commonwealth. However, the rapid growth of organized protest masked huge differences of culture and self-interest.

This story of convergence and growth begins in many places,

including Texas, where at last report C. W. Macune was trying to reunite the warring factions of the Farmers' Alliance. At a peace conference in November 1886, Macune guided the contending parties toward agreement on two bold initiatives, expanding the Alliance beyond Texas and creating a statewide system of cooperative purchasing and marketing.

The expansion campaign began immediately with the absorption of a much smaller Louisiana group into the Alliance (now grandly styled the National Farmers' Alliance and Co-operative Union with Macune as president) and with the formulation of "a method of sending representatives into other States of the Union, for the purpose of organizing and co-operating with other agricultural societies."

Macune left no doubt about the message he expected these representatives to carry across the South. Noting that "all the different classes and occupations of society are engaging in organization for mutual advancement," Macune declared that

> co-operation, properly understood and properly applied, will place a limit to the encroachments of organized monopoly, and will be the means by which the mortgage-burdened farmers can assert their freedom from the tyranny of organized capital.

During its period of rapid growth in 1885 and 1886, the Texas Alliance had concentrated on local cooperation in purchasing and marketing. Now in 1887 the assembled delegates endorsed a plan to appoint a business agent who would purchase supplies and negotiate cotton sales on a statewide basis. To the surprise of no one, the man selected to head the business agency was C. W. Macune.

Macune developed an ambitious scheme of centralized purchasing and marketing that would, unlike the Rochdale-style co-operatives of the Grange, sell goods to members at costs only slightly above wholesale and would extend credit in the form of "joint notes" co-signed by needy members of the various sub-alliances and their more prosperous neighbors. Each member of the Texas Alliance was expected to pay two dollars into a capital fund for the Exchange. Operating on two shaky assumptions (that there were 250,000 active members of the Alliance and that each of them would pay the two dollars), Macune anticipated a capital fund of $500,000.

The hopes of Texas farmers, the rhetoric of Macune, and the early hints of cooperative success emboldened Alliance members to believe that the Exchange might actually break the grip of the middleman and eradicate the crop-lien system. The city of Dallas, hoping to become a regional wholesale hub by whatever means necessary, provided land and promised cash for the honor of hosting the Exchange.

In a bold move to bypass local cotton buyers and the powerful cotton exchanges in Dallas and New Orleans, the Alliance Exchange implemented a system of cotton grading and an elaborate scheme for telegraphically communicating world market prices directly and in secret to local Alliances. By this means Macune was able to arrange for the sale of a significant portion of Alliance members' 1887 cotton crop directly to buyers in New England and Europe. For a tantalizing moment it looked as if large-scale cooperative marketing would allow the Alliance to appropriate for its own use the tools of communication, transportation, and credit employed by "organized monopoly."

However, when the joint-note system was put to the test in 1888 it soon became apparent that the Exchange lacked the capital necessary to finance bulk purchases of supplies or to move the cotton crop. Dallas officials delivered only a small fraction of the promised funds, a mere $20,000 of the anticipated $500,000 had been paid into the capital fund, and bankers refused to issue loans based on the joint notes.

On June 9, Alliancemen gathered in courthouses and meeting halls across the state in a desperate effort to raise sufficient funds to keep the Exchange solvent, but to no avail. The Exchange halted the joint-note program and tried to retrench, but its leaders could not prevent its liquidation in 1889.

Macune and his associates claimed that Texas bankers and merchants had conspired to kill the exchange. Macune's critics within the Alliance blamed the debacle on his mismanagement. Both explanations have merit, but the overwhelming reality was that the Alliance had taken on the impossible task, given their meager capital resources, of attacking head-on the credit system that dominated southern agriculture.

Despite its brief and finally sad career, the Texas Exchange influenced the course of the agrarian movement. Its ambitious plans and the *promise* of relief that it held out were at the heart of the message Alliance organizers took across the Southeast in 1887 and 1888, and its failure was duly noted by Alliance leaders in the southern states before they launched their own statewide cooperatives. Some of those southern leaders responded by acting more prudently with regard to credit. Some of them, like Macune, saw in the failure of the Texas Exchange further proof that the system was rigged against the farmer.

The ambitious cooperative marketing scheme of the Texas Alliance had been necessarily coupled with a second major goal, mobilization of cotton farmers across the South under the Alliance banner. Texas farmers could not alter the terms of trade by themselves. "As the interests of the cotton-producers were identical, and the evils from which they were suffering general," Macune later recalled, "the greatest good could not be effected without uniting the whole cotton belt."

Every fall the cotton South experienced collectively what many thousands experienced individually: the humiliation of being unable to "hold" the crop and bargain for a better price. That loss of control, for one farmer or for the whole South, meant loss of income in an unforgiving world of commercial transactions, and what is more, the loss of *independence* in the republican sense of that word. The serious but ultimately futile attempts of the cooperatives to provide the short-term credit necessary for farmers to hold the crop led many of those same farmers to demand that the federal government provide loans based on the value of their stored cotton and other commodities.

Put in its broadest political terms, southern farmers faced with this economic dilemma envisioned cooperative marketing and political activism as part of the same antimonopoly solution. And though the former was more prominent in the Alliance's strategy for southern expansion, the articulation of political solutions was never entirely absent from the movement. The same gathering of Alliancemen that established the Texas Exchange also reaffirmed the Cleburne demands, even adding planks on nationalization of telephone and telegraph systems, a graduated income tax, and direct election of United States senators. They understood that there was more than one way to "assert their freedom from the tyranny of organized capital."

We should not imagine, however, that the farmers in the grand army that spread across the South in 1887 were all marching to the beat of the same radical drummer. Far from comprising a unified movement, the Alliance's whirlwind campaign of mobilization absorbed two different traditions that were embodied in two distinct kinds of rural organizations.

On the one hand, state agricultural societies, farmers' associations, and the National Cotton Planters' Association represented the interests of the new planter class described in Chapter 1. While planters might rail against the tyranny of *foreign* capital, they did not wish to disturb traditional relationships of social deference or political and economic power at home.

On the other hand, groups like the Agricultural Wheel in the lower Mississippi Valley, the Farmers' Relief in Mississippi, and the rural assemblies of the Knights of Labor in the Carolinas viewed with suspicion elite farmers, even in their own neighborhoods. These grass-roots movements of the rural poor kept alive the tradition of the Reconstruction-era Union League. Initially biracial in membership, they articulated the anger of black and white tenant farmers and laborers. In cooperation with the town-based assemblies of Knights (made up primarily of skilled craftsmen and some textile workers), they formed the core of southern political insurgency in 1886, achieving, among other successes, the election to Congress of John Nichols, State Master Workman of the Knights of Labor in North Carolina.

Let two individuals speak for these genteel and dirt-farmer traditions in the rural South—one a substantial planter, an advocate of scientific agriculture, and a Tarheel born and bred; the other a Canadian-born émigré to Arkansas, a machinist and farmer, and an inveterate organizer of farmers and laborers. Both found their way into the Farmers' Alliance, but by different routes and to different ends.

Elias Carr was born in 1839 on his family's plantation in eastern North Carolina. Educated at the University of North Carolina and the University of Virginia, he took charge of the family estate at the age of twenty and settled into the role of progressive agriculturalist, country squire, and community leader. In 1887, Carr became founding president of the North Carolina Farmers' State Association, an elite-dominated organization whose main function was to lobby for the formation of a state agricultural college. When the college opened (it is now North Carolina State University), Carr was named to its board of trustees.

Just as the Farmers' Association was reaching the height of its appeal for Tarheel farmers, the first Alliance organizers appeared from Texas. Carr and other Association leaders decided to join rather than fight. Technically speaking, the Alliance absorbed the Association, but in fact, much of the old leadership, including Carr, simply exchanged one vehicle for another.

Carr took a personal interest in the cooperative work. He oversaw the establishment of a state business agency that, though aggressive in securing goods at wholesale for Alliance members, operated strictly on a cash basis. The agency may have been fiscally sound (unlike the Texas Exchange), but it was of no use to farmers like the one who wrote to Carr in 1890: "How can a poor, honest, industrious farmer trade through the Alliance without cash?"

Carr was elected president of the North Carolina state Alliance in 1890, at a moment when the farmers' movement of the South and West was facing fundamental choices about cooperation with labor in the cause of antimonopoly politics. Perhaps worried about a resurgence of the Knights of Labor's radical coalition under the banner of the Alliance, Carr refused to admit railroad workers to the order, even those who owned farms.

While endorsing in principle the political demands of the Farmers' Alliance, in 1890 Carr opposed those who fought to make acceptance of the demands a litmus test in the reelection campaign of his friend Democratic senator Zebulon Vance. In 1892, when North Carolina Alliancemen divided among themselves on whether to cast their lot with the new People's Party, Carr stayed with the party of the fathers—the Democratic Party—and was elected governor.

Elias Carr, planter and Democratic Party stalwart, may not have been typical of Alliance leaders across the South, but he did represent an important element in the leadership of the movement. The ready assimilation of local notables like Carr into the Alliance helps to explain how the Texas-based order gained such quick access to existing channels of communication and means of influence across the South. The business and organizational skills of these men contributed to the success of the Alliance in mobilizing a great army of southern farmers. At the same time their presence in the councils of leadership would blunt the sharp edge of the southern farmers' movement.

Isaac McCracken followed a different path to leadership in the Alliance. He was born in Quebec in 1846, but his family moved to Lowell, Massachusetts, when he was eight. Like Terence Powderly and Charles Macune, McCracken tried his hand at a number of trades. He escaped from an apprenticeship as a stonecutter to ship out as a common sailor on a whaling vessel, then returned to Lowell to become a machinist. As a young man he joined the Blacksmiths' and Machinists' Union, where he came to know Powderly. McCracken's craft took him from Massachusetts to Wisconsin and finally to Arkansas, where he worked in the Little Rock machine shops of the Iron Mountain Railroad. In the 1870s he took up farming, and then he began organizing Arkansas farmers and laborers.

In 1882, McCracken founded the Brothers of Freedom, a secret society that merged in 1885 with another grass-roots organization of Arkansas farmers, the Agricultural Wheel. The radical greenback editor Mark L. Pomeroy of Chicago observed of the Brothers of Freedom in 1885 that its "objective is to combine together farmers and laboring men for the purpose of social intercourse and to lessen the burdens of the members by . . . avoiding the crop mortgage system and purchasing supplies as a body corporate." The Declaration of Principles of the Brothers of Freedom marked it as part of a political tradition with which we are already familiar:

> While it is an established fact that the laboring classes of mankind are the real producers of wealth, we find that they are gradually becoming oppressed by combinations of capital, and the fruits of their toil absorbed by a class who propose not only to live on the labors of others, but to speedily amass fortunes at their expense.

The Brothers of Freedom acted on the principles of producerism through political insurgency as well as business cooperation. During its brief career the Brothers of Freedom embraced greenbackism, and after its merger with the Wheel, McCracken steered the combined group toward the Union Labor Party in Arkansas. With McCracken as state party chairman and president of the Wheel in 1888, the Union Labor Party joined with Republicans in supporting a fusion candidate for governor who nearly won election.

Elias Carr and the Farmers' Association, Isaac McCracken and the Brothers of Freedom: their outlooks overlapped in important ways, and in the first optimistic wave of Alliance organizing it seemed as if they would join hands in the grand army of producers. Events would soon bring to light the limits of their common interests.

In 1887 the Texas-based Farmers' Alliance had within its ranks a corps of veteran recruiters ideally suited for organizing the South. Having mastered the art of mobilizing rural people into churches, lodges, schools, and finally the Alliance, scores of them would now retrace the steps that had brought them to Texas and begin organizing in the states (and sometimes in the very neighborhoods) from which they had emigrated.

S. O. Daws, whose organizing skills had saved the Alliance from oblivion in 1882, returned to his native Mississippi, where within six weeks he had organized twenty-three suballiances and had brought into the Alliance fold the Agricultural Relief, a grassroots movement of hill-country farmers. Buck Barry, former Texas Ranger and veteran of the Mexican War and the Civil War, returned to his native North Carolina, from where he soon reported that "the farmers seem like unto ripe fruit—you can gather them by a gentle shake of the bush."

Before setting out from Texas in March 1887, Daws, Barry, and twenty other organizers met with Macune and a "board of examiners" for an intensive discussion of recruiting methods. "The result of this teachers institute," an Alliance paper reported, "has been to lead to more thorough unity of action in the work of organization, and the men who go out into other states will all teach the same thing in the same manner."

The procedures that they employed in every state of the late Confederacy were remarkably similar. Upon entering a community the organizer sought out local farmers (often targeting neighborhood leaders), explained to them the benefits of the Alliance cooperative system, and organized those who were interested into a suballiance. They instructed them in the "secret work" of the order, helped them establish local cooperatives, and collected the initiation fee from each new member (a portion of which they pocketed as payment for their organizing services).

Initially the work of mobilization was like door-to-door selling. One organizer reported from Georgia that he went from "house to house and from field to field at first to get the best men together that I might talk up an interest in the Alliance." But as word spread of the success of local cooperatives and the promise of even greater benefits to be derived from statewide cooperation, neighborhood groups began convening themselves and asking to be initiated. Local farmers' organizations converted en masse to the Alliance. By the end of 1887, the Alliance was well established in North Carolina, Mississippi, Alabama, and Georgia and had begun work elsewhere in the South.

Those who joined came, by and large, from the middle stratum of the rural South. Landowning farmers of modest means were more likely to join than either tenants or planters. Those members were, we must note, all white, for the Alliance explicitly excluded blacks from membership. The ambiguous relationship between Populism and race, both in the South and in the Far West, forms a continuing theme in the story of the movement. At a time when separate and parallel social institutions for blacks and whites were being formalized throughout the South (including churches, lodges, and self-help groups of all kinds), there sprang up a wide variety of rural organizations for blacks, including a Colored Farmers' National Alliance.

Only tantalizing fragments of this organization's history have survived. This much we do know: Two antecedent groups of the Colored Farmers' National Alliance were founded in Texas in 1886, during the period of rapid expansion of the white order. Although the rank and file and most of the leaders were black, the man chosen as General Superintendent of the black group was Richard Manning Humphrey, a white, South Carolina-born Confederate veteran and Baptist preacher.

Despite his origins, Humphrey might best be compared with

the northern white missionaries who participated in the social and political reconstruction of the South. After the Civil War he farmed and served black Baptist congregations in East Texas, and he may well have been involved in biracial political coalitions in East Texas before the establishment of the Alliance. In 1888, he ran for Congress as the Union Labor candidate, backed by a coalition of rural blacks and whites.

In 1888 and 1889 the Colored Alliance spread across the Gulf states and into the Southeast in a recruiting campaign parallel to that of the white Alliance. Like its white counterpart, the black organization emphasized economic and political cooperation. Southern white Alliance leaders typically learned of the black order only after it had established a presence in their states, and as often as not they greeted the news with suspicion. The Raleigh *Progressive Farmer*, published by Alliance leader Leonidas Polk, announced the presence of the Colored Alliance in North Carolina under a headline reading: "A Nigger in the Woodpile."

White Alliance leaders were uncertain how the parallel order would fit into the web of black community organizations, especially in the Carolinas and the lower Mississippi Valley, where remnants of biracial radicalism still existed. The membership of the Colored Alliance *did* overlap with that of the rural assemblies of the Knights of Labor and with other radical groups, although the percentage of rural blacks who belonged to any of them in the 1880s was probably not large.

The Colored Alliance drew much of its leadership from the network of southern black ministers and community leaders, many of whom were veterans of Reconstruction-era and green-backer political battles. For example, the secretary and lecturer of the North Carolina Colored Alliance, Walter Patillo, was a Baptist minister who in the early 1880s had run for local office on an insurgent ticket in Granville County, a stronghold of the Knights of Labor.

Few if any white Alliancemen could imagine accepting blacks into the sacred circle of their own neighborhood suballiances, for to do so would be to affirm the social equality of the races. But economic and political cooperation with a racially separate order might be another matter. Low cotton prices and high interest rates that beggared both were indeed color-blind. To the extent that rural blacks functioned as farm *operators* and not as farm *laborers* (and only a minority of rural blacks did so), their interests coincided with those of their white neighbors. At its 1888 meeting, the white National Alliance encouraged the state bodies to open their cooperative exchanges to members of the Colored Alliance, and most states did so.

For southern farm operators, white and black, the hope of maintaining financial independence by means of economic cooperation was the preeminent reason for joining the Farmers' Alliance. Local trade arrangements, marketing plans, and cooperative stores sprang up behind the Alliance lecturers wherever they went in the South. But for the Texas organizers, local cooperation was only a stopgap measure. Their goal was to help establish a network of statewide exchanges similar to the one founded by Macune, and through the exchanges to bring the cotton producers of the South into a regional alliance for controlling and marketing the annual crop.

After state Alliance business agents conferred in May 1888, statewide exchanges or business agencies were established in most of the southern states. Not surprisingly, since their meeting took place just as the Texas Exchange was experiencing its fatal crisis, the state agents modified the Texas plan, setting for themselves more modest goals than those of the founders of the Texas Exchange.

The strongest of the new exchanges was the one in Georgia, which had its headquarters in an Atlanta office building provided by the Atlanta *Constitution*. The Georgia Exchange served as a purchasing agent for local Alliances, concentrating on fertilizer and a few other basic items that were to be delivered directly to local Alliances on through bills of lading. The exchange operated on a cash basis but encouraged the county Alliances to extend credit to needy members.

The Georgia Exchange, like most of its counterparts outside Texas, concerned itself mainly with purchasing supplies and had only limited involvement in cotton marketing. However, at least ten cotton warehouses, operated by county Alliances, comprised a loose-knit marketing network in the cotton belt of Georgia. The warehouse at Fort Valley was reported to have gotten the lion's share of the local business in 1888, and on Saturdays during market season the Alliance served dinner "to every man, black and white, who carried a bale of cotton to the Alliance warehouse."

Alliances in other states also engaged in cotton marketing, and the Norfolk Exchange of the Colored Farmers' Alliance solicited sales in eastern North Carolina from both black and white cotton farmers. North Carolina Alliancemen established their own tobacco warehouse at Durham to challenge the domination of the American Tobacco Company in auction sales of bright leaf. Florida Alliance organizer Oswald Wilson, the P. T. Barnum of the cooperative movement, established a branch exchange in New York to market the citrus crop of Florida Alliance members. While in New York, Wilson also tried to establish an Alliance journal to be called the *Wall Street Farmer*. Whether that unlikely venture succeeded is unknown.

One deceptively mundane issue triggered a unified response from Alliance cooperatives throughout the cotton belt—the sharp increase in the price of the burlaplike material used to wrap cotton bales. In 1888 and in the following year a cartel of manufacturers acted in concert to raise the price of jute bagging by over 60 percent. The same cartel, incidentally, monopolized the sale of the binder's twine used by western wheat growers, with similar results. The financial impact on cotton growers, though less than that of high interest or freight rates, was significant. And, as a congressional inquiry revealed, the jump in the price of jute was unquestionably the work of a monopoly.

In battling the jute trust the Alliance faced challenges not unlike those facing modern-day Americans determined to counteract huge increases in oil prices. In both cases, two things must happen to break the cartel: a technically acceptable and reasonably priced alternative must be identified and made generally available, and consumers must be persuaded to stick with the alternative, even if in the short run it costs more.

In 1888 the cartel advanced the price of jute just as the crop was about to be harvested, and farmers were virtually powerless to resist. But in 1889, with a network of cooperative exchanges in place and a membership reaching into the millions, the Alliance moved to break the monopoly by persuading farmers to substitute cotton wrapping for jute.

Only a few southern cotton mills were equipped to manufacture the kind of cloth needed, and the major cotton exchanges in the United States and Europe were committed to jute bagging. The Alliance was partially successful in securing supplies of cotton bagging for the 1889 season and in concert with other farm organizations persuaded the New Orleans Exchange to accept the substitute bagging. The influential Liverpool Exchange, however, refused to cooperate.

To get cotton farmers to accept the substitute, Alliance leaders employed every means of communication and persuasion at their disposal. The success of a jute boycott hinged on thousands, even millions, of decisions by individual farmers. Alliance lecturers and Alliance newspapers carried the message to suballiances across the South, with an appeal for the suballiances to enforce the boycott, if necessary by expelling members who refused to cooperate. Alliance members dramatized their support by ceremonially burying rolls of jute bagging and by dressing in suits made of the cotton substitute. At the Piedmont Exposition in Atlanta before thousands of witnesses, an Alliance member and his bride exchanged their wedding vows dressed in cotton bagging. At harvesttime, long lines of farm wagons could be seen hauling cotton to market covered in "the Alliance uniform."

In parts of the South—most notably Georgia and South Carolina—the boycott was remarkably successful, and in the face of it the cartel lowered the price of jute. The Alliance's internal discipline and its apparent success in challenging a real live trust attracted a new wave of recruits, bringing the Alliance to the height of its membership in 1890.

However, the Alliance's very success in forcing down the price of jute (like the reduction in gasoline prices a century later) made it harder to hold members to their pledge to use the cotton substitute, which was more expensive. Furthermore, Alliance leaders could not secure enough cotton bagging for everyone to use at harvesttime, and an appeal for members to hold their crop off the market until it was available was unsuccessful. Once again the problem was credit. Without it, farmers were forced to sell immediately at harvesttime to settle their debts. To make matters worse, several of the Alliance cooperative agencies (most notably the one in North Carolina) had invested heavily in cotton bagging, drawing from their meager capital reserves to make the purchases. When in 1890 most cotton farmers returned to jute, they were stuck with the cotton bagging. The cartel outlived most of the Alliance cooperatives, and after their demise, the price of jute rose again.

Although they were short-lived, the Alliance's cooperative ventures, including the jute boycott, the state exchanges, and the local cooperative stores and warehouses, were principally responsible for the order's success in mobilizing southern farmers. In the end the cooperatives did not transform the institutions of commerce, finance, and marketing, but for a brief moment, both farmers and merchants had reason to believe, or fear, that they would.

Major southern newspapers, attuned to the winds of trade that so influenced the economic life of their own cities, reported on the growth of the cooperatives with amazement and, initially, with approval. National financial papers took a different view. At the end of 1889, *Dun's Weekly Review* noted: "In some Southern

States trade is seriously affected for the time by the operation of Farmers' Alliances, which enlist farmers in co-operative trading and absorb money which might otherwise go to settle indebtedness with merchants. The results in some localities almost paralyze trade."

The favorable response to the fledgling Alliance by major southern newspapers mirrors a somewhat surprising attitude by the South's commercial and political elite. After all, the Alliance was on record in support of a radical political agenda, and the Alliance through its cooperatives was seeking to create alternative channels of trade.

However, in the initial phase of the movement southern organizers generally steered clear of insurgent political campaigns, and local restatements of the Cleburne demands came out sounding like attacks on out-of-state monopolies, such as railroads, the jute trust, and the like, about which there could be broad agreement in southern communities. And the cooperatives themselves, while certainly creating tension with retail merchants, often won the support of civic boosters who saw them as potential vehicles for gaining a comparative advantage over rival trade centers.

The limits of this support from New South boosters would be reached as soon as the Alliance began to be more specific and more militant in its articulation of political demands. In some communities tensions between merchants and Alliance members turned violent as the cooperative movement neared its peak in the summer and fall of 1889.

At Dothan, Alabama, merchants and warehousemen fought to keep an Alliance cotton warehouse out of their town. The town council imposed heavy taxes and fees on the Alliance warehouse, and in a dispute over drayage fees the manager of the warehouse was arrested. An angry mob of Alliancemen descended on Dothan, and in the ensuing fight the town marshal, the warehouse manager, and another Alliance member were killed. In Leflore County in the delta region of Mississippi, merchants fought back when members of the Colored Farmers' Alliance began shifting their business to the white Alliance store in nearby Durant. When a black Alliance organizer named Oliver Cromwell was threatened, blacks staged a protest demonstration. Rumors circulated that blacks were arming themselves for an insurrection, and state troops were called in. When the shooting started, upward of twenty-five blacks were killed, including most of the leaders of the Colored Alliance.

The violence that gripped Dothan and Leflore County in 1889 was, to be sure, the exception in the rural South. More often than not the Alliance's crusade to usher in the cooperative commonwealth could be accommodated within the community and family networks that crisscrossed the countryside. But in an ominous foretaste, the exceptions marked the limits of community.

In the corn and wheat belts of the Great Plains, farmers took a somewhat different road to that moment in 1889 when a grand national alliance of producers seemed about to be born, but as the decade of the 1880s wore on, the southern and western roads bent more and more toward each other. The story of western farmer mobilization is a story of men and women who had knowingly entered the world of commercial agriculture with hopes of making a life, as well as a living, for themselves and their children. Now they, like their southern counterparts, found themselves buffeted by forces beyond their control and their dreams turned to nightmares.

As we have seen, at the same time the Alliance was being revived in Texas (around 1880), a separate organization with the same name was transplanted from Rochester to Chicago, where it was reborn under the leadership of Milton George, the Illinois farmer and editor of a Chicago paper called the *Western Rural*. In 1879 George had called upon midwestern farmers to form neighborhood "cheap transportation clubs." In April 1880 the Cook County Farmers' Alliance was organized at a meeting in the office of the *Western Rural*, whereupon George began publicizing the new organization through his paper, issuing charters to local farm clubs, and, coincidentally, gaining new subscribers. Six months later, George convened a Farmers' Transportation Convention in Chicago. At that meeting, attended by delegates from a dozen states, a "National" Farmers' Alliance was founded "to unite the farmers of the United States for their protection against class legislation, the encroachment of concentrated capital, and the tyranny of monopoly."

Despite appearances, the Chicago-based Alliance did not provide a solid foundation for rural mobilization. Unlike the pioneers of the Texas Alliance, Milton George was more a purveyor of charters than an organizer of rural communities. By inviting local farm clubs to affiliate with his National Alliance and extending honorary memberships to all who requested them, George affirmed a culture of protest, but did not create one. Some of those who joined the Alliance were committed greenbackers. Some sought to establish local cooperative ventures like those of the Grange. Others, like George himself, were primarily interested in broadly based efforts to secure more favorable freight rates.

With little grass-roots structure or program, the Alliance virtually disappeared during the relatively good times of 1882–85. The name Farmers' Alliance would have been erased from the memory of western agrarian protest had it not been for a combination of economic shocks that revitalized the movement.

In the second half of the 1880s the Great Plains agricultural and real estate booms collapsed. Furthermore, railroad freight rates, which had dropped in the 1870s and remained stable in the first half of the 1880s, rose sharply in the late 1880s. The hardships imposed by falling commodity prices, rising transportation costs, and unforgiving indebtedness were compounded by an equally unexpected natural phenomenon, drought. Contrary to what the smooth-talking land agents had promised, rain did not follow the plow; misery did.

In the face of these calamities, a more vigorous movement sprang up from the remnants of Alliance organizations in Nebraska, Minnesota, Iowa, and Dakota Territory. Meanwhile a kindred movement, the Farmers' Mutual Benefit Association, took root in Illinois, and in Kansas veteran farm organizers linked up with the Texas-based Alliance. The result was a massive grass-roots movement, which, though not unified under one organizational banner, was ecumenical in its agenda.

Like the Texas-based Alliance, this new farm movement of the Great Plains was grounded in local and state organizations that simultaneously advocated economic cooperation and an antimonopoly political agenda featuring issues of transportation, finance, and land. To a greater extent than in the South, participants in this western movement believed from the outset that the public policies required to usher in the cooperative commonwealth could only be achieved through third-party politics.

The farmers' movement that swept like a prairie fire across the Great Plains in the late 1880s varied in character and intensity from state to state. To grasp the variety of the movement, let us turn once again to the tier of states and territories that had comprised the heart of the Great Plains boom and would comprise the heartland of western Populism.

Milton George had chartered a Farmers' Alliance in Dakota Territory in 1881, but George's "national" organization was involved only in name with the spectacular growth that accompanied the collapse of the land boom in 1886. Henry L. Loucks, Canadian-born president of the territorial Alliance, along with business manager Alonzo Wardall, a veteran of farm organizations and a locally prominent member of the Knights of Labor, oversaw the development of the strongest Alliance cooperative agencies in the West, and probably in the nation.

In 1887 the Dakota Alliance established a joint-stock company that served members of the Alliance and the Knights of Labor. The company offered reduced prices and extended credit for purchases of coal, barbed wire, farm machinery, and even a specially manufactured "Alliance" wagon. In addition, the Alliance Hail Association offered members a cheap alternative for much-needed hail insurance, as well as fire and life insurance. Under

Wardall's leadership, agents of the Alliance Company and Hail Association doubled as recruiters for the Alliance itself, and in 1888 alone they organized 103 suballiances.

The Dakota Alliance's plans for cooperative marketing of hard winter wheat were equally ambitious, but met with greater resistance. To counter abuses in the grading and handling of the crop, Alliance members first sought to establish grain elevators along the principal rail lines. When railroads and larger processing companies refused to handle wheat shipped through cooperative elevators, the Dakota Alliance prevailed upon fellow members in Minnesota to join in building terminals in Duluth and Minneapolis. They came close to concluding a deal to ship their crop directly to British millers, thus bypassing a host of middlemen.

Both the successes and the near-misses of economic cooperation energized the Alliance in Dakota Territory. During the difficult years 1887–91 cooperative purchasing produced real savings, and the failure of the marketing plans only intensified the demands of Dakota farmers for stringent regulation—even public ownership—of railroads and elevators. In the farming communities of the Dakota wheat belt, control of these necessary links to the world market were effectively under monopoly control, and when, by 1889, Dakota Alliance members had been thwarted in their efforts to establish cooperative alternatives, they declared that "all public necessities, so far as practicable, should be owned and controlled by the government." In the Dakotas, and also in the Prairie provinces of Canada, public ownership of elevators and railroads would be a primary objective of the agrarian revolt.

The Alliance was strongest in those areas of Dakota Territory that had experienced the boom of the 1880s. A careful study of Alliance membership in one such county (in present-day northeastern South Dakota) shed light on who joined the organization. In Marshall County, Alliance members were more likely than their non-Alliance neighbors to be landowners and to have bought their land during the boom period. Alliance members tended to be heads of households rather than single males. Men without property and without wives and children were the least likely to join.

As a group, Marshall County Alliance members carried a heavy load of debt, both on their land and on their personal property, but before the great calamities of the late 1880s this would have been normal for farmers who were moving aggressively into commercial agriculture. The collapse of the boom and the increase in transportation costs left them in a very vulnerable situation, compounded by their responsibilities for supporting their families.

It is unwise to read too much into such a profile: many Marshall County farmers similarly situated did not join, and there is no guarantee that Marshall County is representative of Dakota Territory, much less the whole of the Great Plains. Nevertheless, the evidence from that corner of Dakota seems to square with what we know about those who joined throughout the Great Plains. In the main, the Alliance was an organization of families who had staked a claim to farm ownership but whose hold on that claim was precarious. Farming on the Great Plains had seemed to offer the opportunity for advancement and security, but events conspired to put that at risk.

If the Alliance program in Dakota Territory initially tipped more to the cooperative side than to the political, the reverse was true in Nebraska. The resurgence of the Farmers' Alliance in that state in the late 1880s was led by Jay Burrows, a Gage County farmer, who with his neighbors had organized the first local Alliance chartered by Milton George. The Alliance spoke to the fears of the small landholders who were now at risk. The Lincoln *Farmers' Alliance*, which Burrows founded in 1889, articulated those fears and hinted at solutions:

With corn at from 10 to 15¢; with oats at 8 to 12¢; with the cattle market in the hands of a combine making the feeding of steers a mere lottery . . . the outlook for farmers is unusually gloomy. If a farmer is out of debt, and can remain so, he is master of the situation. But very few indeed are in that fortunate condition. Our financial system, based on debt, and furnishing an entirely inadequate volume of money, forces the business of the country upon a debt basis.

And there was more. Capricious market prices and the risk of foreclosure on mortgaged land threatened personal disaster too great to bear: "Property is ruthlessly sacrificed, and men left with families on their hands—just their bare hands."

What was to be done? The Nebraska Alliance organized a handful of local cooperative stores and sought thereby to regain for the farmer some measure of economic control. But above all, Nebraska leaders pinned their hopes on the adoption of an antimonopoly program by the federal government. They championed governmental control of railroads and a system of federal loans to farmers using land as security. The land-loan scheme, a staple of midwestern reformers, traced its lineage to the antebellum labor movement and in particular to the writings of Edward Kellogg. When linked with a similar program of crop loans that Macune championed as the solution to the crisis of the cotton belt, it would propel the farmers' movement of the West and South into political insurgency. Federal loans on land or crops, depending on local needs, was the final political expression of greenbackism, and the attractiveness of such programs was crucial in the formation of the People's Party.

By 1887, Burrows and like-minded Alliance leaders like Alson J. Streeter (Illinois), August Post (Iowa), and Ignatius Donnelly (Minnesota) had wrested control of the National Alliance from Milton George and committed it to a program of political reform centered on the trinity of transportation, finance, and land. Although this northwestern Alliance never rivaled its southern counterpart in membership or in organizational cohesiveness, it would play a role in the effort to form a unified national movement of farmers and laborers.

The institutional weakness of the northwestern Alliance was demonstrated most conclusively in Kansas. There the collapse of the land boom, and with it the rise of a militant Alliance movement, came a year or so later than in Dakota. Although the economic conditions that called forth the movement in Kansas were much the same as in Nebraska and Dakota Territory, the agents of mobilization were not. The gathering of Kansas farmers into the Alliance in 1889 and 1890 happened with great speed and intensity.

A dedicated band of Kansas greenbackers, chief among whom was a fiery young journalist and agitator named Henry Vincent, identified the Texas-based Alliance as an appropriate vehicle for mobilizing Kansas farmers. In May 1888 one of their number secured an organizer's commission from Texas and set to work. Vincent's paper, grandly named *The American Nonconformist and Kansas Industrial Liberator*, aggressively promoted the order.

From the outset, Kansas organizers followed the double strategy of economic cooperation and political agitation to "throw the rascals out." For example, in Cowley County, the organizers' first target and Vincent's home, the Alliance had by 1889 endorsed independent antimonopoly slates for local office and launched a business exchange that proved to be so successful that one local merchant pledged $2,000 of his own money to put it out of business.

As the run-in with that Cowley County merchant suggests, once the Alliance moved beyond denunciation of his "foreign" capital to addressing local problems it risked retaliation from the town boosters who dominated the economic, political, and social life of Kansas communities. With town-based merchants and professionals controlling local politics, churches and social organizations, as well as local institutions of trade and finance, the Alliance determined to create an alternative set of institutions undergirded by an alternative culture. Economic cooperatives, the social life of the local Alliance, and antimonopoly politics were all part of this cooperative commonwealth.

By the spring of 1889, new suballiances were being organized in Kansas at a rate of more than twenty a week, with the greatest concentration in central Kansas, where farmers had somewhat better prospects of outlasting depression and drought than those farther west. The rapid expansion of the order continued through 1890, with the Alliance claiming over 100,000 members.

By the time of the Kansas organizing campaign the various elements of Alliance mobilization had been packaged and field-tested: a corp of traveling lecturer-organizers, subsidized newspapers and a blizzard of pamphlets, the tightly knit structure of neighborhood, county, and state Alliances, and considerable experience in cooperative purchasing and marketing. When Kansas Alliancemen prepared to launch a statewide cooperative exchange, they were advised by the agents of successful Alliance cooperatives in Dakota, Georgia, and Tennessee, as well as veterans of the Texas experiment.

If Alliance leaders from the South and West could come together in Kansas to help raise an army of producers, why could not farmers and laborers coalesce into a grand *national* army? Such a force seemed to be gathering at just that moment. Well over a million farmers in the South, Midwest, and Great Plains had flocked to the Alliance banner, and the organization was expanding into the Mountain West.

The Texas-based Alliance and the Agricultural Wheel had successfully merged, despite significant disagreement over political strategy. Leaders of the two Alliances, the Illinois Farmers' Mutual Benefit Association, and the Knights of Labor were seriously discussing merger, or at least a coalition based on a common agenda for reform. After Alliance leaders appeared before the General Assembly of the Knights in November 1889, Grand Master Workman Terence Powderly proclaimed, to great applause, "I am willing to lay down the reins of office . . . to pick up the weapons of the private soldier . . . in the ranks of the army of organized producers of America."

When delegates to the Texas-based Alliance convened in St. Louis for their national meeting in December 1889 (and renamed themselves the National Farmers' Alliance and Industrial Union), their goal was nothing less than the unification that Powderly envisioned.

4

Farmers, Laborers, and Politics:

Interest Groups and Insurgency, 1890

The delegates of farm and labor organizations who gathered in St. Louis's Exposition Building on December 3, 1889, represented a national movement, running at full tide, that claimed millions of supporters. Two months earlier the southern Farmers' Alliance and the Agricultural Wheel had merged, and many of those who journeyed to St. Louis expected to participate in yet another round of agreements that would bring into grand union the farmers and laborers of the South and West.

Of the delegates assembled in St. Louis, none were more self-confident than the leaders of the southern Alliance. They had organized the cotton belt, battled the jute trust to a standstill, and launched an aggressive organizing campaign in the Great Plains. They expected to establish cooperative ties with the Knights of Labor and, in effect, to absorb the northwestern Alliance. Representatives of the northwestern Alliance came to St. Louis ready to propose a *confederation* of farm organizations that would have left them with considerable autonomy.

Negotiations between the two Alliances broke down amid considerable acrimony. The differences were partially institutional: many Westerners opposed the tight organization and secrecy of the southern Alliance, while most of the Southerners considered the northwestern order to be a paper tiger. Behind the institutional differences were sectional and partisan cleavages that would loom large in the history of Populism. More than a few of the delegates who gathered in St. Louis were Civil War veterans, for whom the great and bloody issues of 1861–65 were still alive. (One Kansas editor labeled the southern Alliance nothing more than a "rebel yell.")

While some western third-party men lobbied hard for merger (including Alson J. Streeter, Union Labor Party presidential candidate in 1888), the northwestern Alliance was dominated by partisan stalwarts like August Post, a member of the Iowa Republican committee, who had been stung by Alliance attacks on Republicans and "did not want the organization to fuse with any body south of Mason and Dixon['s] line."

Two positive developments outweighed the failure of merger. The first was the admission of the robust Kansas and Dakota Alliances into the southern Alliance—now named the National Farmers' Alliance and Industrial Union (NFA&IU). The Kansas Alliance was partially the product of Texas organizers, and the Dakota Alliance most nearly replicated the cooperative experience of the southern group. The second development was a remarkably broad agreement on political philosophy. While organizational battles captured headlines in St. Louis, the two Alliances, the Farmers' Mutual Benefit Association, and the Knights of Labor all agreed on the necessity of "going into politics" to impose their platform on the federal government.

The NFA&IU adopted a seven-point platform that rehearsed the familiar demands on land, finance, and transportation (this time calling for public ownership of railroads, not just regulation). Charles Macune offered an addendum to the platform that called for the establishment of federal "subtreasuries" that would democratize the marketing and financing of staple crops by providing low-cost federal loans secured by the crops themselves.

With the exception of the subtreasury plan these demands were not new, but they now had behind them the force of a massive social movement—millions of farmers congregated within the community of thousands of local Alliances and assemblies. Theirs was an energy generated by the shared experience of financial distress, of victimization by the trusts, and of hopes for a cooperative commonwealth raised and dashed.

In seeking legislative remedies the farmers' movement challenged the economic and sociological orthodoxy of the day, which decreed that the sorry lot of farmers and workers stemmed from fixed laws of nature. To the contrary, farm spokesmen argued that government—especially the federal government—could and should intervene in economic affairs. It was the rightful duty of government to establish, as historian Norman Pollack put it, a "just polity," in which democratic capitalism prevailed. Government regulation and ownership of the arteries of transportation, communication, and finance was thus the means of restoring a more humane and equitable order.

Faith in democratic capitalism and rough agreement on the means of achieving it constituted a common ground among the Alliances, the Farmers' Mutual Benefit Association, and the Knights of Labor, at least at the level of official pronouncements. Their platforms differed on details (for example, many Westerners favored government loans on land rather than on farm commodities as the subtreasury scheme proposed), but by 1890 they were united in the belief that the dream of commonwealth could be realized politically, whether channeled through the existing parties or a new one.

The values and agendas of the groups represented in St. Louis had been distilled in the statements and platforms of grass-roots farmer and labor organizations over two decades. From discussions in countless labor halls and Alliance meeting rooms had come a language of social criticism that was steeped in the discourse of pre-Civil War America but was focused on the ills of an industrializing nation. The rhetoric of protest acquired meaning and power within the social setting of farm and labor assemblies, and historians of Populism have focused on these organizations as the source of the political whirlwind that became the People's Party.

However, if we are to understand how the language of social criticism found such ready acceptance among so many Americans, it is essential to understand that at the same time that the Farmers' Alliance was spreading its message across America's rural heartland, the West and South were being flooded with the writings of social critics who were not themselves the products of the farmer-labor movement but who had, from other sources, produced a critique of emergent industrial capitalism that resonated with the ecumenical gospel of the producers' organization.

In other words, the language of social criticism came in several dialects. In addition to the rough-hewn phrases of farmers and laborers with their midwestern and southern accents, armchair reformers from the Northeast developed a more genteel form of the same tongue, also drawing on reform traditions from the early years of the Republic and empowered by the same religious fervor as that which caused Populism to be called a "Pentecost of Politics." Two men, in particular, articulated the common sense of many ordinary Americans who felt that the fundamental principles of the Republic were being undermined in the age of industrialization.

Henry George and Edward Bellamy wrote sweeping indictments of industrial America and drafted bold blueprints for the nation's salvation. George's *Progress and Poverty* (1879) and Bellamy's *Looking Backward* (1888) were two of the era's best-selling books. They were enormously influential, less for the specific remedies they offered than for the power of the question they posed: why were so many Americans desperately poor while a handful grew fabulously wealthy?

Though differing in background from the farmers and laborers who comprised the Populist movement, George and Bellamy shared with them a birthright of social criticism, in the form of either Jacksonian antimonopolism (George) or New England social reform (Bellamy). Like the farmers, their critique of industrial America and their vision of the just society were framed by Protestant pietism and a distinctly American reading of history.

Both George and Bellamy possessed in strong measure the spirit of Christian nationalism that fueled moral outrage at the human suffering of the 1870s. The concentration of wealth and power, they believed, left America in danger of following the downward path of ancient Rome from a vigorous republic of small farmers to a decadent empire dominated by the very rich.

An earlier depression had shaped young Henry George's life. The Panic of 1857 drove him from his native Philadelphia to San Francisco, where from a journalist's desk he watched the concentration of wealth and farmland in northern California and where, with the collapse of his own fortunes during the depression of the 1870s, he faced the prospect of poverty and even hunger for his young family.

The explanation for the nation's ills and his own appeared to George in a moment of conversion: "Like a flash it came upon me that there was the reason for advancing poverty with advancing wealth. With the growth of population land grows in value, and the men who work it must pay for the privilege." Monopolization of land for speculative purposes was the root cause of poverty, George argued. His solution was to impose a Single Tax on land—specifically on the value of ground rents which accrued from unearned increases in the value of land. This single solution would, George claimed, restore equality of opportunity, promote harmonious and compact settlement of western lands, and provide all the revenue needed by the federal government, without confiscating private property or introducing a huge bureaucratic state.

Edward Bellamy's indictment of unregulated capitalism led him in the opposite direction from George—toward a vastly expanded government. The problem with capitalism, Bellamy argued, was that it promoted waste: wasteful competition, the wasteful swings of the business cycle, and the waste of human resources in the tragic form of idle labor.

In Bellamy's utopian novel *Looking Backward*, the American economy has by the year 2000 evolved into a system he called Nationalism. As seen from Boston at the turn of the millennium, this prosperous centralized economic system relies for labor on an "industrial army" of the young that is managed by a technological elite whose decisions are shaped by the modern science of statistics.

Bellamy's brave new world is decidedly nondemocratic. Members of the industrial army do not vote, and a council of elders rules by plebiscite. Bellamy's novel was oddly lacking in details about how this socialistic economy would actually produce the life of luxury that awaited veterans of the industrial army. Bellamy, like George, was denounced as a crank by polite and learned society for daring to construct a whole new social system in his head. How would their ideas be received by the farmers and laborers who shared their anger at a world out of joint but whose program of reform was more down to earth?

The works of George and Bellamy were widely advertised in the reform press and widely read in rural households. Both men established organizational ties to the nascent Populist movement, George by way of the Irish Land League (for which he wrote extensively on the evils of enclosure) and the Knights of Labor (which, under fellow Land League member Terence Powderly, embraced the Single Tax). George attracted a following among Kansas farmers for whom the land boom and bust was a major source of discontent. Populist congressman Jerry Simpson of Kansas championed the Single Tax and tried to write it into the legislation governing land distribution in the Indian Territory.

Bellamy's work was also widely read in the rural West and praised by some western farm leaders, including the editor of Nebraska's leading Alliance newspaper. In cities across America, Nationalist Clubs were formed by middle-class reformers and professionals who shared Bellamy's moral outrage and who were grasping for a program of reform. By the end of 1890, Nationalist Clubs had sprung up from Boston to Los Angeles, and Nationalists were being accepted as delegates at the national and state conferences of reformers that would give birth to the People's Party. Despite the broad gulf between Bellamy's utopian blueprint and the Alliances' program of reform, it looked as if the Nationalist Clubs might be the vehicle for recruiting middle-class Americans into the reform coalition of farmers and laborers.

Among the middle-class reformers who flocked to the Nationalist banner were a sizable number of women. In Boston, where the movement began, and in California, its second home, women were everywhere in evidence. Charlotte Perkins Gilman, niece of Harriet Beecher Stowe and forerunner of modern feminism, was a prominent Nationalist lecturer in California. And Frances Willard, president of the Women's Christian Temperance Union, was converted to Christian socialism by means of *Looking Backward*. For many urban women reformers, Bellamy's vision was to be the vital link with the larger reform tradition of which the farmers' movement was a central element.

At the St. Louis meeting of the Alliance, Leonidas Polk of North Carolina beat out Charles Macune and Isaac McCracken for the presidency of the NFA&IU and immediately took as his mandate the forging of just such a unified reform movement. Polk was the southern Alliance leader best qualified to advance the cause of sectional reconciliation. A Whig and Unionist before secession, Polk enlisted as a private in a North Carolina regiment once war came, rising to the rank of lieutenant. (The title of "Colonel" often ascribed to him in the history books was honorific.)

Polk, a substantial farmer but not a wealthy planter, was looked to after the war for leadership in a succession of farm organizations—the Grange, the Farmers' Association, and finally the Alliance. He served as North Carolina's first Commissioner of Agriculture and edited an influential weekly, *The Progressive*

Farmer. A persuasive but not flamboyant speaker, possessed of a flowing beard and stately presence, Polk was the preeminent Alliance leader of the Southeast. An unlikely convert to radical politics, Polk now embraced the Alliance platform, subtreasury and all, and committed himself to the unification of the nation's farmers under the Alliance banner.

Polk threw himself into expanding the Alliance's foothold in the Plains states and leading the march into the Northeast and Far West. During the first of many cross-country tours, Polk brought his message to Winfield, Kansas, home of Henry Vincent, where he spoke in the open air to several thousand farmers assembled on the Fourth of July 1890.

Politicians had kept sectional conflict alive for twenty-five years, said Polk, but "I stand here today, commissioned by hundreds of thousands of southern farmers, to beg the farmers of Kansas to stand by them." "I tell you this afternoon that from New York to the Golden Gate the farmers have risen up and have inaugurated a movement such as the world has never seen."

From New York to the Golden Gate? Almost. The Alliance had established beachheads from coast to coast, and in the Mountain and Pacific states a farmer-labor movement was taking shape with stunning results. On that same Fourth of July, for example, Colorado Alliance leaders met in Denver with Knights of Labor and others to found an Independent Party.

Mountain Populism has often been dismissed as a pseudo-movement trumped up by western silver-mine owners who wanted only to enact the Populists' demand for free coinage of silver so that the value of their product would soar. But since both Democratic and Republican leaders in the Mountain states advocated free silver it is hard to see how this issue would spur the growth of a third party. Thorough studies of Populism in each of the Mountain states reveal a rich and varied movement of farmers, railroad workers, and miners that resembled the movement in the southern and Plains states, with an even stronger dose of labor radicalism thrown in.

Recall that in the 1880s the Great Plains farming frontier and cattle industry had pushed into the front range of the Rocky Mountains from Montana to New Mexico Territory, and that on the arid eastern side of the Rockies irrigation was a necessity for successful farming. At the end of the 1880s, farmers were pushed to revolt by drought, falling prices for crops and land, and the monopolization of vital irrigation systems and railroads. To a greater extent than would happen in either the South or the Great Plains, angry farmers in the Mountain states made common cause with militant workers. Mining camps and railroad settlements became focal points of labor organizing among workers who, like their farmer neighbors, believed themselves to be victims of powerful and distant monopolies.

Colorado epitomizes the diversity of Mountain Populism. It was the nation's leading silver producer, but the farmer-labor base of Colorado Populism was established before the silver crisis of the 1890s. By the end of the 1880s, farmers from the tragically misnamed rain belt of Colorado's eastern high plains, as well as those from the irrigated lands to the north and south, were focusing their anger on absentee capitalists who controlled access to transportation and water. Miners were also seeing the dream of individual success and family security fade in the face of their industry's concentration of capital and technology, which they labeled monopolistic. Alfred C. King, Colorado's blind miner poet, spoke for them:

> The heritage of man, the earth
> Was framed for homes, not vast estates;
> A lowering scale of human worth
> Each generation demonstrates,
> Which feels the landlord's iron hand,
> And hopeless, plod with effort brave;
> Who loves no home can love no land;
> These own no home, until the grave.

Such anger bespoke a tradition of radicalism among western coal and precious-metal miners that was already decades old by the time of the Populist revolt. The glaring discrepancy between the myths of the prospector's instant riches and the hardscrabble reality of the mining camps fanned the flames of protest. The relative isolation and absolute danger of the mines fostered solidarity and radicalism. Nowhere in industrial America were the conditions of labor more harsh and more dangerous than in the underground mines of the Mountain West. When silver miners in Leadville, Colorado, demanded that the mine shafts be shored up, their foreman responded that "men are cheaper than timbers."

Little wonder, then, that miners organized for their own protection: through localized assemblies (such as the union in Nevada's Comstock Lode in the 1860s and the Butte Miners' Union, the first among Montana workers in 1878) and more commonly through the Knights of Labor, miners closed ranks with railroad workers and a host of other laboring people in a formidable western army that was ready to make common cause with angry farmers by the end of the 1880s. Joseph Buchanan, editor of a radical Knights of Labor paper in Denver and member of the Knights' national executive board, spoke for many in the West when in 1883 he proclaimed that "the proletarians have nothing to lose but their chains."

In Colorado, miners and railroad workers flocked to the banner of the Knights of Labor, who won a major strike against the Union Pacific Railroad in 1884. The southern Alliance entered the state in 1888, pushing an aggressive brand of economic cooperation and political antimonopolism. Colorado farmers and laborers increasingly viewed themselves as victims of a colonial economy, their fate determined in London and New York. Their political agenda was fashioned accordingly.

Alliance members dominated the Denver meeting that launched an Independent Party in 1890. They were joined by Knights of Labor, representatives of the Nationalist Clubs, and members of something called the United Order of Anti-Monopolists. The platform they adopted called for protection of the rights of labor, nationalization of railroads and telegraphs, state ownership of ditches and reservoirs, and an end to alien landownership. (The last two planks were aimed at the British-owned firms that controlled much of the state's irrigation system.) Some of its leaders undercut the Independent Party by entering into a coalition of the two major parties, and the Alliance-backed insurgency garnered only a small fraction of the vote. Nevertheless, Republican control over state politics was broken, and the stage was set for a remarkable Populist triumph in 1892.

The elements of the Colorado story were repeated in other Mountain states, sometimes in different proportions and with other local issues playing a decisive role. The roots of Montana Populism were more urban than rural, due to the influence of miners organized by the Knights of Labor and then by the Federation of Western Miners. Antimonopoly and antirailroad sentiment united Montana miners with farmers organized by both southern and northwestern Alliances. In Wyoming, which had little farming or mining, railroad workers and small stockmen combined politically in a movement triggered by monopolistic control of land and water. Similarly, in New Mexico Territory land disputes translated into antimonopolism in ways reminiscent of the beginnings of the Alliance on the Texas frontier.

By 1890 the farmers' movement had reached the Pacific coast. Both Alliances sent recruiters to the Northwest, and by spring organizers commissioned by Leonidas Polk were reporting success in California, Washington, and Oregon. The issues they addressed and remedies they offered looked a great deal like those found on the Great Plains and even in the South.

Twentieth-century Americans have often glimpsed the future by watching the trends in California. Leonidas Polk had reason to hope that California foreshadowed the nation's future when he addressed the delegates who packed Los Angeles's largest auditorium for the state Alliance in 1891. California just might be the place where the Alliance's project would be realized.

Alliance champions in California had vigorously promoted the movement's twin plans for the liberation of small producers: economic cooperation and governmental protection against monopolies of transportation and finance. A speaker who preceded Polk to the rostrum in Los Angeles put it plainly: "The time grows near when the great highways of commerce will be the property of the people; and our Alliance business agency shall bring the producers and consumers together to the exclusion of useless middlemen."

The Alliance entered California at a critical juncture for the state's agriculture. In the 1870s and 1880s wheat farmers had flocked to the central valleys in California's version of the Great Plains land boom, only to see the land consolidated into bonanza farms covering hundreds of thousands of acres. Henry George, observing this massive enclosure movement from San Francisco, had been moved to compose his sweeping indictment of land speculation. Prospects for small family farmers were further dimmed in the 1880s by falling wheat prices and, particularly in the upper San Joaquin and Salinas valleys, by the monopoly power of the Southern Pacific Railroad, which was known locally as the Octopus even before Frank Norris made its practices notorious in his novel of that name.

By 1890 fruit and vegetable production was beginning to replace wheat, a shift made possible by the introduction of irrigation and refrigerated railroad cars. Small farmers could operate fruit and vegetable farms as profitably as the giant agribusinesses, *if* they could process and market the crops cooperatively and *if* water and transportation were cheap and dependable. Under those conditions the American dream of the independent family farm might be realized in California. As one organizer put it: "Let small growers unite in establishing cooperative dryers to handle the small crops of an entire neighborhood. Organization, union, cooperation must be the salvation of the small fruit-grower—unite with your neighbors, join the Farmers' Alliance, and do your duty to your country and your God."

By the spring of 1891, 30,000 Californians had enlisted in the Alliance, making it six times larger than the Grange. A state cooperative exchange was established in Los Angeles, along with local cooperatives for the processing and marketing of wheat, fruit, and vegetables. The fledgling Alliance attracted the attention of Edward Bellamy's disciples who were organizing Nationalist Clubs in San Francisco, Los Angeles, and elsewhere. Nationalists and Alliance members shared an antipathy toward monopolists and agreed on the need for government ownership of railroads. They entered into an informal coalition almost immediately: some Nationalist Clubs transformed themselves into suballiances and embraced the Alliance platform.

This coalition would form the base of California Populism, but the enthusiastic cooperation of Nationalists and Alliance members obscured a fundamental disagreement that would ultimately rend the movement. Where Alliance farmers saw government ownership of railroads and irrigation systems—along with cooperative marketing and processing—as means to restoring free and fair competition, Nationalists thought producer cooperatives were irrelevant and believed that competition itself was the root of the problem. The utopia they imagined was far more centralized and less democratic than the Alliance's vision.

The future of American agriculture was indeed taking form in California in the 1890s, and although that future included echoes of the Alliance's project and even Bellamy's utopia, the outcome would have filled Leonidas Polk with sadness. Cooperative processing and marketing flourished after the demise of the farmers' movement, as did centralized public control of irrigation. But without the Alliance's social criticism, cooperatives became agents of giant agribusiness, and bureaucratically controlled irrigation systems undergirded rather than checked the imperial power of corporate farming.

In the same month that Alliance organizers reached California, others commissioned by Polk pushed into the Pacific Northwest. Wheat farmers in eastern Washington, victimized by freight-rate discrimination and the railroads' monopoly of storage and marketing facilities, were receptive to the Alliance's cooperative plan and its demand for public ownership of the railroads.

Their fledgling movement found allies in the working-class districts of Seattle and Tacoma, where organized labor had agitated for reform since the mid-1880s, first through the Knights of Labor and then through umbrella trades councils. In 1891, Tacoma Knights orchestrated the formation of a third party that embraced the Alliance platform as well as other labor demands. At first Alliance leaders were reluctant to support a farmer-labor party, but the precipitous decline of wheat prices in 1891, compounded by inflexible mortgages and continuing high freight rates, pushed many of them toward insurgency.

Washington's farmer-labor coalition was grounded in traditional principles of labor radicalism, producerism, and antimonopolism, but with one significant addition. The platforms that Washington farmers and laborers hammered together included a demand for the prohibition of Chinese immigration. Sinophobia had deep roots in the farmer-labor movement of the Northwest and in the Rocky Mountain states as well.

In November 1885, two months after Knights of Labor in Wyoming massacred twenty-eight Chinese miners, a Tacoma mob led by Knights organizer Daniel Cronin invaded the Chinese section and forced most of the residents to flee the city. President Grover Cleveland ordered federal troops to put down the "insurrection," and twenty-seven members of the mob were indicted under an 1871 federal law passed to stop Ku Klux Klan violence in the South. Local juries found all of them innocent.

The Tacoma expulsion, reminiscent of the forced removal of blacks from several southern towns at the turn of the century, was an extreme example of the Sinophobia that gripped the Far West in the 1880s. Miners and farmers had no monopoly on anti-

Chinese sentiments (both major parties endorsed immigration restriction), but in the hard times of the 1880s radicalism and racism found common ground in the belief that Chinese immigrants posed a threat to the jobs and farms of honest Americans.

Henry George himself sketched the racial and economic outlines of such an argument in 1869. George argued for expulsion on the ground that the influx of Chinese would depress wages, but his text was peppered with references to the Chinese as "sensual, cowardly, and cruel" and as being addicted to "unnameable vices of the East." In Colorado, the same Joseph Buchanan who incited miners with the revolutionary phrases of Karl Marx also found a scapegoat in Asian workers. The Chinese "vermin," Buchanan wrote, were "like so many leeches, sucking our blood. . . . We feel like going forth and inciting the people to mob and butcher every thieving, infernal Chinaman in the country."

Sinophobia did not constitute a fault line of historical memory to divide western workers like race relations did in the South. There was no equivalent of Reconstruction, no recollection of a time when the ethnic "other" held the balance of political power and might thus become either a threat or an ally against wealth and privilege. Racism posed no *tactical* dilemma for western Populism as it did in the South. In several states insurgents added Chinese-exclusion planks to their platforms with no effect one way or the other. But in the Far West, as in the South, racial antagonism and violence cast a long shadow over the movement.

The farmer-labor movement that spread across the Far West was richly varied and defies simple categorization, but it clearly fit into the mosaic of a national movement. The Alliance in the Rocky Mountain and Pacific coast states shared with its counterpart in the southern and Plains states a twofold project, economic cooperation and political antimonopolism—which Alliance members viewed as complementary. The movement, in its various regional manifestations, shared a morally grounded sense of outrage at the oppression of producers by the forces of capital. In all regions, farmers strove for cooperation with artisans, laborers, and industrial workers—with labor playing the most prominent role in the Far West.

Wherever the movement appeared and flourished, whether in California or Kansas or North Carolina, women and men gathered in their own neighborhoods to establish alternative institutions —intentional communities within which they could imagine a future different from the grim prospects that confronted them. It is to an examination of the Alliance as community that we now turn.

In the summer of 1888 the secretary of the Falling Creek Alliance in North Carolina reported to Leonidas Polk's *Progressive Farmer*: "You cannot imagine what a kindred feeling has sprung among us. We really seem more like the human beings that God made in his own image. Bless the name of the Alliance, long may it continue to grow in strength, it is next to religion with us." In December 1889 a reporter for the St. Louis *Globe-Democrat* described with amazement the gathering of Alliance members at Exposition Hall: "For one solid hour a row of delegates and members filed up the steps and in the corridor before the hall. Each farmer stepped up and gripped the doorkeeper's hand, at the same time placing his mouth close to his ear and whispering the password."

The NFA&IU, like the Grange and the Knights of Labor, was a secret, oath-bound society. Its members gathered on Saturday afternoons in their own neighborhoods to observe the rituals or "secret work," receive instruction and exhortation on subjects ranging from scientific farming to cooperative marketing to federal legislation, elect officers and new members, conduct business by vote of the membership, and enjoy each other's company. Part school, part church, part lodge, the suballiance and its counterpart in other farm and labor organizations were the seedbeds of an autonomous culture of protest.

Though their meetings were conducted behind closed doors, fragmentary images have survived in a handful of yellowed minute books and manuals that describe the workings of the neighborhood suballiances. Assemble those fragments from the South and from the West, and you have a remarkably consistent picture of rural men and women binding themselves together in communities that were as familiar as the churches and lodges to which many belonged, and yet were self-consciously new and purposeful. Whether their meeting place was a schoolhouse on the Kansas plains or a country church in North Carolina, Alliance members believed that in the act of assembling they were forming a new cooperative commonwealth.

Alliance members from the Great Plains or the Pacific Northwest would have felt at home among Leonidas Polk's North Carolina neighbors of the Mount Sylvan Alliance, who during their regular meetings discussed the merits of underwriting the new Alliance exchange in Durham, reported on what was being done to help with the crops of a sick brother, arbitrated a dispute between two members, debated the endorsement of Alliance candidates for the legislature, and passed a resolution "that any young man or Lady . . . caught sparking in time of business be fined to sweep and have water for the next meeting."

Similarly, Alliance men and women from North Carolina who found themselves in the northwest corner of Kansas would have understood perfectly what was about to happen when the president of the Beaver Valley Alliance gaveled the meeting to order and intoned, "Brother Doorkeeper, please secure the door and admit no one during the opening ceremony." After members whispered the password and the chaplain offered an opening prayer, the president ordered that a candidate for initiation be admitted to the schoolhouse that doubled as meeting room. The candidate was ushered in by the steward and conducted around the room, where the various officers instructed him in the duties of membership and invited him to take an oath in which he promised not to reveal the secrets of the order, to act in harmony with his fellow member, and to "assist him in bearing the burdens and crosses of life."

The social life of the suballiances spilled out into the open in ways that dramatized their importance in the larger community. The Alliance conducted its own graveside burial services and held public picnics, horse-drawn parades, and open-air meetings for discussion of public affairs. By 1890, as the farmers' movement loomed as a political power in the South and West, the sight of Alliance processions stretching across the prairie or of massive Alliance rallies that became emotionally charged camp meetings filled those who witnessed them with awe.

Parades, secret passwords and rituals, the routine operations of a suballiance business meeting recorded in the rough hand of a farmer-secretary—these may not seem like the stuff of a radical new political movement. But it was precisely their ordinariness —their ability to bestow upon the assembled members a sense of community—that made these meetings so important. Within the private space of the suballiance and the gathered multitude of state and national meetings like the one in St. Louis, rural men and women found their voice.

Men *and* women. "Show us a sub-Alliance that is progressing and growing with no lady membership," Texas's premier Alliance paper editorialized, "and *The Mercury* will show you a dozen living churches of Christ with no women in them." Or as humorist Josh Billings said of the Populist movement on the Great Plains: "Wimmin is everywhere." Women were an integral part of the Alliance movement, and Alliance women were an integral part of the larger movement of social reform that historian Sara M. Evans has labeled the "maternal commonwealth."

Between the 1870s and the turn of the century, campaigns for temperance, woman suffrage, and economic reform were quite often blended into one righteous crusade that combined a distinctly romantic vision of womanhood with a hardheaded sense of political realities. Mary Elizabeth Lease of Kansas articulated the Populist version of this crusade when, in the midst of the 1892 political campaigns, she said, "Thank God we women are blameless for this political muddle you men have dragged us into.

. . . Ours is a grand and holy mission . . . to place the mothers of this nation on an equality with the fathers."

In the Farmers' Alliance women played a significant role, though one that was less institutionalized than in the Patrons of Husbandry, which had stipulated that certain of the offices in local Granges must be filled by women. At least one-fourth of Alliance members nationwide were women, and local records reveal instances where their numbers were considerably greater. Many, but by no means all, of the women members were wives and daughters of men who belonged. Recall that the Alliance attracted family farmers in much greater numbers than single males. The Alliance's practice of admitting women to membership without payment of dues was in effect a kind of family membership. The rolls of many suballiances contained the names of husbands, wives, and their teenage children of both sexes. Although Alliance women were more visible in the West, they constituted a sizable fraction of total membership wherever the movement flourished.

What was women's role in the Alliance? Bettie Gay of Texas, writing in 1891 on the influence of women in the Alliance, gave two distinct but complementary answers that were echoed throughout the agrarian movement and that clearly located Alliance women within the tradition of the "maternal commonwealth." A woman's position in the Alliance is the same as in the family, she wrote, "the companion and helpmeet of man." At the same time, no one is more interested in reform than women, for they "are the chief sufferers whenever poverty or misfortune overtakes the family."

Annie L. Diggs of Kansas, writing in *The Arena*, echoed Mrs. Gay. The idea that "the home is woman's sphere" is only a half-truth. "The whole truth is that women should watch and work in all things which shape and mould the home, whether 'money,' 'land,' or 'transportation.' So now Alliance women look at politics and trace the swift relation to the home."

Preservation of family values and the cause of economic justice went hand in hand, though for women and men the meaning and balance may have differed. While men were likely to associate the ethical and prophetic foundation of Alliance principles with honest politics and a just public economy, women more often appealed to the economy of the household, to the tranquillity of the home, and to domestic values associated with evangelical religion.

Alliance lecturer Mary Clardy of Texas evoked those values in a fictional account, entitled "The Alliance Fireside," which depicted a well-kept farm home where after supper the young daughter reads an Alliance version of a popular hymn, "The Ninety and Nine." "There were tearful eyes and a long silence when the poem was ended." Then her father "read the 2nd Psalm and led in earnest prayer for all Alliance homes, for their speakers, writers, and papers connected with the cause, and for national political reform. This closed the day." And then the narrator admonishes, "Shall not every farmer's home become a school of Christian political science."

While this vision of the Alliance fireside does not necessarily presuppose that women should have the right to vote, woman suffrage was, especially for many western Alliance women, a "prerequisite for the establishment of the cooperative commonwealth," as historian Mari Jo Buhle put it. Kansas in particular had been a battleground of the suffrage movement since 1867, when Elizabeth Cady Stanton and Susan B. Anthony had led an unsuccessful campaign for equal rights, and many Kansas Populist women were veterans of such battles. Ironically, as we shall see, when the farmers' movement shifted in the 1890s from a community-based movement of social solidarity and economic cooperation to one of political reform, the role of women actually diminished. Despite the much-noted presence of a handful of fiery speakers and effective writers like Mary Lease and Annie Diggs, the high point of women's participation in the agrarian movement was in its early nonpartisan phase.

The Alliance family assembled by a rural fireside, the Alliance community gathered in a country church, the state or national Alliance convened in an urban auditorium—all became part of a "school" for national political reform. The St. Louis convention of December 1889 left no doubt that the farmers' movement was going into politics to transform shared values into public policy. The only question was how—by forming an independent party or by lobbying within the major parties.

The answer, for 1890, was both. In the West, as we have seen in Colorado and elsewhere, farmers and laborers formed state-wide Independent parties—an "Alliance ticket," as it was sometimes known. In the South, Alliance members applied the "Alliance yardstick" to prospective Democratic candidates for Congress and state legislatures. Each was to be asked for their views on the Alliance platform, and only those who measured up were to receive the endorsement of the organization. Both strategies had a certain logic to them, and in 1890 both seemed to meet with remarkable success. But amid the apparent triumph can be seen the root causes of Populism's ultimate defeat.

In the South, more and more farmers had reached the edge of economic disaster by 1890. Alliance cooperatives had offered relief but could not in themselves shield family farmers from the effects of both long- and short-term economic crises. In addition to the slow decline of the cotton economy several unexpected shocks triggered immediate angry responses.

For example, in the old cotton plantation district around Augusta, Georgia, many farmers had taken advantage of rail transportation, refrigerated railroad cars, and modern marketing facilities to diversify into fruit production, a profitable but risky enterprise. One of them was a thirty-four-year-old farm owner and lawyer named Tom Watson, who had already established himself as a spokesman for the beleaguered farmers of Georgia.

In 1890 the Richmond and West Point Terminal Company (forerunner of the Southern Railway) gained a stranglehold over rail traffic in the region and raised freight rates to ruinous levels. Farmers could either pay or watch their fruit rot. Tom Watson and his neighbors paid—and remembered. For them the Alliance's demand for public control over the railroads was now more than a political abstraction.

The southern Alliance consisted mainly of Democrats. Given their strength in the dominant party, they were inclined to use it as a vehicle for gaining relief from the railroads and credit merchants who threatened their financial independence. To those Democrats who complained about the divisiveness of an organized effort to elect Alliance candidates, there was a ready answer. As one South Carolinian expressed it: "How can we divide the Democracy when we are three-fourths of it?"

In the war of maneuver between the Alliance and the Democratic Party in the South, the *initial* response from the party's leadership was generally conciliatory. Rather than attacking the Alliance directly, many waffled on specific issues and smothered the movement with kindness.

North Carolina's Senator Zebulon Vance introduced the subtreasury bill in the Senate at Polk's request, despite his personal and as yet undisclosed opposition. Georgia's influential Democratic editor Hoke Smith made a highly publicized contribution to the Alliance exchange. Josephus Daniels, editor of the Raleigh *State* and like Smith a future cabinet officer in a Democratic administration, spoke for many party leaders when he confided to a fellow Democrat: "I agree with you most heartily that no good can come to the [party] by abuse of Polk or anyone else. I have believed all along that the Democratic speakers and the Democratic press ought to deal with the Alliance candidly and in a conciliatory way."

Applying the Alliance yardstick to Democratic candidates who followed Daniels' strategy was like trying to punch a marshmallow. Nevertheless, local and state Alliances across the South, sensing the power of their numbers, tried to pin candidates down on specific issues. That task was made more difficult by lack of agreement within the Alliance. A few members opposed any involvement in politics, while others were prepared to endorse

Democratic candidates who seemed generally supportive of reform principles, and still others insisted on holding candidates
to the letter of the St. Louis platform.

In four southern states the Democratic Party softened the Alliance's insistence on radical solutions by nominating for governor
men who had ties to the movement but who opposed the St.
Louis platform. In Georgia and Tennessee, conservative state
Alliance presidents were elected governor, as was Texan Jim
Hogg, who advocated railroad regulation but opposed the subtreasury plan. In South Carolina, Ben Tillman, fiery champion
of up-country farmers and a virulent white supremacist, won the
gubernatorial race on the basis of a vague but forcefully argued
attack on "foreign" (non-South Carolina) capital.

When the dust had settled, the Alliance seemed to have won
a great victory in the South. In addition to the four governors,
nineteen of the twenty-seven congressmen elected from the
South were, supposedly, committed to Alliance principles. Furthermore, eight state legislatures elected in 1890 appeared to be
dominated by members or supporters of the Alliance, which
meant, among other things, that U.S. senators to be elected by
legislative vote in 1891 should be held accountable to the Alliance
yardstick.

But it was never that simple, and not just because politicians
sometimes fail to keep their promises. The Alliance yardstick
meant different things in different places. In no southeastern
state was the Alliance completely committed to the St. Louis
platform. It could hardly have been otherwise, since the organization embraced such a wide spectrum of society. The biracial
tradition of radical reform that stretched back through the Knights
of Labor and the Agricultural Wheel to the Union League was,
at best, a minority presence within the Alliance east of the Mississippi, and in many places was excluded altogether.

The subtreasury plan might have provided a clear test of politicians' intentions. If enacted, the plan would have revolution-

ized the financing of the southern cotton crop and provided farmers with low-cost government loans. But in 1890 it was a novelty, not fully explained to the rank and file and hastily introduced in Congress with virtually no chance of passage. (Despite an intensive lobbying campaign led by Polk and Macune it languished in the House Ways and Means Committee and the Senate Agriculture Committee.)

Several state Alliances endorsed the subtreasury, but support from southern congressmen was another matter. In North Carolina, where support for the plan ran high, Senator Vance's opposition nearly cost him reelection, but in the end he wriggled free of a commitment to support it and was returned to the Senate. In Georgia, Governor John B. Gordon openly opposed the subtreasury but the freshly elected "Alliance legislature" nevertheless elected him to the Senate. They did so despite the efforts of Polk and Macune, who endorsed two different challengers. Macune campaigned vigorously for Patrick Calhoun, who, though he endorsed the subtreasury plan, was attorney for the hated Richmond and West Point Terminal Company.

In Texas, Alliance lecturer and future Populist leader Cyclone Davis confided to Ignatius Donnelly of Minnesota that the subtreasury "is the great lever with us among the farmers." But even in Texas the Alliance did not focus its lecturing and educational activities on the subtreasury until August, and then the combined forces of Macune and veteran greenbackers like Davis could not impose it on the state Democratic Party.

What would it take for southern Alliancemen to convince their senators and congressmen to support the subtreasury or other equally radical features of the St. Louis platform? Time enough to mount an educational campaign that would take the platform, subtreasury and all, to suballiances all across the South, a process that was only well begun in 1890. But implicit in that campaign was an even more difficult challenge—persuading the great mass of Alliance members that loyalty to the Alliance platform was more important than loyalty to the Democratic Party, perhaps even more important than the cause of white solidarity.

The political climate of the Great Plains was far different from that of the South in 1890. Outright breaks with the dominant Republican Party appeared, from the Dakotas down to the Oklahoma Territory. Independent slates for local and statewide office (the "Alliance ticket") sprang up along the Middle Border, to the consternation of old-line politicians and town boosters, who feared that "calamity howlers" would scare off prospective settlers and investors.

It was a little late to worry about that. Drought and financial distress had already triggered an exodus of farm families from the western reaches of the Great Plains. As in the South, sudden and unexpected shocks—especially increased freight rates—led farmers to focus their anger on the concentration of wealth and power in the hands of distant "plutocrats."

In 1890 many Plains farmers took the step that most Southerners could not yet contemplate; they founded statewide political organizations for the purpose of unseating Republican officeholders and replacing them with legislators, congressmen, and governors who would enact their program. Why the difference between West and South? Some Plains farmers were no doubt closer to absolute disaster, located as they were in a physically hostile environment and in a social network so new and fragile that community support mechanisms could not be relied upon.

In addition, there were two important differences in the *political* environment of the two regions that help explain why many Plains farmers chose the Alliance ticket over the Alliance yardstick. First, in several Plains states (most notably Kansas) there was a cadre of veteran third-party activists who were committed to the formation of a new party *and* well connected to the mass movement of farmers. In Kansas, for example, editors like the Vincent brothers (Henry and Leo) and Stephen McLallin, along with inveterate reformers like W. F. Rightmire and Annie Diggs, had long experience with the rich mixture of local protest movements that since the 1870s had included greenback radicalism, temperance and woman suffrage, and even spiritualism and other manifestations of religious heterodoxy.

Second, Republican officeholders and editors in the Plains states responded differently to the mass mobilization of farmers than did their Democratic counterparts in the South. Where southern Democrats like Vance of North Carolina waffled on the Alliance platform while trying to sound like friends of the movement, leading Republicans ridiculed the Alliance's leaders and its program of reform. In the opening battle of the war of maneuver between Populism and America's established political parties, Plains state Republicans attacked directly and thus invited a more immediate and decisive counterattack than would be found in the South or in the older midwestern states.

Kansas offers striking examples of both political types, singleminded champions of insurgency and pillars of the establishment who scorned the farmers' movement. During the 1870s and 1880s the Greenback and Union Labor parties had attracted a modest following and had produced a zealous band of perennial reformers who formed a super-secret band called the Videttes, which supposedly acted as a clandestine steering committee for reform politics. The group included the editors of a hard-hitting reform paper called *The American Nonconformist and Kansas Industrial Liberator*—three brothers named Cuthbert, Henry, and Leo Vincent, and William F. Rightmire. After the failure of the Union Labor Party in 1888, they were on the lookout for a vehicle through which to generate popular support for a new party.

According to an account given years later by Rightmire, he and Cuthbert Vincent had gotten themselves initiated into the Texas-based Alliance and had introduced it in Kansas. The Videttes then maneuvered the Alliance into political insurgency. Rightmire's story is questionable. Tales of manipulative inner circles are as old as American politics but often groundless, and Rightmire's claim to have founded the Kansas Alliance does not square with the facts. Nevertheless, Rightmire, the Vincent brothers, and other veteran insurgents did help form an independent party based on the Alliance. As it turns out, they were more adept at translating the anger of Kansas farmers into insurgency than in sustaining the movement.

Senator John J. Ingalls was the kind of enemy that insurgents like Rightmire might have wished for. Completing his third term in 1890, Ingalls proved incredibly insensitive to the plight of the farmers and disastrously frank in his public remarks about the nature of American politics. The hostility of Ingalls and the lesser politicians and editors who followed in his wake pushed many longtime Republicans into the new independent political movement, among them William A. Peffer.

Peffer was the Kansas counterpart of North Carolina's Leonidas Polk, and not just because of the beards that flowed down over both of their chests. Both men were highly respected farm editors and spokesmen, stalwarts of the dominant party in their respective regions, and champions of radical financial plans that could only be enacted by the federal government. At about the same time Polk was discovering Macune's subtreasury scheme, Peffer laid out a similar proposal whereby farmers would receive short-term low-interest loans based on warehouse or elevator receipts for stored crops.

In February 1890, Peffer asked Ingalls to state his views on the issues of concern to farmers. Ingalls haughtily replied that he would make a statement in due course, but through some other medium than Peffer's newspaper. Ingalls' allies vilified Peffer for even asking the question. Meanwhile, grass-roots momentum was building for independent political action. County Alliance presidents, meeting on March 25, called for Ingalls' defeat, appealed to the Knights of Labor for political cooperation, and took the first steps toward channeling the energies of their movement into the formation of a new party.

In April, Senator Ingalls gave his reply in the form of an interview with the New York *World*. To those who sought political reform Ingalls had this to say: "The purification of politics is an iridescent dream. Government is force. Politics is a battle for supremacy. . . . The decalogue and the golden rule have no place in a political campaign." And finally: "This modern cant about the corruption of politics is fatiguing in the extreme." William Peffer, outraged by Ingalls' moral insensibility, cast his lot with the insurgents, taking with him many Republican voters who in the past had been unmoved by the appeals of perennial insurgents like Rightmire.

History is full of what-ifs. Imagine how things might have turned out in Kansas and North Carolina (and by extension in the West and South) had Senator Ingalls and his crowd agreed in 1890 that "no good can come" to the Republican Party by abusing Peffer or other farm leaders, and that they were resolved "to deal with the Alliance candidly and in a conciliatory way," while at the same time Senator Vance and the lesser Democrats had insulted Polk and Tarheel farmers with talk of iridescent dreams.

On June 12, Kansas leaders of the Alliance, Knights of Labor, Farmers' Mutual Benefit Association, and Single Tax clubs assembled in Topeka to found a "People's Party." What followed was a campaign so unlike those that had gone before that it required a different kind of language to describe: "The upheaval that took place . . . can hardly be diagnosed as a political campaign. It was a religious revival, a crusade . . . in which a tongue of flame sat upon every man, and each spake as the spirit gave him utterance."

And so it was, but that dramatic picture needs some down-to-earth explanation, with regard both to the leadership of the movement and to its mass base. Whether or not those who spoke for the movement were filled with the Holy Spirit, they were most certainly prepared for the crusade of 1890 by prior experience in the forces of radical reform and political insurgency. Jeremiah

Simpson (labeled "Sockless Jerry" by a Republican opponent), perhaps the best speaker among Kansas Populists, was a veteran of campaigns on the Greenback, Independent, and Union Labor tickets, as well as a disciple of Henry George. Mary Elizabeth Lease, the most flamboyant of the women who took a public role in the campaign, had previously lectured for the Irish National League and woman suffrage as well as the Union Labor Party. Annie LaPorte Diggs, less strident than Mrs. Lease, had established a reputation as a writer for the temperance and suffrage movements prior to 1890. She would become one of the movement's most effective editorialists.

These and other veteran reformers had never before enjoyed the support of a mass organization such as the Alliance. In 1890 the nascent People's Party had a reciprocal relationship with the Alliance. On the one hand, the new party attached itself to the Alliance to acquire a statewide network of neighborhood organizations. On the other hand, the ongoing organizing campaign of the Alliance was energized by the added imperative of political mobilization. In community after community the Alliance was, simultaneously, a vehicle for social solidarity, a focal point for economic cooperation, and an informal agent of the new People's Party.

The results were dramatic. Five out of seven congressional races went to the Populist candidate, including Jerry Simpson. Almost four-fifths of those elected to the state House of Representatives were Populists, enough to offset a large Republican majority in the Senate and send John Ingalls into retirement, replacing him with William Peffer.

A careful voting analysis by Gene Clanton demonstrates the remarkable success of the new party in its first campaign but also anticipates the difficult choices the party would soon face. The statewide vote for the People's Party—over 100,000 strong—was drawn in almost equal proportions from former Republicans, former Democrats, and former third-party voters. Having mobilized so many voters but having failed to sweep either of the major parties from the field, the party would soon confront the question of whether it could succeed without making common cause with one of the other two.

In 1890 Kansas had the most successful Populist party, but not the only one, or even the first. On June 6, the South Dakota Farmers' Alliance voted to form an Independent Party. The Dakota Alliance had already established the most vigorous program of economic cooperation on the Middle Border, including an innovative crop insurance program. As in Kansas, promotion of cooperatives and creation of a third party went hand in hand. Business agent Alonzo Wardall was a prime mover in the new party. Alliance president Henry L. Loucks won 40 percent of the vote as Independent candidate for governor, and the new party captured enough legislative seats to join with Democrats in sending Congregational minister James H. Kyle to the United States Senate.

In Nebraska veterans of the Union Labor campaign of 1888 were less influential in the Independent movement than in Kansas, and the Alliance leadership was more divided on the issue of insurgency. Nevertheless, an Independent movement did emerge to wage a campaign that one Republican described as "a composite of Hugo's pictures of the French Revolution and a western religious revival." The Independent convention nominated Alliance president John H. Powers for governor, and in the state's three congressional races there were signs of informal cooperation between Independents and Democrats. The Republicans were the big losers in Nebraska. For the first time a Democrat won the governorship, narrowly edging out Powers, and two of the three congressional seats went to Independents. The third was won by a young Democrat who had sought both the Independent and Democratic nominations, and, failing that, had courted Independent voters throughout the campaign. His name was William Jennings Bryan.

The Independent and People's parties of the western states had made an impressive showing and had created momentum for the formation of a national party to contest for the presidency in 1892. By the same token, those Southerners who had applied the Alliance yardstick to Democratic candidates had reason to smile. At a minimum they had gotten the attention and respect of many of the region's leading political figures, as well as a host of smaller fry—state legislators and congressional candidates—who pledged to support Alliance principles.

But there was also reason to be concerned. The goal of the movement, after all, was to enact into law the radical demands most recently revised and reaffirmed in St. Louis. But how knowledgeable were the rank-and-file members about the platform, and how deep was their commitment to its enactment?

Both the western and southern strategies, as they played out in 1890, produced an extremely rapid mobilization of rural people whose anger at incumbents and generalized antimonopoly beliefs were beyond dispute. But it is doubtful that many of the members both knew what the platform contained and embraced its every plank, including nationalization of the railroads, abolition of the national banks, and transformation of the credit system through the subtreasury. To be sure, the movement included many who were steeped in greenbackism and some who were true believers in the gospels of Henry George and Edward Bellamy. But politically, the movement had gotten ahead of itself. A massive campaign of education and exhortation would be required if the grand army of farmers and workers was to storm the ramparts of American politics.

In addition to the lack of informed consensus on a platform, the would-be Populists displayed a curious but thoroughly American ambivalence about political parties. They insisted, time and again, that principle counted for more than party, and some would have agreed with a contemporary New York reformer (not a Populist) that parties were "only combinations for the purpose of getting place and power." What would happen to a body of true believers such as this one when it turned out that some of their leaders were just as intent on self-aggrandizement as Democratic or Republican hacks, or when the movement's principles could be implemented only by making deals with one of the two hated major parties?

These potential pitfalls for the nascent political force that was coalescing in 1890 were internal to the movement. Populism was also constrained by its position within the larger culture and subject to unexpected or unanswerable moves by the major parties. What if midwestern Republicans decided to co-opt the movement rather than ridicule it? What if southern Democrats shifted from courtesy to violent opposition? And what if those southern Democrats played the racial card? Could a fledgling movement of potentially radical dimensions withstand the combination of brute force and debilitating appeals to white solidarity? The future, which looked so bright for the movement, was also fraught with danger.

Both the dramatic success of the movement and the causes for alarm were on display when the annual meeting of the NFA&IU convened in Ocala, Florida, in December 1890. Even the location of the meeting spoke to the growing national diversity of the farmers' movement. Central Florida, though geographically southern, was not part of the cotton South. Its emerging fruit and vegetable farms, made possible by modern transportation and marketing systems, made the Ocala region more like the California valleys than the older staple-crop regions of cotton, tobacco, corn, and wheat, from which the Alliance had arisen.

The same mix of boosterism and social criticism that characterized the California Alliance was to be found among the Floridians who hosted the Ocala meeting. As in California, the Florida Alliance had developed an aggressive cooperative marketing network (complete with a New York office) in an effort to direct the state's agricultural growth toward the interest of family farmers. The NFA&IU was drawn to Ocala by the promise of free accommodations and reduced railroad fares, which were offered to advertise the opening of Ocala's Semitropical Exposition—a kind of mini-World's Fair complete with agricultural and commercial exhibits and a mammoth carnival. (Ocala is less than sixty miles from the present-day site of Disney World.)

Despite the excursions and the hoopla, the participants in the Ocala meeting had serious business to attend to, and they knew it. Delegates from twenty-five states were seated, along with observers from a half dozen farmer and labor organizations.

The great issue at Ocala was how—not if—the Alliance and kindred organizations should enter national politics in 1892. Delegates from the West and the South had different answers, buttressed by the events of 1890. The Kansans, spurred on by the Vincent brothers and other third-party advocates, urged the Alliance to endorse a national People's Party to continue the work begun in the Plains states in 1890. Most Southerners stuck by their strategy of the Alliance yardstick and at the very least cautioned delay in the formation of a national third party.

Westerners who had forsaken the Republican Party in 1890 had a very practical concern. If Southerners refused to join their western brethren in insurgency and the net effect was to strengthen the Democratic Party nationally, the Westerners would be under intense pressure to return to the GOP. Southerners argued, with equal logic, that having committed themselves to a strategy of promoting the reform agenda within the Democratic Party they must at least give that approach time to succeed or fail in the legislative sessions upcoming in 1891.

Western insurgents at Ocala, led by the Kansas delegation, called for a national conference, to be held early in 1891 in Cincinnati, to form a national party. Southern delegates (still in the majority) objected, and the Kansans did not force the issue on the floor of the convention. The Alliance did, however, endorse a proposal by Macune to enter into a confederation with other reform organizations that would conduct political education based on the Alliance platform in 1891 and convene a national conference in early 1892.

For Alliance delegates of all stripes, "political education" was the watchword at Ocala. Virtually the entire spectrum of Alliance leadership embraced President Leonidas Polk's call to field paid lecturers in each congressional district in 1891. Delegates approved both the district lecture system and a network of Alliance and labor newspapers (the National Reform Press Association), which, jointly, would provide the informational base of a third party, with or without the name.

The text of that educational campaign was to be a revised version of the Alliance's platform, which was agreed to almost without exception by supporters and opponents of a third party. The Ocala demands modified earlier platforms by incorporating western land-loan schemes into the subtreasury plan, proposing stronger governmental regulation of railroads and telegraphs (with public ownership to be a last resort), and calling for direct election of United States senators and the establishment of a graduated income tax. With only slight alterations, the Ocala demands would be the banner of Populism in the 1890s.

Despite agreement on the platform and an agreement to disagree about forming a third party, there were ominous signs of disharmony at Ocala. Both Polk and Macune faced charges of interfering with the Georgia senatorial election. Macune's enemies claimed he had taken money from Patrick Calhoun in exchange for his support (it was not the first time charges of malfeasance had been leveled at the Texan), and although an investigative committee found no proof of the charges, Macune's reputation was sullied and his relations with Polk strained.

Even more ominous than the squabble over the Georgia Senate election was the interjection of a volatile racial issue. A Mississippi delegate introduced a resolution putting the Alliance on record in opposition to the Lodge Election Bill, then pending in Congress. The Lodge Bill (known as the "Force Bill" in the South) would have reestablished federal protection for black voting rights in the South. The Mississippi resolution passed by voice vote, but on the last day of the convention Alonzo Wardall called for it to be stricken from the minutes. His motion was tabled, with voting divided mainly along sectional lines.

The potential political alignment of West and South in a new party, already fragile, was now even more at risk even before the Year of Education had begun.

5

Creating a
Political Culture:

The People's Party, 1891–92

In 1891 and early 1892, champions of a new reform party labored
on two fronts to create a viable national organization. In a series
of highly publicized conferences reformers of all stripes argued
the merits and tactics of launching a new party. There was, in
essence, a traveling continuation of the Ocala debate. Simultaneously, veterans of the reform crusade began a massive educational campaign, conducted through a network of reform
newspapers employing new technologies of mass communication
and through a disciplined lecturing system designed to mobilize
grass-roots support for political insurgency. By means of these
and even more dramatic forms of persuasion, the farmer-labor
movement hoped to fashion an irresistible force in American
politics by the time of the 1892 elections.

In January 1891, the northwestern Alliance, meeting in
Omaha, endorsed a set of demands similar to the Ocala platform
and called for the formation of a new party in 1892. Later that
month, representatives of the NFA&IU, the Colored Farmers'
Alliance, the Knights of Labor, and the newly formed Citizens'
Alliance met in Washington to confirm plans for a conference of
industrial organizations to be held in February 1892. Representatives of the Colored Farmers' Alliance and the Citizens' Alliance
were ready to get on with the new party, but Macune and his

allies insisted that the issue remain open until the 1892 conference.

Frustrated by the delays and uncertainties, a band of western insurgents headed by the original leaders of the Kansas People's Party reissued the call for a May convention in Cincinnati that they had originally made in Ocala. They were determined to proceed with the formation of a new farmer-labor party, whether the Alliances were ready to move or not.

"Founding" conventions had become something of a regular event in the Midwest: four meetings held during the past two decades had launched new parties, with no lasting results. This time, however, the perennial reformers had tapped into the massive Alliance movement of the Plains states. If they were to succeed in forming a national party they would need to bring Southerners into the fold. Thus the significance of another confrontational gathering, one that nominally involved only one state, Texas, but in fact had larger implications.

In early 1891 while most Southerners still clung to the hope of reform within the Democratic Party, Alliance radicals were maneuvering closer to insurgency, their cause strengthened by the actions of supposed friends of the movement in high places. In Texas, the reform agenda of newly elected Governor Jim Hogg began and ended with the establishment of an appointed railroad commission. When the Alliance's legislative watchdog committee pressed for more, Hogg blasted the committee and the subtreasury plan, warning that those who insisted on the subtreasury yardstick were third-party troublemakers.

Hogg had it about right. Veteran Texan insurgents like William R. Lamb (an early leader of Alliance radicalism), Evan Jones (an architect of the Cleburne demands), and "Stump" Ashby (a one-time Methodist minister whose sermons proved too radical for his superiors) had been busily organizing a new lecturing system to spread the subtreasury message across the Lone Star State.

In April, Jones summoned Alliance lecturers from across the state to a meeting in Waco. Noting the political import of the conference, Macune rushed back to Texas, inviting leading Alliance Democrats from Georgia and South Carolina to come and help him block a third-party move. They were met by a phalanx of Texas insurgents and national leaders of the third-party movement—Henry Vincent of Kansas, Alonzo Wardall of South Dakota, and Ralph Beaumont, the socialist lecturer of the Knights of Labor who, representing the Citizens' Alliance, had challenged Macune's delaying tactic in January.

This "educational" conference might well be considered the beginning of the People's Party in the South. Debate was courteous but intense, and in the end the insurgents prevailed. The conferees strengthened the lecturing system, established Texas affiliates of the National Reform Press Association and the National Citizens' Alliance (Lamb was named president of the former and secretary of the latter), and voted to send a delegation to the "National Union Conference" in Cincinnati. In a gesture that affirmed the continuity between this new departure and the farmers' movement, Captain L. S. Chavose of Lampasas presented the triumphant insurgents with the banner of the first Farmers' Alliance.

On May 18, 1891, banner headlines in the Cincinnati *Enquirer* heralded the arrival of "THE GREAT INDUSTRIAL ARMY." The delegates and self-styled representatives of a kaleidoscope of reform organizations—1,400 strong—were not exactly an army: Single Taxers, Bellamyites, prohibitionists, and woman suffragists mingled in Cincinnati's Music Hall with the more numerous representatives of the Alliances and other farm organizations.

With Senator Peffer of Kansas chairing the meeting, advocates of prohibition and woman suffrage received a hearing for their causes (Peffer favored both), but the focus of the conference was on how and when to form a third party, not on adding new planks to a platform. A vocal minority of the delegates opposed immediate action. They included not only a handful of southern Alliance leaders and (in absentia) Leonidas Polk but also several third-party stalwarts, including Congressman-elect Jerry Simpson of Kansas, William Lamb of Texas, and former Greenback presidential candidate James B. Weaver of Iowa. Why the hesitation? None could fail to notice the lack of southern participation in the Cincinnati meeting. Fewer than forty representatives from the former Confederacy showed up, and most of them were from Texas. The ceremonial embrace of Confederate veteran Cyclone Davis of Texas with a Union counterpart from Indiana merely highlighted the fact that the southern battalions of the industrial army were missing from the ranks. The most powerful argument for delay was that it would increase the prospects for southern participation, without which the new party was doomed.

In the end, the Cincinnati conference virtually endorsed the Ocala platform, voted to establish a provisional Executive Committee of a new party (to be styled the People's Party of the United States), and instructed that committee to attend the conference previously announced for February 1892. If that conference launched a national party, they were to join forces with it. If not, they were to issue an independent call for a presidential nominating convention. Herman E. Taubeneck of Illinois was elected chairman of the provisional committee, which was to include three members from every state represented at Cincinnati. Thus, for all the foot dragging, the People's Party now had a nucleus of leadership for mobilization in the states during 1891.

Around that same time the party also acquired the nickname by which it has been commonly known. The name was conceived, by one account, on the train ride home from Cincinnati, when leaders of the Kansas delegates discussed the need for a more succinct label for members of the People's Party. From the Latin *populus*, for "people," they invented the term "Populist." And it stuck.

So the new party had a name and a skeletal organization, but it did not have the South. The political direction of the former Confederacy depended, in no small measure, on the Farmers'

Alliance, which had recruited more white Southerners than belonged to the Baptist or the Methodist Church. There would be no mass defection of Alliancemen to Populism before the yardstick strategy had been fully tested. The test was not long in coming. Before cotton-chopping time in the spring of 1891 it was clear that the southern Democracy would not embrace the Ocala demands.

One southern legislature after another declined to enact the Alliance's legislative program. Mississippi and Florida followed the example of Georgia and North Carolina, where popular politicians who opposed the subtreasury were elected to the United States Senate. In state after state where members of the Alliance comprised majorities of the legislature, reform proposals went down to defeat.

Nowhere was the failure of the Alliance yardstick more dramatic than in Georgia. Late in 1890 the legislature had elected John B. Gordon to the Senate. (This Democratic stalwart, who opposed almost all elements of the order's legislative agenda, had himself initiated into the Alliance before the legislative session.) When the legislators reconvened in the spring of 1891 they passed a bill that increased creditors' power to collect from debt-ridden farmers and killed bills that would have strengthened regulation of railroads and out-of-state corporations. After intense debate within the Alliance caucus, the legislature gutted instructions to the Georgia congressional delegation that they support no one for Speaker of the House who did not endorse the Ocala demands. All this left J. T. Olive, author of the anticorporation bill, complaining to Terence Powderly about the *"pseudo* reform leaders here."

Why did the Alliance fail so miserably to work its will in southern legislatures in 1890–91? Certainly the entrenched power of banks, railroads, and Democratic regulars presented formidable obstacles. Southern Democrats and their journalistic allies unleashed the same venom against the Alliance as western Republicans had in 1890. During the pivotal year of 1891 there were also violent incidents reminiscent of the Ku Klux Klan terror a generation earlier. In Mississippi, arsonists burned the offices of the state's leading reform paper, and few doubted that the attack was the work of Democratic regulars.

But outside enemies were not solely to blame. Many legislators elected in 1890 with Alliance backing had only tenuous connections to the order, and when push came to shove the so-called Alliance legislatures did not turn out to be so different from those that had preceded them. Furthermore, in most southern states the Alliance itself was deeply divided over the Ocala demands, despite the fact that they had been ceremonially ratified by most of the state Alliances.

The real question was whether, once reform through the Democratic Party had failed, the great mass of southern voters could be persuaded of the logic of insurgency: *if* Alliance principles took precedence over partisan loyalty and the Democratic Party rejected those principles, *then* men of integrity must leave the party of their fathers. But to act on that logic was, as one anguished Virginian put it, "like cutting off the right hand or putting out the right eye." To bring Alliance voters to such a drastic step and to enfold them in an alternative culture of American politics called for an unprecedented campaign of political education.

In his presidential address at Ocala, Leonidas Polk identified education as "the greatest and most essential need" of the movement. The Alliance had *always* been an educational institution, in which suballiances were the classrooms, Alliance newspapers and tracts the textbooks, and Alliance lecturers and organizers the teachers. In the critical months following the Ocala meeting, Alliance leaders committed to fixing the order's political demands onto the national agenda agreed on the need for a more organized and sophisticated educational program. While not aimed exclusively at the South, this campaign had no more important target in 1891 than the states of the former Confederacy.

To some modern readers, the reformers' appropriation of the term "education" may seem out of place: education is what goes on in schools, while *propaganda* is the stuff of political campaigns. One is objective and factual, the other subjective and emotional. But the distinction has never been that clear, and the reformers knew it. Then as now, schools' curricula were not immune to social conflicts. Indeed, as the political struggles of the Populist era approached their zenith, the nation's educational system itself became a cultural and political battleground.

Populists claimed that the "textbook trust" not only inflated the price of educational materials but, more importantly, controlled their content so as to present a politically correct version of history and economics—a Whiggish telling of the story that celebrated the rise of industrial capitalism, denied the loss of economic and political liberties among farmers and laborers, and ignored the erosion of traditional family and community values.

The aim of the reformers' educational campaign was thus twofold: *politically*, to recruit and energize a grass-roots army capable of capturing both state and federal governments, and *culturally*, to rewrite the "curriculum" through which Americans were instructed in political economy. Both goals would be pursued by means of the written word and a kind of Socratic dialogue within the schoolroom of the local Alliance.

Reform newspapers, books, and tracts had provided a richly varied stream of news and information since the beginning of the movement. The spread of new printing technologies in the 1870s and 1880s made it easier for every community to have its own newspaper—often edited, composed, and printed by one person. Would-be reform journalists needed only a little cash and a big appetite for writing and typesetting to get started. Endorsement as the "official organ" of a county or state Alliance increased the odds of survival.

The job of publishing a country newspaper was made easier by the national distribution of "boiler plate" (metal plates containing columns of printed material) and "ready print" (paper stock already printed on one side). By means of these new technologies local readers could receive timely information about events in the wider world. However, the principal distributors of commercial boiler plate were hardly sympathetic to the reform movement and its view of political economy.

At Ocala, leaders of the reform movement took steps to co-ordinate the work of the hundreds of local reform papers and to provide an alternative source of national news by establishing the National Reform Press Association. Macune, editor of the NFA&IU's official organ, *The National Economist*, was named president of the NRPA, but its other officials were committed third-party men—W. Scott Morgan of Arkansas, Cuthbert Vincent, Ralph Beaumont, and William Lamb.

Local editors could join the Association by submitting back copies of their papers for examination, agreeing to support the political demands of the NFA&IU, the Farmers' Mutual Benefit Association, and the Knights of Labor, and paying a small initiation fee. In return they received each week "plates of carefully edited matter, including an original cartoon." The stream of statistics and analysis, along with the weekly political cartoon, bolstered grass-roots understanding of the movement's political agenda. As one historian of Populism has noted, in 1891–92 the National Reform Press Association served as "the basic internal communications agency" for the formation of a national People's Party.

Both the NRPA and several of the larger reform papers developed whole series of lessons for use by suballiances and local political clubs. In 1891–92 Macune's *National Economist* produced scores of exercises on political economy, complete with pedagogical instructions. Macune's lessons turned the Whiggish version of history on its head: from ancient Greece to contemporary America, history was on the side of the producers, not of the holders of concentrated capital. As one observer has noted, "for Macune, history became a kind of laboratory in which he tried to demonstrate the elemental laws of social and political change."

In addition to distributing educational materials with the

weekly editions of reform newspapers, the Alliance recruited and trained new cadres of lecturers, whose task was to convey in a uniform way the message of the Ocala demands and to promote discussion of political issues within the local Alliances. Unlike the early organizers, the new lecturers were to be paid from a central fund rather than depending on a portion of initiation fees.

The lecture system, like the educational exercises prepared for the suballiances by the reform press, promoted discussion and questioning rather than passive learning, or so the fragmentary remains of Alliance proceedings would indicate. The suballiance-as-school was a protected space within which rural men and women could find their own voices and explore the meaning of an alternative political culture. In regions where the NFA&IU was just establishing a presence in 1891 (parts of the Pacific Northwest, the old Midwest, and the Northeast) lecturers openly combined Alliance recruiting and political education with the formation of a partisan organization. In the South, most of the county and congressional district lecturers were veteran organizers and political activists, and by 1891 many of them were moving toward the third party.

Such was the case in the desolate hill country west of Austin, Texas, where Samuel Early Johnson boldly signed his name to the Gillespie County Alliance's political resolutions (they endorsed the Ocala demands and denounced the "subsidized press" and the monied interests that controlled it) and was elected county lecturer. The next year Johnson, grandfather of the thirty-sixth President of the United States, would become a Populist candidate for the state legislature.

Populism's campaign of political education employed materials and methods that came readily to hand—newspapers and tracts, neighborhood gatherings, even the archetypal religious institution of rural America, the camp meeting. In Kansas, Texas, Georgia, and even Pennsylvania, the Alliance and kindred organizations appropriated the form of religious encampments for their own purposes. Observe one such gathering at the precise moment when the Alliance movement is being transformed into the People's Party.

It is late July 1891, after crops have been laid by and rural families are free to leave their farms for the customary round of camp meetings. Traveling on a dusty road in northeastern Texas, you find yourself approaching one such gathering. It is early morning in the shady grove outside the town of Sulphur Springs. The smoke of cooking fires hangs in the trees, and the smell of breakfast is in the air. You add your wagon and team to the hundreds already filling the grove. Thousands of rural men, women, and children have assembled from surrounding counties for five days of singing, praying, and speechmaking.

By 9:30 a huge crowd is gathering at the speakers' stand, and those just arriving can make out the strains of a familiar hymn. The assembled congregation stands for prayer. The Reverend S. J. Brownson takes the rostrum, reads from scripture, and begins the morning sermon. But this is no ordinary camp meeting. Brownson explicates his scriptural text "to show the right and necessity of preachers taking an active part in the politics of the country." The speaker, editor of a Populist newspaper, leaves no doubt that the clerical activism he has in mind is of a radical variety. The country is in the grip of plutocrats, Brownson explains. "We are now in the dark night of slavery. . . . Sixty millions are in absolute slavery today, but the Alliance will emancipate them."

The exhortations, songs, and prayers continue all day and into the evening. Speaker after speaker lays bare the evils of the nation's financial system and holds out the promise of legislative relief. The speakers include Texas Alliance-Populist stalwarts like Sulphur Springs's own Cyclone Davis, as well as visiting luminaries of the movement like William Peffer of Kansas and C. A. Post of Indiana. After the camp meeting was over and the twelve thousand or so participants returned to their homes, a nervous Democrat reported that "the seeds of discontent have been sowed and it will take considerable speech-making to heal the wounds of [the Democratic Party] in this section, not that the speeches of the new party have really been convincing, but their assertions have been of a most sweeping character."

Sweeping indeed. One Populist spokesman proclaimed that "Christ himself was the author and President of the first Farmers' Alliance." Others claimed scriptural support for their cause. For these men and women biblical history was continuous with and directly relevant to contemporary events; thus the message of the Hebrew prophets, the ministry of Jesus to the poor, and the biblical vision of the coming kingdom gave the formulators of Alliance-Populist dogma a historical vantage point from which to judge the ills of industrial capitalism.

The carefully orchestrated camp meetings (as carefully orchestrated as those which Methodists and Baptists used to channel converts into local church membership) gave the third-party movement a powerful means of creating community and mobilizing a committed following. By just such means as these did rural Americans find themselves in the summer of 1891 drawn to the People's Party.

The orchestration of the camp meetings by third-party leaders illustrates an important point about how the People's Party came into being, a point easily obscured by the metaphors that liken the movement to a prairie whirlwind. Populism didn't just happen. In 1891 and 1892 insurgent leaders mounted an intensive campaign to create an organized social base for a new party in almost every region of the United States. Prominent Populists and Populist-leaning reform leaders crisscrossed the nation in a frantic effort to replicate the successful Populist mobilization in Kansas. For example, Peffer's appearance at a camp meeting in Texas was the final stop on a long swing that began in West Virginia.

The campaign varied according to the organizational needs in each region. In the band of vote-rich states from Pennsylvania westward to Michigan and on the Pacific coast, third-party champions spearheaded recruiting drives for the NFA&IU that were more or less openly linked to partisan mobilization. In the Plains states and Texas they created or revived membership organizations that paralleled the Farmers' Alliance—a Citizens' Alliance for urban workers, a Women's Alliance, and new and reactivated assemblies of the Knights of Labor. And in the South, where enough farmers were already mobilized in the Alliance to create a major party, they skillfully employed the Southerners' own logic of the Alliance yardstick to drive a wedge between farmers and the Democratic Party.

What followed was a political war of maneuver, or more accurately a series of such wars, played out in the individual states. Political parties in nineteenth-century America, for all their national trappings, were in fact collections of state and local bodies, and the success of the new People's Party would depend both on its ability to mobilize people state by state and on the tactics of local Republican and Democratic parties at the moment they confronted Populism.

In the summer of 1891, Kansas Populists flooded neighboring Iowa, organizing local affiliates of the NFA&IU, helping to found a state People's Party, and campaigning vigorously for its slate of nominees in Iowa's off-year elections. The Greenback Party had seriously eroded Republican domination in Iowa in the mid-1880s, and a credible Populist showing there in 1891 could have established the viability of the new party in the Midwest. But the organizing campaign did not produce the kind of movement that had swept Kansas, and the Populist ticket captured a mere 3 percent of the vote.

Populism never enjoyed the success in Iowa and the Midwest that it did in the Plains states. Scholars have usually explained this by pointing out differences in the agricultural economies of the two regions or in the type of farmer organization: the Midwest was not as hard hit by depression or drought as the Plains, and the NFA&IU had no significant presence in the region prior to 1891.

Economic and organizational differences may help account for the failure of midwestern Populism, but recent studies of Iowa politics suggest that these differences have been overstated. Falling farm prices hurt farmers in Iowa as well as in the Dakotas, and while the drought-induced suffering of western Kansas and Nebraska surpassed anything in the Midwest, western Iowa was as hard hit as the contiguous regions of eastern Kansas and Nebraska. Although the southern Alliance (the NFA&IU) was a Johnny-come-lately to Iowa, the northwestern Alliance had established local and state cooperatives—even a mutual insurance company—before such agencies of "movement culture" were established in Kansas and Dakota.

What distinguished Iowa from its neighbors to the west was its recent political history. While conservative Republicans dominated politics in Kansas and Nebraska until 1890, the GOP in Iowa had faced a serious challenge in the 1880s from a coalition of antimonopoly Democrats and Greenbackers, including James B. Weaver, one of several fusion candidates to wrest congressional seats away from the Republicans. Faced with the prospect of losing their jobs, most Republican officeholders saw the wisdom of the antimonopoly and Alliance demands for stricter state control over the railroads.

In a stunning defeat for the railroad-dominated Republican leadership, the Iowa legislature in 1889 imposed maximum freight rates and made the state railroad commission elective rather than appointive. In Iowa, with both major parties actively bidding for farm support, the Alliance yardstick had worked. Why then, Iowa farmers asked, join the Populists? Few did.

If Plains state Populists were anxious to establish a presence in the nearby Midwest, they were desperate to mobilize the South. The Alliance's strong base of support in the mostly rural South convinced western Populists that the South offered the greatest opportunities for victory in 1892. More importantly, Kansas Populists badly needed to draw Southerners away from the Democratic Party to counteract damaging criticism at home. Kansas Republicans were scoring points by claiming that the People's

Party was nothing more than a conspiracy to destroy the GOP by luring western farmers away from their traditional home while Southerners stayed within the party of their fathers.

Kentucky offered an immediate opportunity to silence the critics. Like Iowa, Kentucky was to elect a governor and state officials in 1891. It had both a sizable Farmers' Alliance and a People's Party organization in place to challenge the Democrats. Kansas Populists, including Peffer and Congressman-elect John Otis, moved in to help organize the state, and national chairman Taubeneck took personal charge of the campaign. Making full use of the persuasive techniques described earlier, the Populists urged Kentuckians to rally behind the one party that fully upheld the Alliance principles, including the subtreasury.

Kentucky, like Iowa, enjoyed robust competition between the two major parties. In the most recent presidential campaign, Republican Benjamin Harrison had won 45 percent of the popular vote in narrowly losing the state to Grover Cleveland. Democrats and Republicans could see clearly the danger of ignoring the ground swell of agrarian discontent. One leading contender for the Democratic gubernatorial nomination was advised: "Anything you can do to soft-soap the Alliance will go down to your interest." The eventual winner of the Democratic nomination, John Y. Brown, was by no means a farmer candidate, but he courted rural support by promising to get tough with the powerful Louisville & Nashville Railroad.

Brown won the governor's race with a bare 50 percent majority. Kentucky Populists fared better than their counterparts in Iowa (9 percent of the vote as compared to 3), and Taubeneck declared: "The 'solid south' is broken." But elections are not won with 9 percent of the vote. The farmers' movement in Kentucky, though large and well organized through the Alliance, was not united in its view of political insurgency. Both major parties, as well as the infant People's Party, garnered substantial votes in the elections of 1891. It would take more than a whirlwind campaign to break the domination of the Democratic Party in the South.

The *real* break in the Solid South would come only if the Populists could gain a foothold in the Carolinas and the Deep South. Nowhere did their prospects seem brighter than in Georgia. During the summer of 1891, William Peffer, Jerry Simpson, and Mary Lease toured the state, speaking on behalf of the Ocala platform and, by indirection, the third party. Democratic leaders, recognizing the threat, excoriated the Kansans and their Georgia hosts. One editor referred to Mrs. Lease as a "watery-eyed, garrulous, ignorant and communistic old female from Kansas."

Democrats had good reason to worry about the continued support of the "wool-hat boys," as Georgia's dirt farmers were commonly known. The state legislature, dominated by Democrats supposedly sympathetic to the Alliance, had rejected the Ocala demands and had elected a foe of the subtreasury to the Senate. Escalation of freight rates by the Richmond and West Point Terminal Company threatened ruin for farmers in the eastern part of the state. A healthy Alliance organization that blanketed the state could readily become the structure for mobilizing farmers into the third party, and a pair of farm leaders seemed poised to make the leap into insurgency.

Lon Livingston and Tom Watson had both been elected to Congress as Alliance Democrats in 1890. Livingston, president of the state Alliance and an ally of Charles Macune in the ill-fated campaign to elect Patrick Calhoun to the Senate, could lambast anti-Alliance Democratic politicians with the best of them, but when push came to shove he worked to keep rural Georgians within the Democratic fold, not to lead them out of it.

Tom Watson, a wiry thirty-five-year-old redhead who could "talk like the thrust of a bowie knife," had already developed a statewide following among embattled small farmers. He was, to be sure, an unlikely Populist. Descended from wealthy planters but impoverished in his youth, Watson had taken up the law and had made a small fortune at it. With earnings from his law practice and judicious investment in farmland (he owned 3,000 acres and had twenty-one tenant families on his place), Watson was one of the wealthiest men in his part of the state. But no one could more effectively articulate the anger and fear of the small farmer than Watson, and although as a lawyer he was ineligible for membership in the Alliance, he became its champion, combining in great oratorical flourishes a defense of his beloved Southland against the onslaughts of northern capitalists and a critique of the financial and transportation systems that threatened to impoverish farmers regardless of race or standing.

In later life Watson recalled, "I did not lead the Alliance; I followed the Alliance, and I am proud that I did follow it." Allowing for a certain false modesty, the Farmers' Alliance in Watson's congressional district *did* lead him toward the third party. Farmers were outraged by the actions of the Richmond Terminal and the seeming collusion between the Democratic Party and big business. Watson's own sense of outrage at the inaction of the state legislature—and Livingston's questionable role in the senatorial election—was bolstered by the sober calculation that the Ocala demands counted for more among his rural constituents than loyalty to the Democratic Party.

Watson and his Populist-leaning allies battled the Livingston forces for control of the state Alliance and lost. Searching for a platform and a means of discrediting Livingston among rank-and-file Alliance voters, Watson began publication in October of a newspaper boldly entitled *The People's Party Paper*, and in November he dispatched a trusted ally, Mell Branch, to the NFA&IU's national meeting in Indianapolis with a simple but startling proposal. With Livingston and the other Georgia delegates looking on in horror, Branch introduced a motion that instructed all congressmen elected with Alliance support to enter no party caucus that did not require endorsement of the Ocala platform. (It was through caucuses held at the beginning of each Congress that the majority party selected a Speaker and in effect organized the House of Representatives.)

The Fifty-second Congress was scheduled to convene within

a few weeks, with a large majority of Democrats. If Branch's motion passed, Livingston, Watson, and the forty-odd Southerners elected in 1890 with Alliance support would be instructed not to take part in the Democratic caucus, where an antisubtreasury Georgian, Charles F. Crisp, was expected to be nominated for Speaker, but rather to join with western Populists in a new party caucus.

The fate of Branch's resolution not only had a tremendous bearing on southern politics; it was also a good barometer of the pressures building within the NFA&IU. Leonidas Polk, by now a Populist in all but name, had been easily reelected president, and western Populists held many of the key positions at the Indianapolis convention. Over Livingston's objections Polk referred the resolution to the Committee on Demands, chaired by James B. Weaver. The committee, and then the whole convention, ratified Branch's motion by a comfortable margin, doing so in the sober realization that it made the national Alliance virtually an adjunct of a new political party.

Branch's motion proved to be the means by which the Alliance yardstick was decisively applied. Just before the new Congress was to convene and elect a Speaker, Alliance congressmen met in the Washington office of Macune's *National Economist*. The southern contingent had shrunk to seventeen, of whom sixteen —led by Livingston—rejected the Indianapolis ruling and announced their intention to vote with the Democrats. The seventeenth, Tom Watson, looked Livingston in the eye and shouted at him, "The farmers trusted you, and now you want to betray them for your own personal interest."

With tempers flaring, Livingston and all but one of the Southerners trooped off to join the Democratic caucus. The nine remaining members (Watson and eight Westerners) adjourned to Senator-elect Peffer's rooms, where they held the first congressional caucus of the People's Party. The eight Westerners agreed to nominate Watson for Speaker.

Back in Georgia, at the call of the Populists' provisional ex-

ecutive committee (all associates of Watson), Alliancemen and
other rural Georgians began organizing from the grass roots up,
precinct by precinct, county by county, often simply transforming
local Alliances into People's Party committees. By the beginning
of 1892, economic distress, rejection of Alliance demands by the
Democrats, and the internal dynamics of the Farmers' Alliance
had combined to create the People's Party in Georgia.

On February 22, 1892, the long-awaited conference of industrial organizations convened in St. Louis. The mood of that gathering demonstrated just how much the political balance had
shifted since the Ocala convention had accepted Macune's compromise suggestion for holding such a conference on Washington's birthday in 1892. Farmer, labor, and reform leaders of all
stripes were present for what, in fact, was more like a mass
meeting than a representative assembly. By far the largest contingent was from the NFA&IU, and for the first time many of
the Alliance's southern delegates were prepared to embrace the
third party. The temperance and woman suffrage movements
were also well represented, directly by delegates from the WCTU
and the Women's Alliance and indirectly by delegates from other
organizations that championed one or both of their causes.
Frances Willard, president of the WCTU, had labored before
the conference opened to lay the foundation for a merger between
Populists and prohibitionists in a broadly based reform party.

Leonidas Polk, already being mentioned as a possible presidential candidate for the People's Party, was elected permanent
chairman of the meeting, and Frances Willard was selected vice
chair. The assembled delegates reaffirmed the platform of the
NFA&IU, strengthening it by reasserting the demand for public
ownership of railroads rather than government *regulation* as in
the Ocala demands. A separate set of resolutions (not formally
part of the platform) included an endorsement of the proposition
that "the question of female suffrage be referred to the legislatures of the different states for favorable consideration." Prohi-

bition, an even more volatile issue in the West than woman suffrage, was not mentioned.

After approval of the platform itself, the delegates were brought to their feet, cheering wildly for a full ten minutes, by the reading of a preamble written by Ignatius Donnelly of Minnesota, veteran reformer and one of Populism's most powerful orators. Donnelly's preamble, which was subsequently incorporated into the People's Party platform at the national convention in Omaha, is a crucial document in the history of Populism. The preamble denounced the two major parties for their insensitivity to the sufferings of the American people and unequivocally called for a new national party to implement a reform program. As a philosophical statement, Donnelly's powerfully worded preamble was a succinct distillation of Populist thought as it had been developing in the Alliance and labor halls of America for the past two decades. It evoked the moral outrage of rural and working-class Americans at the conditions that surrounded them and articulated their shared sense of the proper role of government in addressing the nation's ills.

Imagine Donnelly's words being read to the hundreds of delegates packed into St. Louis's Exposition Music Hall, who had already been stirred by two days of singing and oratory. Standing under a banner that read: "We do not ask for sympathy or pity. We ask for justice," Donnelly proclaimed:

> We meet in the midst of a nation brought to the verge of moral, political and material ruin. Corruption dominates the ballot box, the legislatures, the Congress, and touches even the ermine of the bench. . . . The newspapers are subsidized or muzzled; public opinion silenced; business prostrated, our homes covered with mortgages, labor impoverished, and the land concentrated in the hands of capitalists. . . . the fruits of the toil of millions are boldly stolen to build up colossal fortunes, unprecedented in the history

of the world, while their possessors despise the republic and endanger liberty. . . .

In this crisis of human affairs the intelligent working people and producers of the United States have come together in the name of justice, order and society, to defend liberty, prosperity and justice. We declare our union and independence. We assert one purpose to support the political organization which represents our principles.

We charge that the controlling influences dominating the old political parties have allowed the existing dreadful conditions to develop without serious effort to restrain or prevent them. They have agreed together to ignore in the coming campaign every issue but one. They propose to drown the outcries of a plundered people with the uproar of a sham battle over the tariff, so that corporations, national banks, rings, trusts, "watered stocks," the demonetization of silver, and the oppression of usurers may all be lost sight of. . . . We assert that a political organization, representing the political principles herein stated, is necessary to redress the grievances of which we complain.

Assembled on the anniversary of the birth of the illustrious man who led the first great revolution on this continent against oppression, filled with the sentiments which actuated that grand generation, we seek to restore the government of the republic to the hands of the "plain people" with whom it originated. Our doors are open to all points of the compass. We ask all men to join with us and help us.

After the cheering had subsided, Lon Livingston moved the adoption of the platform *without* the preamble, but the delegates would have none of it and endorsed both, clearly signaling their approval of the third party. Just as the meeting was adjourning, Charles Macune took the floor and shouted for the delegates to stay in their seats for a mass meeting to be chaired by James B.

Weaver, the purpose of which was to coordinate with the Executive Committee of the People's Party the call for a national nominating convention. A committee was formed for that purpose, and in conjunction with Taubeneck's Executive Committee it announced that the convention would be held on July 4 in Omaha, Nebraska. All those in sympathy with the movement were urged to meet in their respective communities in March, ratify the St. Louis demands, and elect delegates who would, through a progression of county, district, and state conventions, select delegates to the Omaha convention.

This selection process outlined in St. Louis was intended not only to name convention delegates but also to mobilize a national party, precinct by precinct. Since national political parties were in fact loose confederations of state parties. Populist success in 1892 would depend, in part, on recent political history in the various states. On the Great Plains the success of state-level insurgency in 1890 and 1891 prepared the ground for nationally oriented organizing in 1892. Conversely, in midwestern states like Iowa where the two major parties had more successfully co-opted the Alliance movement, the Populist organizing campaign made little headway.

In the West, the character and intensity of Populist mobilization varied from state to state. In Colorado, labor editor Davis W. Waite, a committed antimonopolist, organized a state People's Party in September 1891. Waite's party was strongly connected to the national movement and its entire platform (reflecting the influence of Alliance and labor veterans), although by early 1892 the decline of silver prices gave particular urgency to the agitation for currency reform. In Nevada, the third-party movement, in the form of a Silver Party organized by former Republicans, focused entirely on the remonetization of silver and identified itself with national Populism only as a matter of convenience.

In Wyoming, where stock raising, not silver mining, dominated the economy, the St. Louis appeal for third-party mobilization had almost no impact until a dramatic confrontation in the Powder

River region galvanized support for the People's Party. Large landowners, backed by agencies of state government, dominated the local cattle industry and controlled most of the rangeland. In April 1892 their organization, the Wyoming Stock Growers Association, hired twenty-five Texas gunmen to suppress a rival organization of small stock raisers in Johnson County.

Accompanied by a band of ranch foremen and cattlemen, the gunmen rode into Johnson County for the stated purpose of rooting out rustlers, but with the clear intent of intimidating small stockmen. (Some said they carried a list of those marked for execution.) After the invaders had burned several homes and killed two alleged rustlers, they were intercepted and surrounded by angry Johnson County stockmen. The mercenaries were rescued by federal troops from nearby Fort McKinney, who were ordered into action by President Harrison upon the urging of Wyoming's governor and U.S. senators. The invaders and those who had sent them into Johnson County went unpunished.

The collusion of Republican state and federal officeholders with the Wyoming Stock Growers Association and its hired gunmen unleashed a storm of protest against the GOP and pushed small stockmen into alliance with the fledgling Laramie-based People's Party. Knights of Labor and Populist organizers Henry Breitenstein and Shakespeare Sealy persuasively explained the Johnson County war as a struggle between producers and monopolists. Republicans deserted to the new party in droves, and when Wyoming delegates arrived in Omaha they were able to persuade the national party to condemn the "invasion of . . . Wyoming by the hired assassins of plutocracy, assisted by federal officials."

In the South no single event equaled Wyoming's Johnson County war in defining the gulf between Populists and non-Populists, but the internecine struggle at St. Louis between Populist-leaning Southerners like Polk and die-hard southern Democrats like Livingston foreshadowed a debate that would divide communities, churches, and even families in 1892. Up until that point, the farm movement had brought together a wide social and economic spectrum of rural white Southerners who had accepted, if somewhat uneasily, an alignment with black farmers similarly organized in a parallel Jim Crow Alliance. The Democratic Party had embraced or at least tolerated the movement in an effort to keep southern white farmers within the majority party.

This would all change after the Populists' grass-roots mobilization campaign moved into high gear at St. Louis. In Texas and Tennessee, Democratic officials required Alliance members to renounce the order's political agenda before participating in party conventions. Elsewhere Democratic spokesmen heaped ridicule on Populists and their leaders, much as Republicans had done in Kansas two years earlier.

Upon returning to Georgia from St. Louis, Lon Livingston warned that the new party was dangerously unorthodox on matters of race. His close associate in the Alliance, Governor William J. Northen, took up the cry and added to it the charge that leading Georgia Populist Charles C. Post (a recent émigré from Chicago) was an infidel and an anarchist. Prominent churchmen in Georgia and other southern states branded Populism as a threat to property and good order and thus anathema to the region's prevailing religious values.

Potential Populists in the South now faced hard choices. Standing with the Alliance's demands and the People's Party meant setting oneself in opposition to the region's prevailing culture and might well mean cutting oneself off from family and friends. As Milford W. Howard, Alabama's lone Populist congressman, later recalled: "My own father would not hear me speak and said he would rather make my coffin with his own hands and bury me than to have me desert the Democratic Party." A century later it is difficult for Americans to conceive of a time when partisan conflict could drive such a wedge between father and son, but 1892 was just such a moment.

In June 1892, less than a month before the Omaha convention, two events occurred that had substantial and opposite effects on the course of Populism in the South. On June 11 Leonidas Polk, the party's probable presidential nominee, died of cancer. His death deprived the national party of its most articulate spokesman for sectional reconciliation, and it removed from consideration the one candidate who could have made it possible for many Southerners to join the Populists without seeming to desert the South (though Polk's nomination would not have mollified the likes of the elder Howard).

On June 22 the Democratic National Convention in Chicago spurned appeals to incorporate farmers' demands in their platform and nominated former President Grover Cleveland for President. Cleveland had been unpopular when he left office in 1889, and nowhere more so than in the South, in part because of his unyielding opposition to currency reform. For all their posturing and feigned support for the farmers' movement, southern Democratic delegates to the Chicago convention voted overwhelmingly for Cleveland's nomination.

For thousands of wavering and desperate Southerners this was the last straw. Among them was Virginian Edmund Cocke, a large landholder and member of a prominent family, who had concluded that "a very short duration of existing conditions will reduce all Virginia farmers to serfdom." Grover Cleveland had contributed to this sorry state of affairs by supporting the "monstrous combination of capital" that controlled the volume of money. Cocke wrote to his cousin, a Democratic congressman, to explain how he had reached a political decision that would force Cocke "to separate myself from many near and dear to me." Cocke recalled that "on the 23rd June at 2 P.M. I [received] the papers giving me the [Democratic] platform and the nomination of Cleveland. In one hour I was en route to the Peoples Party Convention in Richmond."

Thus by many routes did Populists from the various states reach the first national convention of the People's Party in Omaha. The call for the Independence Day convention had set the number of delegates at 1,776. (Around 1,400 actually came.) Beginning their work on July 2 so as to ratify a platform and make nominations on the Fourth of July, the delegates distilled the key points of farmer-labor platforms from the past two decades into a document that they referred to as a "Second Declaration of Independence."

The Omaha platform—the clearest and most unadulterated expression of Populist political thought—began with Donnelly's apocalyptic preamble, slightly reworked to take full advantage of the Independence Day theme. The heart of the platform was a succinct statement of the movement's position on the venerable trinity of issues—money, transportation, and land, with particular emphasis on the first.

The financial plank was a recapitulation of greenbackism, and included the following demands: government control of the currency and its distribution to the people without the use of banking corporations by means such as the subtreasury "or a better system," "the free and unlimited coinage of silver and gold at the present legal ratio of sixteen to one," an increase in the supply of money to no less than $50 per capita, a graduated income tax, limitation of government revenues to that which is needed for necessary expenses (a jab at the protective tariff), and the establishment of postal savings banks.

The transportation and land planks were brief but contained truly radical demands—public ownership of railroads and of telegraph and telephone systems and an end to monopolistic control and alien ownership of land. Appended to the platform was a list of ten resolutions, including demands for adoption of the "Australian" or secret ballot, various plans for the protection of labor, and denunciation of large corporations' use of private armies (referred to collectively as Pinkertons) to suppress strikes and intimidate Western stock raisers.

This last point had special urgency for the delegates, not only because of the recent memory of the Johnson County war but also because at the very moment the platform was being drafted an army of Pinkerton agents was descending on the Carnegie

Steel Works at Homestead, Pennsylvania, to do battle with workers who had been locked out of the mill the week before. On July 6 a pitched battle between steelworkers and the Pinkertons would leave sixteen dead and would make the name Homestead synonymous with industrial conflict.

The Omaha platform was drafted quickly and with little controversy, with the exception of the missing plank on woman suffrage. (The platform's architects had deleted the controversial suffrage plank from the St. Louis demands in an effort to broaden the party's appeal, but in doing so they drew sharp rebukes from women delegates, including Mary Lease's daughter, Louisa.) The completed document was enthusiastically received by the delegates, who applauded, sang, and waved banners for what seemed like hours. One observer noted, "This dramatic and historical scene must have told every quiet, thoughtful witness that there was something at the back of all this turmoil more than the failure of crops or the scarcity of ready cash."

The "something more" was, in fact, the encapsulation of decades of agrarian and radical thinking. Through the Alliances and labor organizations, through the writings of social critics like Henry George and Edward Bellamy, Americans of the industrial age had reworked and reaffirmed the antebellum principles of producerism and republicanism. In the new age of monopolism the Jacksonian slogan of "equal rights for all, special privilege for none," took on a new meaning. The survival of democratic capitalism now required governmental action on behalf of ordinary citizens. As Donnelly's preamble put it: "We believe that the powers of government—in other words, of the people—should be expanded . . . as rapidly and as far as the good sense of an intelligent people and the teachings of experience shall justify, to the end that oppression, injustice, and poverty shall eventually cease in the land."

The platform adopted at Omaha reflected decades of thought and debate. By contrast, the selection of presidential and vice presidential nominees was the work of the few frantic weeks since Polk's death. Some wished they could nominate Jerry Simpson, but the Canadian-born Kansan was constitutionally ineligible. After the death of Polk much of the talk centered on Walter Q. Gresham, originally from Indiana but by 1892 a federal judge in Chicago. Though not an announced Populist, Gresham was reported to be an advocate of free silver and a champion of labor. He would have added an air of respectability to the ticket and might have helped the party in the vote-rich midwestern states of Indiana, Illinois, and Iowa, but his own equivocation and the opposition of many Populists to nominating a man from "outside the ranks of the workers-in-the-vineyard" removed him from consideration by the time the delegates convened in Omaha.

It seemed as if by process of elimination the nomination would go to James B. Weaver, Greenback presidential nominee in 1880 and a perennially available third-party candidate. Some delegates, seeking a fresh face, turned to the forty-year-old senator from South Dakota, James H. Kyle. Some Southerners, anxious to have a candidate not so strongly identified with the Union Army as General Weaver was, initially backed Kyle. But when the ballots were counted Weaver won by a four-to-one margin. The Populists balanced the ticket by selecting as Weaver's running mate a former Confederate major (called "General" as a courtesy) named James G. Field, who had lost a leg in combat. Field "knew the oratorical language of the South and could speak it well" as one classic study of Populism notes, but he had never joined the Alliance in Virginia, and as recently as three weeks before the convention had not decided whether to join the People's Party!

Thus the People's Party left Omaha with a ticket headed by a man who carried the stigma of being a perennial third-party candidate and seconded by one who had no serious connection to the Populist movement. In all likelihood no candidate short of George Washington could have produced a Populist victory in

1892, but a ticket headed, for example, by Polk and Peffer could have generated a fuller representation of Populism's true strength.

The Populist campaign of 1892 was, in the view of those who waged it, a continuation of the crusade to mobilize American farmers and workers in a righteous cause. But now the crusade turned political party would run headlong into some sobering realities of American politics. In the West, the issues of prohibition and woman suffrage divided Populists along traditional party and ethnic lines. In the South, the specter of race haunted the new party, as did the ever-present prospect of election fraud by the ruling Democrats. In the Northeast—home to well-oiled political machines—the Populists lacked the organizational base necessary to mobilize voters. Nationally, the Populists would find that the major parties, however ponderous and loosely connected they might be, had a remarkable capacity for coalescing every four years to mount effective and well-financed presidential campaigns.

As the Populist crusade evolved into a national political party seeking to prevail in national as well as state campaigns, the issues of prohibition and woman suffrage—closely linked in the public mind—presented tactical dilemmas. Many Populist women and not a few of the party's male leaders had a long association with the temperance and prohibitionist movements. Annie Diggs, for example, began her political career in Kansas as a poll watcher for the Prohibition Party. But in the West, where Populists were already cooperating with Democrats against a common Republican foe, association with the prohibitionist cause would mean certain rejection by the Democratic Party, for whose immigrant supporters antiprohibition was an article of faith. At the national level, the People's Party sidestepped the prohibition issue altogether, much to the dismay of Frances Willard and others who had hoped to create a grand union of economic and moral reform.

Populism's relationship to woman suffrage is more complex. Southern Populists opposed it and helped to keep the issue out of the Omaha platform. The People's Party in Kansas, Idaho, Oregon, and Washington endorsed woman suffrage, and Populists in those and other states supported it in their respective legislatures. In Kansas, however, the introduction of enfranchising legislation in 1891 sharply divided the Populist forces. Kansas Populist women were joined by Stephen McLallin and other radical third-party advocates in support of the measure, but it was opposed by the Populist leader in the state House of Representatives and several of his colleagues, who joined with Republicans in defeating it.

The Rocky Mountain West had a more progressive tradition on woman suffrage than either the Great Plains or the South. Women had first received the right to vote in Wyoming and Utah territories in 1869 and 1870. In 1890, Wyoming became the first state to grant women the vote, and elsewhere in the region Populists supported the measure. With Governor Waite's blessing Colorado Populists joined with Republicans to adopt woman suffrage in 1893. In Montana, the popularity of Ella Knowles, Populist candidate for attorney general, attested to the overall support of the suffrage issue. The historian of Mountain state Populism is certainly correct in claiming that Populists there "played a notable part in the crusade for woman suffrage." In the nation as a whole, however, Populists were not of one mind on the issue.

Of all the stumbling blocks to Populist success, none would prove more vexing for the Populists themselves and more troublesome to students of the movement than the issue of race, particularly in the South. White Populists (indeed, white Americans) from *all* parts of the country operated within a culture that assumed the racial superiority of Northern European peoples. Farmer-labor coalitions in the Pacific Northwest championed the exclusion of Chinese workers. Alliance members in the South participated in an economic system that had exploited slaves and continued to exploit their descendants. If Great Plains Populists seemed more tolerant on matters of race, it was largely because, except for a few pockets of emigrants from the South, blacks were largely absent from their communities.

Nevertheless, in the South, where over 90 percent of all African-Americans lived and where they potentially held the balance of power, the possibility of a biracial coalition of the poor stirred hopes—and fears—as it had since the days of Reconstruction. In a few corners of the rural South there was a continuous and vital tradition of biracial cooperation, often stretching back through the Knights of Labor and the Agricultural Wheel to the Republican coalitions of the 1870s. Elsewhere in Dixie, when the Alliance moved decisively into the political arena in 1891 and 1892, its leaders sought cautiously to establish ties with their counterparts in the Colored Farmers' Alliance, and through them their black constituencies.

Sometimes working through that organization's president, R. M. Humphrey (a white Southerner and an early advocate of the People's Party), and sometimes striking out on their own, white Alliance leaders gingerly courted black leaders like John B. Rayner of Texas and Walter A. Patillo of North Carolina. Rayner (a teacher) and Patillo (a Baptist preacher) were part of a network of black community leaders long active in Republican politics and, in their cases, the rural organizing efforts of the Knights of Labor.

In the 1880s and 1890s quiet courtship of black voters by way of influential community leaders was commonplace among Democratic officeholders, who, despite the rhetoric of racial solidarity, often relied upon black votes to remain in power. It is difficult to know exactly how the Alliance-Populist liaisons with the black community in 1891–92 differed from Democratic practice: white participants were circumspect in what they said and wrote, and few life stories of black participants have survived in the historical record. Nevertheless, when we see one or two black delegates in southern Populist conventions, when we hear white Populists awkwardly pledging to respect the political (not social) equality of blacks, and when we encounter sustained cooperation between

Populists and biracial Republican state organizations, it would seem that we are glimpsing something more than southern politics as usual.

Certainly the Democrats thought so. When the Populist mobilization began, bringing with it the prospect of a biracial challenge for control of local as well as national office, Democratic spokesmen unleashed a devastating racist barrage and a persuasive appeal for white solidarity. As Tom Watson put it in the summer of 1892, "The argument against the independent political movement in the South may be boiled down into one word—nigger." Ironically, in hotly contested races such as Watson's own bid for reelection to Congress, Democrats also used race in a very different way: by fraud or intimidation they rounded up enough black votes to beat the Populists.

This is the conventional story of race and southern Populism: a courageous Populist attempt to build a coalition of the have-nots was snuffed out by a relentless racist attack and by the manipulation of black votes. There is much truth to the story. Such coalitions did appear in many communities across the South, only to be beaten down with words and with more powerful weapons. In one East Texas community the black and white Populist movement lasted until the end of the decade and was wiped out only by a deadly hail of bullets.

But then as now, the interplay between economic and racial interest, between movements of reform and of reaction, is not quite so straightforward as the story would suggest. While we may never know exactly what most black Southerners thought about the prospect of forging an alliance with rural whites, we can infer certain grounds for skepticism on their part. For one thing, many of the leaders of the Alliance and of southern Populism looked frighteningly familiar: they were among the landed elite who had managed the plantations and made the laws that kept many blacks in a state of near-slavery. (Georgia planter William L. Peek, Populist candidate for governor in 1892, had once introduced a bill in the state legislature that would have sent farm tenants to jail for failing to fulfill their contracts with landlords.) Furthermore, the economic interests of black farm laborers and sharecroppers did not coincide with those of white landowners, and thus there were differences in their preferred remedies. The Colored Farmers' Alliance, for example, endorsed Henry George's Single Tax plan and was less than enthusiastic about the subtreasury.

The interests of black laborers and white farm owners diverged dramatically in the fall of 1891 when Humphrey called for a South-wide strike of cotton pickers, the goal being to increase wages from fifty cents to one dollar per day. Few blacks actually responded to the strike call outside of East Texas and the delta plantations of eastern Arkansas, where fifteen strikers were lynched, but the white agricultural press reacted with cries of outrage not appreciably different from the reactions of other southern journalists.

And what of the white Southerners who in 1891–92 dreamed of a Populist movement that embraced all producers regardless of skin color? By the end of the decade many of them, beaten down by the double-edged Democratic attack, were demanding the disfranchisement of black voters as a means of ending political corruption and restoring social harmony.

Even in 1892 the dream was severely circumscribed. White Populists were careful to distinguish between black political rights, which they initially supported, and social equality between the races, which they uniformly opposed. In Alabama and North Carolina, the Populists' alliance with the Republican Party fostered the free exercise of voting rights by blacks, but in Georgia, Populists were themselves guilty of Klan-like activities to discourage blacks from voting anything other than the Populist ticket. Even in 1892, the historian of Georgia Populism concludes, "there can be no doubt that Georgia Populists used terror and intimidation to influence state elections."

Assessing Populism's experiment with interracial politics in the South is like asking whether the glass is half empty or half full.

This much we can say: for a brief moment the People's Party, made up of various strands from the region's social fabric, included threads of a quarter-century-old biracial tradition and a new and fragile multihued skein, but it also included older and uglier strands woven tightly into the life of the region and the nation.

Even while southern Populists wrestled with the complexity of a biracial coalition, the People's Party as a whole confronted a second conundrum that they would never fully resolve, the issue of cooperation with one of the two major parties. Here the logic and history of Populism as a *movement* collided with the ultimate *political* question: how to get more votes than the other guy. Having once crossed the line between interest group and insurgent movement, Populism set itself in opposition to traditional political dealmaking. We stand on principle, the Populists proclaimed, and we will have nothing to do with the corrupt old parties. When they talked that way they sounded for all the world like religious enthusiasts of the "come-outer" or Restorationist traditions in American religion, who believed that by shunning the corrupt old churches they were restoring Christianity to its original purity.

As a political tactic, however, that stance could doom the People's Party to perpetual minority status. The alternative was "fusion" with the smaller of the two major parties in a particular state—an agreement to divide the slate of offices and presidential electors between the two. In Kansas, where the independent movement achieved its greatest success in 1890, many Populists had already interpreted those election returns to mean that only by cooperating with the Democrats could they expect to defeat the Republicans. And they did so in 1892, along with Colorado and Wyoming Populists. In the South, where the relative positions of the major parties was reversed, Populists considered fusion with Republicans, but except in Alabama they rejected it, for the moment.

In subsequent years the debate between "fusionists" and "mid-roaders" (those who avoided both old parties and stuck to the middle of the road) would divide and fatally wound the People's Party. In 1892 the key questions in that debate were already on the table: could Populists cooperate with Democrats in the West and Republicans in the South without abandoning the principles upon which their movement was founded, and, conversely, could they ever actually win elections without such cooperation?

Candidate Weaver, whose political career in Iowa had included Democratic-Greenback collaboration, was fully prepared to accept fusion at the state level, but his own task was to mount a credible nationwide campaign in direct competition with a sitting Republican President, Benjamin Harrison, and a former Democratic chief executive, Grover Cleveland. Between them the Democrats and Republicans would spend nearly $4 million on the national campaign, while the Populist national committee was virtually broke. And although the Populists were better organized in some parts of the West and South than their major-party rivals, both had shored up their grass-roots organizations since the vigorously contested election of 1888 in which Harrison had defeated Cleveland by fewer than 100,000 votes.

Playing David to the major-party Goliaths, Weaver broke with tradition and took his campaign directly to the people in a grueling cross-country speaking tour. Neither Cleveland nor Harrison campaigned personally, relying instead on surrogate speakers and on the mass circulation of campaign literature by their parties. Although he promised to campaign in every state, Weaver focused on the West and South, where there was reason to believe the Populists had a chance of winning.

Accompanied by his wife, Clara, Mary Lease, and other leading Populist speakers from Kansas and South Dakota, Weaver toured the Far West and the Great Plains, where he received enthusiastic welcomes. But even accompanied by his vice presidential running mate, Weaver was less well received in the South. The Democratic press kept up a steady attack on his war record, alleging that he had committed atrocities against Confederate prisoners, and local Democratic organizations heckled him wherever he appeared.

Weaver's tour of Georgia was particularly perilous. In Macon an angry crowd hurled insults and rotten eggs at Weaver and his traveling party, leading Mary Lease to tell a Kansas audience some months later that "Mrs. Weaver was made a regular walking omelet by the southern chivalry of Georgia." The next day in Atlanta, upon learning that even Tom Watson had required police protection to escape from an angry mob, Weaver cut short his campaign tour, citing "a spirit of organized rowdyism."

The candidate's reception in the South foreshadowed the election returns. Cleveland swept the South on his way to regaining the presidency. In no southern state except Alabama did Weaver receive more than a third of the vote. Fraud, intimidation, and outright violence accounted for part of the poor showing, but more importantly, the Alliance's educational campaign failed to convert the great mass of rural white Southerners to the third-party cause, and the halfhearted courtship of black voters yielded little.

Results from the West were more heartening. Weaver carried Kansas, Colorado, Nevada, and Idaho, and shared in the electoral votes of North Dakota and Oregon. His twenty-two electoral votes were the first won by a third party since the Civil War. Populist-Democratic cooperation also produced gubernatorial victories in Kansas and Colorado, while elsewhere Populist candidates won a significant number of state and local offices.

Western Populists could not hide their disappointment at the failure of their southern brethren to add any numbers to Weaver's electoral total, even though the Populist ticket had made a respectable showing in six southern states. Their criticism is less useful as an analysis of the national election returns than as a statement about their political troubles at home, where they were vulnerable to Republican charges of indirectly helping to elect Cleveland.

Far more important than the Populists' failure to carry the

South, and more ominous for the future of the party, was the result in the vote-rich northeastern quadrant of the nation, where Weaver had not even campaigned. East of the Mississippi and north of the Ohio River—in states that contained twice as many electoral votes as the former Confederacy—Weaver received less than 5 percent of the vote, and in much of the old Midwest (including his home state of Iowa) he did no better.

Cleveland, not Weaver, received most of the protest votes of those who were out of sorts with Harrison, including the votes of many industrial workers. As former President Rutherford B. Hayes explained it: "The labor vote, holding the balance of power and better organized than ever before, joined the Democrats." With the Knights of Labor now reduced to a corporal's guard, Populists in 1892 had little entrée into the organizational world of industrial workers. It remained to be seen whether the People's Party could yet forge a national farmer-labor coalition.

Just as the decline of the Knights of Labor spelled trouble for one wing of the farmer-labor coalition that had shown such promise in the 1880s, so too the virtual collapse of the Farmers' Alliance signaled a dangerous erosion of the social movement that undergirded the People's Party. As early as 1891 most of the Alliance cooperatives in the South and West were dead or dying, and with them died the fundamental reason why many had joined the order.

The campaign of 1892 virtually put an end to the Alliance. Hundreds of suballiances were converted into local People's Party clubs, few of which survived the fall campaign. Members who objected to the Alliance's embrace of the new party simply abandoned the order, and despite lingering efforts to revive it on a nonpartisan basis, the Alliance was effectively finished.

Proof of the Alliance's moribund condition—and of Populism's need for an underlying membership organization—can be seen in the efforts of national chairman Herman E. Taubeneck to create a successor. No sooner was the election over than Taubeneck set about promoting a new organization called the Industrial Legion. Modeled on the Grand Army of the Republic (the Union veterans' organization) and "commanded" by GAR official Paul H. Vandervoort of Nebraska, the Industrial Legion had, not surprisingly, little success in the South, and not much more in the West.

The election of 1892 was only the first national campaign for the People's Party. There would be chances for greater success amidst the economic crisis that struck soon after Cleveland's inauguration, and the closely balanced competition between the major parties would create space for the third party to maneuver. But the character of Populism would not be the same. The white-hot emotions of a protest movement would begin to give way to the calculations of one more political party, and the community-based organizations through which rural men and women had come to imagine the possibility of the cooperative commonwealth simply melted away.

6

The Crisis of Populism,
1893–98

On May 1, 1893, the newly inaugurated President of the United States, Grover Cleveland, opened the World's Columbian Exposition in Chicago with the press of a button. Touching an ivory telegraph key, President Cleveland turned on the Exposition's 10,000 electric lights and started up the machinery in buildings throughout the "White City" that had been built on the shores of Lake Michigan to commemorate the 400th anniversary of Columbus' voyage to the New World.

The fair, with its technological marvels, cultural beauty, and commercial vitality, proclaimed the bright promise of America's future. Even Populists and other critics of industrial capitalism were captivated by the fair. Eugene Debs called it "the sublimest testimony the world has ever heard or seen . . . of the civilizing, elevating, liberalizing force of labor." Henry Demarest Lloyd thought that it "revealed to the people possibilities of social beauty, utility, and harmony of which they had not even been able to dream." In far-off Texas, veterans of the Lampasas Farmers' Alliance disassembled the cabin in which they first met for shipment to Chicago, anticipating that it would be part of their state's exhibit at the fair. And after touring the Exposition, Hamlin Garland dashed off a note to his father back on the Dakota farm: "Sell the cook stove if necessary and come. You *must* see this fair."

Four days after Cleveland opened the Exposition, the New York stock exchange crashed, signaling the onset of a depression that was, until the 1930s, the nation's worst. By the end of 1893, 15,000 businesses had failed—including five of the nation's largest railroads—and as many as 20 percent of the nation's industrial workers were unemployed. In Chicago alone, 75,000 were out of work by winter, and a young reporter named Ray Stannard Baker wrote to his parents from Chicago, "There are thousands of homeless and starving men in the streets. I have seen more misery in this last week than I ever saw in my life before."

At harvesttime farm prices in the rural South and West dropped below the costs of production, and on the Great Plains drought added to the misery. The desperation on the western Plains jumps out at us from this matter-of-fact message of a Kansas farm woman to Populist governor Lorenzo D. Lewelling in 1894:

> I take my pen in hand to let you know that we are starving to death. It is pretty hard to do without anything to eat here in this God forsaken country. . . . My husband went away to find work and came home last night and told me that we would have to starve. He has been to 10 counties and did not get no work.

A century removed from this human tragedy we can analyze the systemic sources of this collapse: the ripple effect of a European depression underway since 1890, the cumulative impact of declining farm prices that had racked the South and West since the late 1880s, frenzied speculation and unsound borrowing on the part of industrial and railroad giants, and a currency system that lacked the volume and elasticity to meet the demands of a growing economy. But for those who experienced the depression firsthand, a more immediate explanation came to mind: Cleveland and the Democrats were to blame.

Imagine what the reaction of that Kansas woman would have been to Cleveland's Secretary of Agriculture, who proclaimed: "The intelligent, practical, and successful farmer needs no aid from the Government. The ignorant, impractical, and indolent farmer deserves none." In California, unemployed men began referring to the soup kitchens that kept them from starving as "Cleveland cafes." In South Carolina, Governor Ben Tillman bellowed, "Send me to the Senate, and I'll stick a pitchfork in Grover Cleveland's old fat ribs." In Colorado, where free silver was a matter of local jobs before it was a plank in the Populist platform, Governor Davis Waite promised to fight Cleveland on the currency issue through the ballot box and with stronger means if necessary: "If the money power shall attempt to sustain its usurpation by the 'strong hand,' we will meet that issue when it is forced upon us, for it is better, infinitely better that blood should flow to the horses' bridles than our national liberties should be destroyed."

Unemployed workers and destitute farmers—and the millions of Americans who feared they might soon join them—threatened to sweep the Democrats from power. Who stood to benefit from the Democrats' misfortune? The Republican Party, though weakened by Cleveland's victory in 1892 and by Populist gains in the West, was still a national power to be reckoned with, particularly since Republicans had the good fortune of being out of power when the depression hit.

But the depression seemed tailor-made for the Populists. It was their platform that had spoken of "a nation brought to the verge of moral, political, and material ruin," and had outlined a program of governmental action to curtail the special privileges of the wealthy and protect the equal rights of working people.

If hard times alone make Populists, then the economic collapse of 1893 would most assuredly usher in the Populist moment. But the fate of the Populist crusade depended on other forces as well, including (as the elections of 1890 and 1892 attest) the interplay among political parties and programs and the credibility of Populist officials in those states where they had actually won office.

The response of President Cleveland to the economic crisis of 1893 seemed to play into the Populists' hands, but in the long run it would create for them a profound dilemma. Cleveland called Congress into special session on August 7 to repeal the Sherman Silver Purchase Act of 1890. The President's action riveted national attention on an issue that, up until that time, had been of secondary interest to the Populists. To understand how the battle over the Sherman Act affected the career of the People's Party, let us step back from the political combat of 1893 to review the history of the silver issue.

The question at hand was whether the government would purchase and coin silver and at what price (expressed as a ratio of silver to gold). From the founding of the Republic until 1873, both gold and silver had been theoretically part of the money supply, at a traditional ratio of 16:1. But since the 1830s the high price of silver relative to gold had encouraged silver miners to sell their product on the open market rather than present it to the mint for coining. In 1873 the little-noted Coinage Act removed silver from the list of U.S. coins, but by the mid-1870s increased silver production had dropped prices to the point where coinage was profitable. The Coinage Act was denounced as a monstrous conspiracy, and political demands were heard for the remonetarization of silver.

By the 1890s the demand for free and unlimited coinage of silver at a ratio of 16:1 was a standard part of the Populist platform and was championed by many Republicans and Democrats from the South and West. The silver issue had become, in the eyes of some farmers and other debtors, a panacea for increasing the money supply and (they believed) for reversing America's long deflationary slide. Free-silver advocates appropriated some of the same arguments for a flexible and expansive currency that greenbackers had employed for two decades. Populists from the antimonopoly greenback tradition, however, would contend that any specie-based currency—even one based on silver—would afford only palliatives, as compared to the fiat money that they proposed as part of the subtreasury or land-loan plans.

Radical antimonopolists had a point, but in the 1880s the silver issue largely supplanted greenbackism as a rallying point for advocates of inflation. The Bland-Allison Act of 1878 and the Sherman Silver Purchase Act of 1890 appeased the silver forces somewhat by allowing the government to purchase silver, but their actual effect on silver prices and the money supply was modest. Government had not gone far enough, silverites argued, and repeal of the Sherman Act would make a bad situation worse.

On the other side of the coin, President Cleveland blamed the Silver Purchase Act for the panic and for a sharp decline in the nation's gold reserves. Treasury notes, with which the government paid for the silver it bought, were being redeemed in gold, thus pushing the gold reserve below the $100 million level that financiers believed necessary to maintain the nation's international credit.

Both sides framed the issue in moral terms. Silverites blamed a conspiracy of politicians and international bankers for the "Crime of '73" which kept the nation in poverty, while goldbugs (so called by their opponents) spoke of an "honest dollar." J. Laurence Laughlin, a leading academic economist of the day, recoiled in indignation: "The eagerness of the advocates of free silver is founded on an appeal to dishonesty and cheating on the part of those who would like to repudiate and scale one-half of their obligations."

This, then, was the climate of opinion when President Cleveland called Congress into special session. Setting aside tariff reform and other issues dear to him, Cleveland backed the repeal effort with the full authority of his office, including the threat to withhold patronage appointments from congressmen who voted the wrong way. The repeal measure easily passed the House of Representatives, even though a third of the Democrats and all of the Populists voted against it. One of the principal speakers in opposition to repeal was thirty-three-year-old William Jennings

Bryan of Nebraska, who asked his fellow Democrats: "Does any one believe that Mr. Cleveland could have been elected President upon a platform declaring in favor of the unconditional repeal of the Sherman law? Can we go back to our people and tell them that, after denouncing for twenty years the crime of 1873, we have now at last accepted it as a blessing?"

In the Senate, where the rules provided for unrestricted debate, opponents managed to delay a vote until October. Then, angrily brushing aside a compromise measure proposed by his own floor leader, Cleveland pushed for outright repeal, and got it.

Cleveland's decision to focus his response to the depression on repeal of the Sherman Act and the acrimonious congressional debate that followed clothed the silver issue with greater importance than it deserved and forced it to the center of policy debates within the People's Party. Advocates of the Omaha platform and other radical reformers argued that even free coinage of silver would leave unresolved the structural ills confronting the nation's economy. Silver's champions within the party were equally quick to note the persuasive way in which the issue rhetorically framed the conflict between "the money power" and the people. They noted as well that the silver issue seemed to offer a common ground for political cooperation with those in the South and West who had felt threatened by the Omaha platform, not the least of whom was the young Nebraska congressman who had spoken so eloquently in opposition to repeal.

In 1896, Henry Demarest Lloyd, social reformer and architect of a Populist-labor coalition in Illinois, would denounce the silver issue as "the cow-bird of the Reform movement," which "waited until the nest had been built by the sacrifices and labours of others, and then laid its eggs in it, pushing out the others which lie smashed on the ground." More recently the historian Lawrence Goodwyn has called the silver crusade a "shadow movement," an opportunistic collection of office seekers that mimicked and finally supplanted genuine Populism. If free silver was a shadow movement, then Grover Cleveland was as much its father as William Jennings Bryan; if a cowbird, then it was hatched in 1893 in the debate over repeal of the Sherman Act.

Concentration on free silver and cooperation with silverites in one or both of the major parties marked one option for the People's Party. A very different path would put the Populists in step with the small armies of the unemployed then converging on Washington and with industrial workers who were challenging not only their employers but the power of the federal government.

As the depression deepened in 1894, urban and industrial protest escalated, seemingly increasing the prospect of forging the coalition of farmers and laborers that had eluded the Populists in 1892. In the late spring and summer "industrial armies" of the unemployed converged on Washington by rail and on foot from New England, the Midwest, and the Pacific coast to petition Congress for relief. The San Francisco contingent included an eighteen-year-old Jack London and an Alliance lecturer named Anna Ferry Smith. The most highly publicized group, calling itself the Commonwealth of Christ, left Massillon, Ohio, on Easter Sunday under the command of Jacob S. Coxey, a well-to-do businessman and greenbacker.

While visiting the Columbian Exposition the previous year, Coxey had met up with a West Coast radical named Carl Browne, who introduced him to the idea of industrial armies. A marching protest movement was the perfect vehicle for publicizing Coxey's scheme to end the depression: a massive public works program to engage the unemployed in building roads at a rate of $1.50 per day, to be financed through congressional issue of $500 million in legal-tender notes.

Coxey's army never included more than 600 of the faithful (among them Kansas Populist Annie Diggs and Coxey's wife and their infant son, Legal Tender Coxey), but that was not the point. "What Coxey and Browne did," notes historian Carlos Schwantes, "was to create an unemployment adventure story that the press found irresistible." As they made their way across the depressed industrial belt of western Pennsylvania, the colorful band of true believers drew huge crowds of well-wishers and a contingent of reporters almost as large as the army itself.

Once in Washington, the Commonwealth of Christ paraded through the city to the Capitol, with Coxey's seventeen-year-old daughter riding on a white horse and the "General" and his wife following in their carriage. Coxey mounted the Capitol steps and prepared to speak. He was arrested for trespassing and sentenced to twenty days in jail. Other "armies" arrived in the capital by midsummer, but they were brutally dispersed by the authorities. Coxey returned home to Ohio to run for Congress as a Populist.

Coxey would never win a congressional seat, but his dramatization of the plight of the unemployed helped focus the attention of the small band of Populist congressmen on this new and disturbing feature of industrial America. Though their ability actually to pass legislation was nil, Populist congressmen had already introduced bills to enact much of the Omaha platform, including banking and currency reform and nationalization of the railroads. By 1894 they were also introducing bills aimed directly at the effects of the depression. Congressman John Davis of Kansas introduced a major public works program similar to Coxey's scheme. Senator Peffer supported a system of old-age pensions that anticipated the Social Security system. And Populist congressmen took the lonely but courageous view that Coxey and his followers had every right to petition Congress in person. A reading of the Populists' record in Congress during the depression of the 1890s led historian Gene Clanton to identify them as early champions of the idea "that in an advanced urban-industrial society the federal government has a role to play in cushioning the impact of economic collapse and in restoring and maintaining prosperity."

Within days after Coxey's arrest on the Capitol steps, a labor struggle broke out in Illinois that would dramatize the Cleveland administration's reflexive support for big business and create a new opportunity for a Populist-labor coalition. On the southern edge of Chicago, George Pullman had laid out a model town to provide both shelter and culture for the workers who built railroad sleeping cars for the Pullman Palace Car Company. All was not well in Pullman. Workers chafed at the social control of the planned community, and when Pullman cut wages by 25 percent with no corresponding reduction in rents, they went out on strike.

The Pullman workers were persuaded by the increasingly powerful American Railway Union, headed by Eugene V. Debs, to declare a boycott of all trains containing Pullman cars. The General Managers Association, representing all Chicago-based railroads, met the boycott with a well-coordinated plan to fire and blacklist all railroad workers who refused to handle Pullman cars. But when the boycott spread beyond the Chicago region and virtually paralyzed rail traffic in most of the West, the GMA was powerless to stop it. Railroad officials then turned to Washington for help, knowing they had friends in high places.

Cleveland's Attorney General, Richard Olney, was former legal counsel to the Chicago, Burlington & Quincy Railroad. Olney secured a federal injunction against Debs and the ARU that forbade the union from interfering with the U.S. mail or with interstate commerce. Responding to exaggerated reports of strike violence, President Cleveland ordered federal troops to Chicago over the objections of Illinois's prolabor Democratic governor, John Peter Altgeld. When troops marched into the city on Independence Day there *was* violence, much of it involving mobs of nonstrikers. Railroad equipment was destroyed, and six buildings on the grounds of the closed Columbian Exposition were burned to the ground.

Federal authorities broke the strike and arrested Debs and other ARU leaders, charging them with contempt of court for ignoring the injunction and with violation of the Sherman Antitrust Act. (Cooperation among labor unions was interpreted as a conspiracy in restraint of trade.) Debs was quickly convicted, but his case was appealed to the U.S. Supreme Court. The argument presented there by his young attorney, Clarence Darrow, was addressed not only to the learned justices (who to no one's surprise upheld the guilty verdict) but also to potential adherents of a radical labor-Populist coalition.

Darrow's argument combined the familiar principles of producerism and equal rights with advanced arguments about the need for class solidarity under the new conditions of large-scale industrialization. Although laborers are theoretically equal to their employers, he said, "the present system of industry," in which thousands of workers are beholden to one employer who controls both capital and technology, makes it imperative for workers to cooperate as a class, regardless of their particular craft or occupation. The immediate point of the argument was to defend the ARU against charges that it had illegally "conspired" with Pullman's workers, but the larger point was an appeal for the "industrial classes" (including farmers) to join in political alliance. Before surrendering to authorities to serve his sentence, Debs urged ARU members to support a broadly based coalition with the People's Party, and from jail he predicted a Populist victory.

The central figure in the effort to forge an electoral alliance of farmers and laborers in Illinois was Henry Demarest Lloyd, a professional reformer of the same generation and background as Henry George and Edward Bellamy. Lloyd is best remembered for his muckraking attacks on big business, most notably the 1894 exposé of Standard Oil, *Wealth Against Commonwealth*. As an editorial writer for the Chicago *Tribune* in the 1870s Lloyd gained a reputation as an ardent antimonopolist. Contact with the Independent Labour Party and the Fabian Society in England gave him a frame of reference for developing his own brand of morally grounded moderate socialism.

Throughout the 1880s Lloyd's spacious home in suburban Winnetka had been a haven for reformers of all stripes: Jane Addams and her fellow social workers from Hull-House, Chicago labor leaders like Debs and Tommy Morgan, Populists like Donnelly and Weaver, reform-minded social scientists like Richard T. Ely and John R. Commons, and black leaders including Booker T. Washington. Although initially skeptical of the farmer-dominated People's Party and convinced that the Omaha platform did not go far enough, by 1893 Lloyd was seeking to forge a coalition of reformers as broad as his guest list.

Populism had made little headway in Illinois in 1892, but with the onset of the depression the tiny People's Party redoubled its effort. Henry Vincent, of Kansas Populist fame, moved to Chicago and began publishing a Populist newspaper, *The Searchlight*, which joined the ranks of the sizable reform press in the city. Lloyd, Vincent, and their associates began the delicate task of forging an alliance among rural Populists, craft unions of the American Federation of Labor (whose president had no use for Populism), socialist unions (heavily German in membership), Single Taxers (whose leader had no use for socialists), and Bellamyite Nationalists.

The goal was to field unified slates of candidates for legislative and local office in 1894 on the People's Party ticket. Two statewide Populist conferences actually coincided with the Pullman boycott (delegates to the second were stranded in Springfield by the boycott), a circumstance that added a sense of urgency to the enterprise. After once failing to agree on a platform, delegates adopted the Omaha platform and papered over their differences on the socialists' demands for "the collective ownership by the people of all means of production and distribution."

Although downstate farm support for the labor-Populist coalition was always shaky and cooperation between socialists and Single Taxers tenuous, it appeared that the new party might do well in Chicago and Cook County. As the campaign headed into its final weeks, Ignatius Donnelly, Eugene Debs, and other coalition leaders spoke to a massive rally of enthusiastic supporters at the Central Music Hall. A second and climactic rally two weeks later featured Clarence Darrow, Illinois's revered former senator

Lyman Trumbull (a venerable champion of the equal rights tradition), and Henry Demarest Lloyd.

Lloyd spoke, as historian Chester M. Destler put it, "as the chief architect of the labor-Populist alliance." Focusing on the moral imperative of their movement and ranging from Jefferson to the new socialist parties of Britain and Germany in search of analogies for this new movement, Lloyd "sought to define the common meeting ground of the old, antimonopolistic democratic tradition of America with the newer, non-Marxian Socialism of the British Fabians and labor leaders, and of such American writers as Edward Bellamy and Laurence Gronlund." Lloyd appropriated the title of Gronlund's non-Marxian socialist tract *The Cooperative Commonwealth* (1884) to articulate the new vision of America represented by the union of republican farmers and socialist industrial workers. Once in power, Lloyd proclaimed, the People's Party would wipe away the "centralized corporate despotism" of Cleveland's administration and would use the powers of eminent domain and public control over financial policy to usher in the cooperative commonwealth.

But Lloyd's stirring rhetoric could not hold the fragile coalition together. On October 10, Henry George himself spoke in Chicago, and instead of endorsing the coalition as anticipated, he expressed his "indifference or even hostility" to the Populists, whereupon many of the Single Taxers broke ranks. Equally damaging was the opposition of Samuel Gompers, president of the American Federation of Labor, who warned trade union leaders against becoming embroiled in partisan politics.

In 1892, James B. Weaver had won about 22,000 votes in Illinois, less than 3 percent of the total and fewer than even the Prohibitionist candidate. In 1894, Populist totals in local and statewide elections improved only slightly on Weaver's total, and no Populist actually won office. Even allowing for some of the creative ballot counting for which Cook County was famous, this was not enough to make a serious impression on state politics. What had gone wrong?

To begin with, few farmers had joined the ranks of the People's Party. This has been attributed, variously, to the lack of effective Alliance organizing in the state and to the relative prosperity of Illinois farmers. While both explanations have some merit, it is also likely that most of them had no use for the internecine squabbles of Chicago's socialists and trade unionists and saw no serious prospects of a victory for the fractured People's Party in Illinois. In spite of significant support among members of the ARU, relatively few industrial workers had voted Populist either. For some of them, the *state* Democratic Party, under prolabor Governor Altgeld, was still a safe haven. But the big winner in Illinois, as elsewhere, was the Republican Party, which reaped the harvest of farmers' and wage earners' disgust with Cleveland's administration. A reform paper's postelection assessment applied equally well to Chicago and to downstate Illinois: "The people turned to the republicans for relief from hard times . . . with a unanimity . . . scarcely ever paralleled in political history."

Lloyd and his associates had believed their labor-Populist coalition could provide the basis for a national coalition of farmers and laborers. In Wisconsin, Minnesota, Missouri, and New York and even Oklahoma Territory there were signs in 1894 that this might actually happen. Oklahoma Populism, shaped largely by the leaders of the movement in neighboring Kansas, was now blessed with two outstanding Populist-labor editors, Leo Vincent, brother of Henry and former editor of *The American Noncon-formist*, and Ralph Beaumont, the onetime architect of the Knights of Labor's national political strategy. But the disastrous results in Illinois demonstrated the implausibility of such an alliance. The world had changed since the pre-Haymarket days when grand coalitions of producers were at least imaginable. In the new industrial America, both the new Republicanism and socialism constituted "modern" alternatives for labor, but it was not clear that Populism could play such a role.

"There ought to be two first-class political funerals in this country in 1896," Lloyd had told the cheering throngs at the Central

Music Hall, meaning, of course, the Democratic and Republican parties. Instead, it now appeared, one might well be that of Populism.

Likewise, in the Populist heartland of the Great Plains states and the Mountain West the returns in 1894 gave little comfort to the champions of the new party. Populists were badly beaten everywhere, and Republicans were the big winners. In Kansas, Governor Lewelling and all but one of the Populist congressional candidates went down to defeat, as did Governor Waite in Colorado. In Nevada, where the Silver Party had cooperated with the Populists in 1892, silverites went their own way and swept the state. In Nebraska, William Jennings Bryan, elected to Congress with Democratic and Populist backing, chose not to seek reelection and lost all hope for a Senate seat when Republicans captured the legislature. In Iowa, James B. Weaver lost badly in his bid for Congress.

What happened to western Populism? One explanation is that, unlike 1892, the Populists fielded their own slates of candidates rather than cooperating with the Democrats. But in bellwether states like Kansas, the Republicans would have won even if the Populist votes had been combined with those of the Democrats, who were now saddled with the unpopular Cleveland. As in Illinois and the Midwest, the Republican Party of the Plains states regained its traditional position of dominance by making itself the serious alternative to the party of Cleveland.

Another explanation for the poor showing of western Populists is that in several states they now had a record of their own to defend. It was not an altogether attractive record. To be sure, in no state did the Populists control both houses of the legislature, and much of the Populists' record was interpreted for the voters by a partisan Republican press, but in Kansas, Colorado, and a handful of other states, the highly visible and controversial acts of Populist elected officials in 1893–94 became a liability.

In Colorado, where shrill rhetoric and radical politics were commonplace, many voters were frightened by the Populist governor (whose remarks about repeal of the Sherman Act had given him the nickname "Bloody Bridles Waite"), and while his support for striking miners at Cripple Creek won him renewed labor support, it stirred mine owners to redouble their attacks on him. In North Dakota, where Populists had promised that if elected they would establish state-owned terminal elevators, Populist legislators won passage of such a bill, but it was so clumsily drawn that the elevator was never built. A similar Populist plan in Minnesota met with the same fate.

These setbacks paled in comparison with the disasters that befell the Populists in Kansas, where the People's Party had won the governorship, a majority of the state Senate, and enough seats in the House of Representatives to challenge the Republicans for control. With both Republicans and Populists claiming a majority in the House, conditions deteriorated into what the papers quickly labeled a "legislative war." In its early stages the struggle resembled a comic opera (Republicans occupied the legislative chamber in the mornings, Populists in the afternoons), but the situation turned nasty when Republicans forcibly drove the Populists from the hall.

Governor Lewelling ordered the militia to oust the Republicans, but the commander, a loyal Republican, positioned his troops and Gatling guns to support the small army of Republican "deputies" in and around the capitol. Bloodshed was averted through a compromise that left the Republicans in control of the House, but the political damage fell largely upon the Populists, thanks to the Republican press through which most Kansans received their news of the events.

Leaving aside the legislative war, Kansas Populists did not cover themselves with glory. Infighting was intense (including a highly publicized feud between Governor Lewelling and Mary Lease), and the governor's attempts to hold the Populist-Democratic coalition together with the glue of patronage opened the People's Party to charges that it was now no better than the old corrupt parties it had sought to replace.

Intraparty strife was so fierce among Kansas Populists (who had no leaders approaching the statesmanlike stature of Lloyd, Darrow, or Debs in Illinois) that Democratic and Republican editors often simply reprinted their attacks on each other verbatim. James C. Malin, pioneering student of Kansas Populism, noted half a century ago, "No one outside the Populist party said any harsher things about [the] Populist leadership than the Populists themselves."

After the 1894 elections, Kansas Republicans held a mock funeral to mark the death of Populism. Indeed, as historian Peter Argersinger has noted, "Populism in its original form, creative nature, and radical motivation was dead. . . . Populism, as Kansas had known it in the days of its pentecostal fervor to remake society, was no more."

But what of the South? The economic and political events of 1893 seemed to bode well for Dixie Populism. The depression ravaged the cotton belt, afflicting not only farmers but also the tradesmen who handled and marketed the crop. In Alabama and elsewhere, strikes of miners, railroad workers, and dockhands echoed the upheavals of the Midwest and drew similar expressions of solidarity from the Populists.

Meanwhile, the elite leaders of the Democratic Party not only suffered the embarrassment of Cleveland and his policies; they were also faced with explaining why so many southern congressmen and senators had done Cleveland's bidding in the repeal of the Sherman Act, including Speaker of the House Charles Crisp of Georgia. In September 1893, Governor William J. Northen of Georgia, an Alliance Democrat, wrote frantically to the President: "The conditions of this State are fearful and threatening, and are creating a lack of confidence in the party in power. . . . Ex-Congressman Watson, the leader of the Populists, has taken advantage of the conditions, and is speaking over the State to assemblies never less than 2,000, and sometimes as many as 50,000 people."

Across the South, the ranks of the People's Party were swelled in 1893 and 1894 by angry middle-class Democrats. With little or no understanding of the Omaha platform or of antimonopoly greenbackism, they were simply mad at Cleveland and eager to vote for free silver. In almost every southern state (Texas, the bellwether of greenbackism was an exception), Populists in 1894 concentrated on winning more of these middle-class voters to the cause.

Georgia Populists nominated for governor one such recent convert, Judge James K. Hines of Atlanta. Descended from distinguished Virginia families, Hines was a Harvard-trained lawyer and chairman of the board of trustees of Emory College. For reasons of his own, Hines had endorsed the Ocala platform in 1890, and he was widely considered to be friendly to the agrarian cause. Respected by businessmen and farmers alike, he was the ideal candidate to test the new strategy. (Tom Watson had promoted his candidacy over that of an old-line Alliance leader.) On the campaign trail Hines talked mainly about free silver and the evils of the Cleveland administration, while Watson and others kept alive the tradition of the Omaha platform.

According to the first election returns, Hines appeared to have won a stunning victory, but when the "official" tally was completed he had been counted out by election officials. "We had to do it!" said one Democrat. "Those d—— Populists would have ruined the Country." To make matters worse, Watson was again cheated out of his old congressional seat. In Richmond County alone, where 11,240 were registered to vote, 13,740 ballots were cast. Looking beyond the thievery and outright violence of the 1894 elections, Populists in Georgia and elsewhere in the South faced another problem: when Democrats learned how to be for free silver and against Cleveland, who would need to be a Populist?

North Carolina Populists took another road to moderation. There the radical greenback tradition had never been as strong as in Georgia or Texas, and so downplaying certain aspects of the Omaha platform in favor of free silver came rather easily for leaders like Marion Butler, a youthful lawyer who had left the Democratic Party after the nomination of Cleveland in 1892. Quickly assuming leadership of Tarheel Populists, Butler devised a strategy for attracting middle-class support by cooperating with North Carolina's large Republican Party. The basis of cooperation in North Carolina and elsewhere in the South (similar but less formal measures were adopted that year in Alabama and Georgia) was common hatred of the Democrats and agreement on "a free ballot and a fair count."

The results of fusion in North Carolina were stunning: a Republican and Populist sweep rolled up large majorities in the legislature and sent four Populists and three Republicans to Congress. Governor Elias Carr, another Alliance Democrat, escaped only because he was not up for reelection. The newly installed fusion legislature promptly elected Butler to the U.S. Senate.

In the Byzantine world of fusion politics, Republicans and Populists maintained their own identities at the local level, while agreeing (sometimes) to combine their votes in support of specific candidates. While these arrangements resuscitated black political life in the state between 1895 and 1901, they did not constitute a Populist commitment to racial equality, as Helen G. Edmonds emphatically notes: "Fusion politics was . . . based upon the arithmetic of political bargaining. The Populist movement in North Carolina was not a revolt against 'White Supremacy,' and to think for one moment that the party fused with the Republican party to inaugurate an era of political or social equality for the Negroes . . . is failure to understand the confusion and complexity of the 1890s."

Populists in North Carolina, Georgia, Alabama, and elsewhere in the South made substantial gains in 1894, in part by trimming their sails on the party's agenda. One can also detect the beginnings of a similar shift in their stance on race. Most southern Populists maintained their support for equal voting rights (although in Alabama they toyed with a proposal for an all-white primary), but to counteract the mounting Democratic attacks they became more vocal in their denunciation of social equality, claiming, for example, that the hated Cleveland was promoting racial integration. Simultaneously denounced by the Democrats for supposed racial unorthodoxy and crippled by Democratic manipulation of black votes, southern Populists edged away from their commitment to a biracial coalition.

Thus, while it would appear that the People's Party in the South had fared better than elsewhere in 1894, there was a very real question of exactly what Populism had come to mean in the region. In the nation as a whole, Populist votes had increased to almost a million and a half as compared with one million in 1892, but the vitality of the party was waning. In every region but the South, the Republican Party had shown decisively that it, not the People's Party, was the beneficiary of Cleveland's woes.

To be sure, in the aftermath of the 1894 elections Populists did not recognize their party's marginal status or concede national preeminence to the Republicans. Populists spoke bravely of representing two million voters, and they confidently expected their numbers to swell to a majority after the impending collapse of one or both of the major parties. Populists did, however, acknowledge that their party had reached a critical juncture in its struggle for national recognition.

The Populists' dilemma stemmed from a basic fact of politics: the objective of parties and candidates is to win at least 50 percent of the vote. By the time of the Populist crusade there was a diminished opportunity for "minor" parties to influence *national* policy by gaining a foothold in Congress. In contrast to British and European parliaments, Congress by the 1890s had come close to institutionalizing the two-party system by granting enormous powers to the presiding officers and chairmen of the various committees. Populist congressmen were often prohibited even from speaking on the floor, and their chances of actually enacting the planks of the Populist platform were virtually nil.

Even in the South and West, Populism had been able to garner no more than 25 to 45 percent of the vote, and whatever their other limitations, Populists could count. There seemed only two options, both with serious drawbacks: either fuse with one of the major parties, in hopes of achieving a majority, or go it alone, in hopes that worsening conditions and the intransigence of the major parties would produce a Populist majority.

By 1894, fusion meant agreeing on a platform of the lowest common denominator, and that was free silver. To the core group of true believers—those committed to the Omaha platform and even to more direct support for the cause of labor and to woman suffrage—such an agreement was unacceptable, even though, as they could plainly see, the core had not grown appreciably.

As soon as the 1894 election results were in, national chairman Herman E. Taubeneck announced that the party would concentrate on the "financial question" (silver), to the exclusion of many of the more radical elements of the Omaha platform. Taubeneck went on to decry the attempted "takeover" of the People's Party by socialists in his home state of Illinois, a direct challenge to the labor-Populist coalition that Lloyd had forged in the preceding elections. Taubeneck's appeal (which carried at least the suggestion of fusion with the Democrats) was echoed by James B. Weaver, by Nebraska's Democratic-Populist senator William V. Allen, and by several other prominent western Populists. Howls of outrage erupted from two overlapping but not synonymous groups: southern Populists (most of whom had recently left the Democratic Party, at great personal cost), and the true believers in the Omaha platform (who rehearsed the familiar explanations of silver's inadequacy as the singular focus of reform).

The struggle between fusionists and mid-roaders would continue throughout the brief and unhappy time remaining to the People's Party, but that internal conflict must be understood in relation to the growth of the free-silver cause in the larger public arena. Although the silver campaign of the 1890s was grounded in the inflationist ideology of an earlier day, it gained focus and power through several well-orchestrated initiatives after the repeal of the Sherman Act.

One such initiative was a well-organized and well-financed lobbying effort on behalf of western silver-mining interests. The American Bimetallic League was the centerpiece of that effort. Through the League, silver interests quietly funded prosilver newspapers, conferences, speaker bureaus, and a public relations office headed by one William H. Harvey. "Coin Harvey" churned out silver tracts in 1894. One, called *A Tale of Two Nations*, depicted in barely fictional form a plot by British bankers with Jewish names to destroy the United States by demonetizing its silver. In another, entitled *Coin's Financial School*, the young Professor Coin confounds the goldbugs by demonstrating, in a series of dazzling lectures, the unassailable logic of free silver and the conspiracy behind the gold standard.

Coin's Financial School was an immediate hit, becoming by 1895 the *Uncle Tom's Cabin* of the silver movement. Harvey's tracts on silver were far more simplistic than the Populist platform, which located free silver within a larger critique of industrial capitalism. But his writings touched a nerve, much like the sensationalist literature of a century later that purports to explain the economic decline of the United States by depicting a Japanese conspiracy. Many Americans, especially in the debt-ridden regions of the rural South and West, were prepared to accept not only the economics of silver but also the conspiratorial underpinnings of the silver campaign.

A second free-silver initiative, not unrelated to the efforts of the American Bimetallic League and its star publicist, was the building up of the silver wing of the Democratic Party. Southern Democrats fleeing the political fallout of Cleveland's unpopularity had championed the cause of silver, often as a way of appeasing the rising Populist forces in their states. Silver was, of course, popular in the Mountain West and increasingly so among Democrats of the Middle Border. Veteran silverites like Richard P. Bland now found themselves sharing the stage with younger converts like William Jennings Bryan of Nebraska.

As late as 1892 Bryan was quoted as saying, "I don't know

anything about free silver. The people of Nebraska are for free silver and I am for free silver. I will look up the arguments later." By 1893 Bryan had looked up the arguments, and by 1894 he was crisscrossing the South and West, speaking for the silver cause and polishing the phrases that would bring more converts to the fold. One that he used often and with great effect was: "I will not help to crucify mankind upon a cross of gold."

In 1895 Bryan took part in a giant conference of the Bimetallic League in Memphis, which, though nominally nonpartisan, was managed by Democrats, for the purposes of strengthening the silver wing of the party and of bringing Populists into the silver campaign. The southern participants in the Memphis conference represented a Who's Who of the Democratic establishment in Dixie, the very people whom southern Populists had renounced when they joined the People's Party. The one Populist conspicuously present was Marion Butler of North Carolina.

It was clear to Senator Peffer and other opponents of fusion that Bryan and the silver Democrats had no intention of forsaking their own party to form a new one based on currency reform, and they were cautious about getting too close to them. When the Fifty-fourth Congress convened late in 1895 the six Populist senators held the balance of power between Democrats and Republicans in the upper chamber. Rather than acquiesce in the Democrats' appeals to join them, Peffer and his colleagues refused to vote with either party, thus allowing the Republicans to organize the Senate.

Despite a good deal of maneuvering by fusionist Populists, silver Democrats, and a handful of silver Republicans, it is clear that Peffer and the mid-roaders had it right. The Democrats' idea of fusion, as Tom Watson later put it, is that "we play Jonah while they play whale."

It was against the backdrop of the American Bimetallic League's sophisticated public relations campaign and the growing strength of the silver Democrats that the Populist leadership made a fateful decision. In January 1896, at the urging of Bryan himself, Taubeneck and Weaver persuaded the Populist National Committee to postpone their nominating convention until after the Republicans and Democrats had met. The idea was that if both nominated opponents of free silver, then the People's Party would reap a windfall of silver support. In the unlikely event that one of them should nominate a silverite, Populists could join in a union campaign on the silver issue. Despite strong protest from mid-roaders, the schedule held. Populists would meet in St. Louis on July 22, after the two major parties had settled on their candidates.

The Republicans behaved as expected, nominating former congressman William McKinley of Ohio. More flexible on issues that mattered deeply to farmers and laborers than most Republican leaders, and certainly more so than Cleveland, McKinley was nevertheless identified with the gold standard. The GOP had followed the script.

The Democrats did not. During the spring and early summer, state Democratic conventions in the South and West committed themselves to the cause of silver and to the defeat of a sitting President. The delegates who gathered in Chicago for the Democratic National Convention ended Cleveland's hopes of renomination by adopting a platform that embraced free silver and rejected most of Cleveland's other policies as well.

The presidential nomination was very much in doubt when the platform was presented. Ben Tillman of South Carolina spoke first, and immediately dashed his own hopes of being nominated. In a rambling speech that mixed free silver with southern vituperation and virulent racism, Tillman managed to offend many of the delegates. William Jennings Bryan followed with a speech that electrified the delegates and helped win him the nomination. It was a recapitulation of the stump speech he had been delivering across the South and West for the past eighteen months, and it ended with this now famous peroration: "You shall not press down upon the brow of labor this crown of thorns." (Bryan's fingers traced imaginary trickles of blood from his own temples.) "You shall not crucify mankind upon a cross of gold." (He stood silent, arms outstretched.) The speech alone did not win him the nomination, but it certainly helped, and it identified him as an orator to be reckoned with.

McKinley and his managers were surprised by Bryan's nomination and adjusted their campaign plans to deal with a formidable foe. The Populists were dumbfounded by it and found themselves in an impossible situation. "If we fuse," Lloyd lamented, "we are sunk. If we don't fuse, all the silver men we have will leave us for the more powerful Democrats." The Populist delegates who convened in St. Louis were deeply divided, and the events of the convention would drive even greater wedges between them.

Probably a majority of the delegates came to St. Louis ready to nominate Bryan. They included many Westerners and a substantial number of eastern delegates (the East was overrepresented at the convention, on the basis of Populist strength in the states). A sizable and vociferous minority opposed fusion with the Democrats. They included most of the Southerners, a significant number of western mid-roaders, and a handful of labor delegates and socialists. The fusionists demonstrated their strength by electing as convention chairman Senator Allen of Nebraska, a "Demo-populist," as Peffer called him, and a well-known Bryan supporter.

The mid-roaders showed their own resilience by beating back an attempt to dilute the platform. Instead, the document adopted in St. Louis retained almost all the planks of the Omaha platform (the subtreasury and land-loan programs were not mentioned by name) and added an endorsement of a public works program for the unemployed and a denunciation of "the wholesale system of disfranchisement adopted in some states" (Tillman's South Carolina had already adopted such a system), coupled with an appeal for the states to "secure a full, free and fair ballot and an honest count." Mid-roaders further demonstrated their strength by forcing the convention to vote first on the vice presidential nominee and rejecting Bryan's Democratic running mate, Arthur Sewell, a banker from Maine, in favor of Tom Watson, who accepted in the mistaken belief that Sewell would be withdrawn from the Democratic ticket.

The vote on the presidential nominee was another matter. Once Debs and Peffer had declined invitations to be nominated, the mid-roaders had no major figure of their own with which to counter the Bryan bandwagon; all they had was their insistence that fusion with the Democrats meant the death of the People's Party. They settled upon S. F. Norton, a little-known greenbacker and Populist editor from Chicago.

Amid shouted questions to the chair as to whether Bryan would accept the Populists' nomination without Sewell on the ticket (the morning papers reported that he would not), General Weaver rose to place Bryan's name before the convention. At the close of his speech a parade of Bryan supporters snaked its way around the hall. Mid-road delegates began to coalesce around the large Texas delegation. As the demonstration made its way past their stronghold, a Bryan supporter tried to seize the Texas banner, whereupon a fight broke out among the delegates, and according to one account revolvers were drawn. The party was literally coming apart on the floor of the convention. Once order was restored Bryan easily received the nomination (the vote was 1,042 to 321), but it was a gesture that would probably do him more harm than good in the election.

Small wonder that Bryan managed to avoid acknowledging his nomination on the People's Party ticket. The Democratic national chairman bluntly stated that Sewell would stay on the ticket and that the Populists "could go with the Negroes, where they belong."

It fell to North Carolina's young senator, Marion Butler, to "manage" the Populists' national campaign, Butler having been selected to replace Taubeneck as party chairman. An architect of Populist-Republican fusion in North Carolina and champion of national fusion with the Democrats, Butler at least knew what he was trying to do, but the implausibility of the situation became clearer as fusion arrangements were hammered out state by state. In some states Democrats and Populists actually divided the presidential electors, leaving open the possibility that Bryan could be elected but his running mate defeated. In Kansas and Colorado, Populists agreed not to challenge the Bryan-Sewell ticket, in return for Democratic support of their state candidates. Watson's name was not even on the ballot in his home state of Georgia!

In several southern states Populists were supposedly fusing with Democrats at the national level and with Republicans for state offices. In the Midwest, where fusion was more widely accepted, the Populist-Democratic alliance was not quite so traumatic, though veterans like Senator Peffer could not bring themselves to endorse it. In Illinois, even the residue of the ill-fated labor-Populist coalition stayed with Bryan, including Eugene Debs, who would announce his conversion to socialism two months after the election. Whatever one can make of the (con)fusion of the Populists in 1896, it was a far cry from the Politics of Pentecost.

And it was also a sideshow. Taking little notice of the Populists, McKinley and Bryan battled it out in a closely contested race in which both men identified the band of industrial states from Ohio to Wisconsin as the ground upon which the election would be won or lost. McKinley's well-organized and lavishly financed campaign triumphed over Bryan, who traveled 80,000 miles and made 600 speeches. In the end, Bryan could not convince urbanites and industrial workers that he understood their concerns, while McKinley successfully presented himself as the "Advance Agent of Prosperity."

In retrospect, the presidential election of 1896 marked the beginning of a Republican ascendancy in national politics that would continue until the 1930s. But in the short run, the elections of 1896 provided for a curious wave of Populist successes and near-successes at the state level. In Kansas and Colorado, Populists traded their party's vice presidential nominee for fusion victories in state and congressional races. Similarly, fusion candidates prevailed in Nebraska, South Dakota, Montana, Idaho, and Washington. In Georgia, Alabama, and Texas, Populist-Republican tickets got over 40 percent of the vote, despite massive fraud and considerable violence. In North Carolina, Republicans and Populists made a clean sweep of the elections. Nationwide, fusion in congressional races actually gave Populism—of sorts—its greatest representation in Washington, with a total of seven senators and thirty congressmen who were either Populists, fusionists, or Silver Party members.

But these gains were illusory. Most of the fusion victories lasted only one term. While local pockets of Populism might hold out for another year or two, and in some cases until the end of the century, the party was moribund. In 1898 an agreement between fusionists and mid-roaders collapsed, with disastrous results at the polls. A corporal's guard of Populists renominated Bryan for President in 1900, and in 1904 and again in 1908 Tom Watson was chosen as the standard bearer, winning, in that last year, only 28,000 votes.

By then virtually all of those who had once dreamed of the cooperative commonwealth had drifted to other parties or out of politics. In the West, many found their way back into the Republican Party, although a vigorous socialist tradition sprang up from Populist roots in states from North Dakota to Texas. (In 1912, the high point of the Socialist Party, the largest socialist organization was to be found in Oklahoma.) In the South, while a few Populists stuck with the Republicans, most either returned to the party of their fathers or dropped out of politics, sometimes the victims of the very disfranchising laws that their national convention had abhorred in 1896.

The role of Populists and former Populists in the disfranchisement of southern blacks is still a matter of debate among scholars. While conservative Democrats took the leading role in the systematic exclusion of blacks from the voting process around the turn of the century, it is clear that Populists were sometimes involved. The difficulty of sorting out how and why this happened is illustrated by the experience of two nearly contiguous counties in Texas, each of which had a strong Populist organization and a substantial black population. In Grimes County, a biracial Populist coalition survived the collapse of the national party and was rooted out only by the superior firepower of the local Democratic militia. In nearby Milam County, to which Charles Macune had returned after falling from grace in the farmers' movement, Populists decided by 1898 to join with Democrats in establishing an all-white primary. Barely a dozen years after Macune had joined the Farmers' Alliance in Milam County and had gone from there to help fashion American Populism, the movement was dead.

At a crucial point in *Intruder in the Dust*, William Faulkner has one of young Chick Mallison's uncles explain to the Mississippi teenager:

> For every Southern boy fourteen years old, not once but whenever he wants it, there is the instant when it's still not yet two o'clock on that July afternoon in 1863, the brigades are in position behind the rail fence . . . and Pickett himself . . . looking up the hill waiting for Longstreet to give the word and it's all in the balance, it hasn't happened yet. . . . [T]hat moment doesn't need even a fourteen-year-old boy to think "*This time. Maybe this time* with all this much to lose and all this much to gain."

For many of us who write about Populism there is a special version of this dream. It's always 1896, or 1892, or 1886. With the success of Populism hanging in the balance, as the cause of the Confederacy did on the eve of Pickett's charge at Gettysburg, we can think, whenever we want: "This time, maybe this time." Could things have turned out differently for the People's Party? And if so, could Populism have altered the direction of American politics?

Some who have studied the movement would answer no to both questions. For Richard Hofstadter and those who viewed Populism as an expression of status anxiety, the natural progression of Populism is toward George Wallace and even David Duke, not toward a sustained critique of industrial capitalism and the liberal welfare state. For some who have examined the crusade of the 1880s and 1890s with one eye on social movements of the late twentieth century that were co-opted by the powers that be, Populism was doomed by an "iron law of oligarchy" to be manipulated and destroyed by leaders who had no common interest with the farmers and working people who believed in the cooperative commonwealth.

Some of the scholars who believe that Populism could have changed the shape of twentieth-century America are at pains to describe the conditions under which the People's Party could have succeeded at the ballot box. For Lawrence Goodwyn, if only the Farmers' Alliance had more thoroughly organized rural America and introduced it to the cooperative ideal, and if genuine Populism had not been undercut by the "shadow movement" of free silver, things could have been different in 1896. For Gene Clanton, if the Republicans had won the presidency in 1892 and were thereby saddled with the liabilities that befell Cleveland and his party when the depression hit, then perhaps the Populists would have had a better shot at national prominence.

Could the Populists' political crusade have turned out differently? The odds of success, it seems to me, were lower than Pickett's. The organizational base of the movement was limited to regions that could not, in themselves, carry a presidential election: the South, the Great Plains, and the Far West. The industrializing states that Bryan and McKinley contested so vigorously in 1896, and upon which hinged one of the great shifts in American politics, were beyond the reach of the People's Party.

Not only was Populism regionally isolated; it was also caught in a cross fire between Democrats and Republicans at a time when the two-party system was being institutionalized. A young

Woodrow Wilson had already documented this crystallization in Congress, and even as the Populist movement spent its fleeting moment on the political stage, election laws were being reshaped in the states in such a way as to make insurgencies far more difficult to mount. At the state level, "wars of maneuver" in which Populists operated between the lines of the two major parties could sustain viable movements for a time, but even there Populists were always at risk of being "counted out" by the party strong enough to control the electoral process.

Furthermore, the very organizational network that allowed Populism to sweep across the rural South and West in 1890–92 did not long survive the birth of the People's Party. The precipitous decline of the Alliance and before that the fall of the Knights of Labor stripped the new party of the protected space within which rural and working-class Americans could congregate and, in the sharing of ritual and ideology and cooperative action, imagine an alternative world.

Finally, and in a related vein, Populism was sustainable only so long as it was perceived to be above the common traffic in partisan bickering and dealmaking that permeated Gilded Age politics. Having identified itself as a Pentecost of Politics, it had no language with which to articulate a sense of itself in the brokered world of partisanship.

If the Populist crusade could not itself survive the tumultuous 1890s, what was its legacy? Early students of the People's Party, most notably John D. Hicks, saw a continuity between Populism and the two great currents of twentieth-century liberalism—progressivism and the New Deal. Populism was, in this telling of the story, the seedbed of liberal reform. We can certainly find among the platforms and resolutions of the People's Party specific ideas that were later enacted into law. But the progressives and New Dealers accommodated themselves to the new corporate order in ways that true believers in the Omaha platform would have had difficulty accepting. Theirs was a movement of producers, rooted in the political and cultural values of the nineteenth century. Theirs was a vision of democratic capitalism that did not, in the end, fit well with the political and bureaucratic structures that accompanied industrial capitalism.

One hundred years after the birth of the People's Party, conservative columnist George F. Will took note of a clamorous field of Democratic presidential hopefuls—including one senator from Weaver's home state of Iowa and another from Bryan's Nebraska, along with a governor from Isaac McCracken's Arkansas—and blasted them for appropriating the old name. Entitling his essay "A Pox on Populists," Will anointed George C. Wallace of Alabama as "the most successful populist of this half century."

It is as much a critique of twentieth-century liberalism as of Populism itself that a century after the movement flourished, its name is more readily associated with those who view the liberal welfare state as an irritating repository of "special privilege" than as a bulwark of "equal rights," specifically with a tradition of "conservative" Populism stretching from Wallace and Barry Goldwater to Ronald Reagan and David Duke, a tradition that has gained force during the economic upheavals of the past two decades. To be sure, as with the American Bimetallic League's campaign of 1894–96, this new conservative Populism has been well financed and has addressed only selectively the anger that people feel, but its strength and persistence tell us something about the distance between Populism and liberalism.

Does conservative Populism represent the sum of the movement's legacy? The evidence suggests that it does not. Most studies of the last quarter century have depicted American Populism as a movement that advanced a serious critique of monopolism and offered alternative visions of democratic capitalism. Populism represented "the humane preference" in American politics (Gene Clanton), a search for "the just polity" (Norman Pollack), or America's "democratic promise" (Lawrence Goodwyn).

Neither proto-fascists nor proto-New Dealers, the Populists fashioned a powerful movement out of the cultures of nineteenth-century reform and out of their own shared experiences. In the end they failed to bend the forces of technology and capitalism toward humane ends, and many of them shared with other Americans of their time a myopic view of equal rights, one still distorted by racism and sexism. But for all their failures and limitations, the Populists fashioned a space within which Americans could begin to imagine alternative futures shaped by the promise of equal rights. Theirs is a legacy waiting to be fulfilled.

Bibliographical Essay

This essay concentrates on books and articles that have been particularly helpful in the writing of *American Populism*. For a comprehensive bibliography of the literature, see Henry C. Dethloff and Robert W. Miller, *A List of References for the History of the Farmers' Alliance and Populist Party* (Davis, Calif., 1989). William F. Holmes provides a thorough and balanced analysis of books and articles published since the mid-1960s in "Populism: In Search of Context," *Agricultural History*, 68 (1990): 26–58. Steven Hahn and Jonathan Prude provide an excellent overview of recent trends in rural social history in their editors' introduction to *The Countryside in the Age of Capitalist Transformation: Essays in the Social History of Rural America* (Chapel Hill, 1985).

Introduction

The dramatic events of 1877 have been much written about. The stories of the end of Reconstruction and of the Great Strike are well told in Eric Foner, *Reconstruction: America's Unfinished Revolution, 1863–1877* (New York, 1988); and Nell Irvin Painter, *Standing at Armageddon: The United States, 1877–1919* (New York, 1987).

The accounts of the New York and Texas beginnings of the Farmers' Alliance given here follow Lee Benson, *Merchants, Farmers, and Railroads: Railroad Regulation and New York Politics, 1850–1887* (Cambridge, Mass., 1955); and Robert C. McMath, Jr., *Populist Vanguard: A History of the Southern Farmers' Alliance* (Chapel Hill, 1975). For a social and economic description of the Genesee Valley and the Texas frontier, see Paul E. Johnson, *A Shopkeeper's Millennium: Society and Revivals in Rochester, New York, 1815–1837* (New York, 1978); and Robert C. McMath, Jr., "Sandy Land and Hogs in the Timber: (Agri)cultural Origins of the Farmers' Alliance in Texas," in Hahn and Prude, eds., *The Countryside in the Age of Capitalist Transformation*, pp. 205–29.

For a look at the way the Alliance wrote its own history, see Nelson A. Dunning, ed., *Farmers' Alliance History and Agricultural Digest* (Washington, 1891), and W. Scott Morgan, *History of the Wheel and Alliance, and the Impending Revolution* (Hardy, Ark., 1889, reprinted 1967).

Four general works on Populism that were not discussed in the Introduction have been particularly helpful. One is Carl C. Taylor, *The Farmers' Movement, 1620–1920* (New York, 1953, reprinted 1971). The rural sociologist Taylor began work on his encyclopedic study of farm movements in the 1920s. His study is a useful if little-known resource. A second is Norman Pollack, *The Just Polity: Populism, Law, and Human Welfare* (Urbana, 1987). In the 1960s Pollack wrote eloquently on the radical nature of Populist ideology. This exegesis of Populist texts, which revises his earlier interpretation, is a valuable contribution to the field. The third is Gene Clanton, *Populism: The Humane Preference in America, 1890–1900* (Boston, 1991). This brief general history summarizes Clanton's earlier work on Kansas and provides valuable insights on Populists in Congress. Finally, the story of Populism as told by one of its principal leaders, published serially in 1899, is now accessible in a volume thoroughly annotated by a leading Populist scholar: William A. Peffer, *Populism: Its Rise and Fall*, edited and with an introduction by Peter H. Argersinger (Lawrence, Kans., 1992).

The four major works on Populism that *were* assessed in the Introduction are John D. Hicks, *The Populist Revolt: A History of the Farmers' Alliance and the People's Party* (Minneapolis, 1931, reprinted 1961); C. Vann Woodward, *Tom Watson, Agrar-*

ian Rebel (New York, 1938, reprinted 1963); Richard Hofstadter, *The Age of Reform from Bryan to F.D.R.* (New York, 1955); and Lawrence Goodwyn, *Democratic Promise: The Populist Moment in America* (New York, 1976). A thoughtful assessment of Hicks's impact on the field is found in Martin Ridge, "Populism Redux: John D. Hicks and *The Populist Revolt*," *Reviews in American History*, 13 (1985): 142–54. C. Vann Woodward conceded that his "critics have scored several telling points" concerning Watson's racial views and gives a balanced assessment of his own work on Populism in *Thinking Back: The Perils of Writing History* (Baton Rouge, 1986). Woodward provides a gentle critique of Hofstadter, with sharper barbs for less cautious scholars of the status anxiety school in "The Populist Heritage and the Intellectual," in Woodward, *The Burden of Southern History*, rev. ed. (Baton Rouge, 1968). See also Alan Brinkley, "Richard Hofstadter's *The Age of Reform*: A Reconsideration," *Reviews in American History*, 13 (1985), 462–80; and Robert M. Collins, "The Originality Trap: Richard Hofstadter on Populism," *Journal of American History*, 76 (1989): 150–67. For assessments of Goodwyn's work from different perspectives, see David Montgomery, "On Goodwyn's Populists," *Marxist Perspectives*, 1 (1978): 166–73; and Stanley B. Parsons et al., "The Role of the Cooperatives in the Development of the Movement Culture of Populism," *Journal of American History*, 69 (1983): 866–85.

Sociologists who have applied resource mobilization theory to Populism are not of one mind on the subject. Writing from a neo-Marxian viewpoint, Michael Schwartz concludes, contra Goodwyn, that the Alliance's move into politics was a profoundly conservative shift in *Radical Protest and Social Structure: The Southern Farmers' Alliance and Cotton Tenancy, 1880–1890* (New York, 1976). In *Farmers in Rebellion: The Rise and Fall of the Southern Farmers' Alliance and People's Party in Texas* (Austin, 1984), Donna Barnes reaches a different conclusion. See also Scott G. McNall, *The Road to Rebellion: Class Formation and*

Kansas Populism, 1865–1900 (Chicago, 1988). For a review of this theoretical approach, see J. Craig Jenkins, "Resource Mobilization Theory and the Study of Social Movements," *Annual Review of Sociology*, 9 (1983): 527–53.

1. Populist Country Before Populism

Social and economic historians are still arguing about the relative significance of subsistence and commercial agriculture in American history, and about the corresponding significance of a republican or capitalistic outlook among farmers. The arguments are summarized and points of convergence noted in Allan Kulikoff, "The Transition to Capitalism in Rural America," *The William and Mary Quarterly*, 3rd series, 45 (1989): 120–44. Similar issues are addressed for the early twentieth century in a case study from North Dakota: Harriet Friedmann, "Simple Commodity Production and Wage Labour in the American Plains," *The Journal of Peasant Studies*, 6 (1978): 71–100.

There is a voluminous literature on the social and economic history of the Great Plains. I have relied particularly on four books: Brian W. Blouet and Frederick C. Luebke, eds., *The Great Plains: Environment and Culture* (Lincoln, Nebr., 1979); Gilbert C. Fite, *The Farmers' Frontier, 1865–1900* (New York, 1966); Craig Miner, *West of Wichita: Settling the High Plains of Kansas, 1865–1900* (Lawrence, Kans., 1986); and Herbert S. Schell, *History of South Dakota*, 3rd ed. (Lincoln, Nebr., 1975).

Two scholars who have helped us understand the interplay among culture, environment, and market forces in the West are James C. Malin and Allan Bogue. For present purposes, see, especially, Malin, *Winter Wheat in the Golden Belt of Kansas: A Study in Adaption to a Subhumid Geographical Environment* (Lawrence, Kans., 1944); and Bogue, *From Prairie to Corn Belt: Farming on the Illinois and Iowa Prairies in the Nineteenth Century* (Chicago, 1963).

The best work on the connection between technology and culture in western agriculture is J. Sanford Rikoon, *Threshing in the Midwest, 1820–1940: A Study of Traditional Culture and Technological Change* (Chicago, 1988). Also important for this study was Thomas D. Isern, "Folklife of the Threshing Outfit," *South Dakota History*, 16 (1986): 18–34. See also Wayne Rasmussen, "The Impact of Technological Change on American Agriculture, 1862–1962," *Journal of Economic History*, 22 (1962): 578–91.

Agricultural conditions in the Rocky Mountain states are outlined in Fite, *The Farmers' Frontier*, and in Robert W. Larson, *Populism in the Mountain West* (Albuquerque, 1986). Donald Worster develops the notion of the "hydraulic society" and analyzes the political economy of western irrigation in *Rivers of Empire: Water, Aridity, and the Growth of the American West* (New York, 1985).

As with the West, agricultural history in the New South is a well-plowed field. The indispensable beginning point is still C. Vann Woodward, *Origins of the New South, 1877–1913* (Baton Rouge, 1951), but see, contra, Jonathan Weiner, *Social Origins of the New South: Alabama, 1860–1885* (Baton Rouge, 1978). Among the economic studies of southern agriculture that I have found most useful is Gavin Wright, *Old South, New South: Revolutions in the Southern Economy Since the Civil War* (New York, 1986). See also Gilbert C. Fite, *Cotton Fields No More: Southern Agriculture, 1865–1980* (Lexington, Ky., 1984); and I. A. Newby, *Plain Folk in the New South: Social Change and Cultural Persistence, 1880–1915* (Baton Rouge, 1989), from which I drew the quotation from Steve and Josie Lee.

Outstanding studies of the two New Souths include Michael Wayne, *The Reshaping of Plantation Society: The Natchez District, 1860–1880* (Baton Rouge, 1983); and Steven Hahn, *The Roots of Southern Populism: Yeoman Farmers and the Transformation of the Georgia Upcountry, 1850–1890* (New York, 1983). The latter should be compared with David Weiman, "Farmers and the Market in Antebellum America: A View from the Georgia Up-Country," *Journal of Economic History*, 48 (1987): 627–48; and Lacy K. Ford, "Rednecks and Merchants: Economic Development and Social Tensions in the South Carolina Upcountry, 1865–1900," *Journal of American History*, 71 (1984): 294–318.

On the agricultural development of the Texas frontier, see Rupert N. Richardson, *The Frontier of Northwest Texas, 1846– 1876: Advance and Defense of the Pioneer Settlers of the Cross Timbers and Prairies* (Glendale, Calif., 1963); and Terry G. Jordan, *Trails to Texas: Southern Roots of Western Cattle Ranching* (Lincoln, Nebr., 1981).

The notion of community as a two-dimensional set of social networks has been adopted by historians from the work of anthropologist Robert Redfield. See especially Richard R. Beeman, "The New Social History and the Search for 'Community' in Colonial America," *American Quarterly*, 39 (1977): 422–43; and Darrett B. Rutman, "The Social Web: A Prospectus for the Study of the Early American Community," in William L. O'Neill, ed., *Insights and Parallels: Problems and Issues of American Social History* (Minneapolis, 1973), pp. 57–89.

On the black family in the rural South, see Orville Vernon Burton, *In My Father's House Are Many Mansions: Family and Community in Edgefield, South Carolina* (Chapel Hill, 1985). The studies of Great Plains agriculture cited above all contain rich descriptions of community life, including both the rounds of visitation and the organizational activities. For the South, see Joe Gray Taylor, *Eating, Drinking, and Visiting in the South: An Informal History* (Baton Rouge, 1982); and John T. Schlotterbeck, "The 'Social Economy' of an Upper South Community: Orange and Greene Counties, Virginia, 1815–1860," in Orville Vernon Burton and Robert C. McMath, Jr., eds., *Class, Conflict, and Consensus: Antebellum Southern Community Studies* (Westport, Conn., 1982), pp. 3–28. On the development of "voluntary communities," see Don Harrison Doyle, *The Social Order of a Frontier Community: Jacksonville, Illinois, 1825–1870* (Urbana, 1978);

and John Mack Faragher, *Sugar Creek: Life on the Illinois Prairie*, (New Haven, 1987).

On the development of transportation and market institutions, see, in addition to works already cited, Morton Rothstein, "The International Market for Agricultural Commodities, 1850–1873," in David T. Gilchrist and W. David Lewis, eds., *Economic Change in the Civil War Era* (Greenville, Del., 1956), 67–72; Harold D. Woodman, *King Cotton and His Retainers: Financing and Marketing the Cotton Crop of the South, 1800–1925* (Lexington, Ky., 1968); and Alfred D. Chandler, *The Visible Hand: The Managerial Revolution in American Business* (Cambridge, Mass., 1977).

Three articles that provide systematic evidence concerning the immediate economic causes of farmer unrest are Robert Higgs, "Railroad Rates and the Populist Uprising," *Agricultural History*, 44 (1970): 291–97; Mark Aldrich, "A Note on Railroad Rates and the Populist Uprising," *Agricultural History*, 54 (1980): 424–32; and Robert A. McGuire, "Economic Causes of Late-Nineteenth-Century Agrarian Unrest: New Evidence," *Journal of Economic History*, 41 (1981): 835–49.

2. Cultures of Protest, 1867–86

The following four studies provide a useful introduction to the meaning and intellectual roots of "producerism" and related concepts: Bruce Laurie, *Artisans into Workers: Labor in Nineteenth-Century America* (New York, 1989); Richard Oestreicher "Terence V. Powderly, the Knights of Labor, and Artisanal Republicanism," in Melvyn Dubofsky and Warren Van Tine, eds., *Labor Leaders in America* (Urbana, 1986) pp. 30–61; Harry Watson, *Liberty and Power: The Politics of Jacksonian America* (New York, 1990); and Chester McArthur Destler, *American Radicalism, 1865–1901* (Chicago, 1966).

On the fencing controversy and its relation to the antimonopoly tradition, see, in addition to works cited above for Chapter 1,

Roscoe Martin, *The People's Party in Texas: A Study in Third Party Politics* (Austin, 1933); and Robert W. Larson, *New Mexico Populism: A Study of Radical Protest in a Western Territory* (Boulder, Colo., 1974). Southwestern social banditry, including the career of the James brothers, is discussed in David Thelan, *Paths of Resistance: Tradition and Dignity in Industrializing Missouri* (New York, 1986).

On the Grange, see D. Sven Nordin, *Rich Harvest: A History of the Grange, 1867–1900* (Jackson, Miss., 1974); Joseph G. Knapp, *The Rise of American Cooperative Enterprise, 1680–1920* (Danville, Ill., 1969); and Robert A. Calvert's forthcoming history of the Grange in the South. A brief treatment of the roles of both the Grange and the Union League in the rural South appears in Foner, *Reconstruction*. A full treatment of the latter appears in Michael W. Fitzgerald, *The Union League Movement in the Deep South: Politics and Agricultural Change During Reconstruction* (Baton Rouge, 1989).

For the role of the Knights of Labor in farmer-labor politics, see, in addition to the previously cited works of Laurie and Oestreicher, Leon Fink, *Workingman's Democracy: The Knights of Labor and American Politics* (Urbana, 1983); and Melton McLaurin, *The Knights of Labor in the South* (Westport, Conn., 1978). The Reading preamble is reprinted in John R. Commons et al., *History of Labour in the United States*, Vol. 2 (New York, 1926). On the railroad strikes of 1885 and 1886, see Ruth A. Allen, *The Great Southwest Strike* (Austin, 1942); and Michael J. Cassity, "Modernization and Social Crisis: The Knights of Labor and a Midwest Community, 1885–1886," *Journal of American History*, 66 (1979), pp. 41–61. Leon Fink stimulates our imagination about alternative outcomes of the 1886 strike in "The New Labor History and the Power of Historical Pessimism: Consensus, Hegemony, and the Case of the Knights of Labor," *Journal of American History* 75 (1988): 115–36.

The expansion of the Texas Farmers' Alliance is described in previously cited works by Lawrence Goodwyn, Donna Barnes,

Robert McMath, and Michael Schwartz. The interpretation advanced by Schwartz differs from the others in arguing that the politicization of the Alliance was the result of a takeover by conservative planters. The early career of Charles Macune is described by his namesake and great-grandson in Charles W. Macune, Jr., "The Origins of a Populist: Dr. C. W. Macune Before 1886," *Southwestern Historical Quarterly*, 90 (1986): 139–58.

3. The Farmers' Alliance in Search of the Cooperative Commonwealth, 1887–89

The most detailed account of the Texas Exchange is to be found in Goodwyn, *Democratic Promise*. The economic dilemma of southern cotton farmers who sought to market their crop cooperatively is analyzed in Wright, *Old South, New South* and in Knapp, *The Rise of American Cooperative Enterprise*.

The Brothers of Freedom and the Agricultural Wheel were chronicled by the agrarian movement's own historians, Dunning and Morgan, but these and other radical farm groups in the South have only begun to attract scholarly attention. See Paul Horton, "Testing the Limits of Class Politics in Postbellum Alabama: Agrarian Radicalism in Lawrence County," *Journal of Southern History*, 57 (1991): 63–84.

The exemplar of Alliance conservatism is described in Lala Carr Steelman, "The Role of Elias Carr in the North Carolina Farmers' Alliance," *North Carolina Historical Review*, 57 (1980): 133–58; and in Steelman, *The North Carolina Farmers' Alliance: A Political History* (Greenville, N.C., 1985). The spread of the Alliance across the South and the formation of the Colored Farmers' Alliance is described by Goodwyn and McMath and in Theodore Saloutos, *Farmers' Movements in the South, 1865–1933* (Berkeley, 1960). Donna Barnes provides the fullest account of the Texas beginnings of the jute-bagging fight. The violent reactions to Alliance cooperatives in Alabama and Mississippi are described in William Warren Rogers, *The One-Gallused Rebellion: Agrarianism in Alabama, 1865–1896* (Baton Rouge, 1970); and William F. Holmes, "The Leflore County Massacre and the Demise of the Colored Farmers' Alliance," *Phylon*, 34 (1973): 267–74. Roy V. Scott touches on the formation of the northwestern Alliance in "Milton George and the Farmers' Alliance Movement," *Mississippi Valley Historical Review*, 45 (1958): 90–109. Jeffrey Ostler provides a fresh treatment of early Alliance activities in Kansas, Nebraska, and Iowa in *The Fate of Populism* (Lawrence, Kans., forthcoming).

The analysis of Alliance members in Marshall County, Dakota Territory, is based on John Dibbern, "Who Were the Populists? A Study of Grass-Roots Alliancemen in Dakota," *Agricultural History*, 56 (1982): 677–91. Several articles and graduate theses have been written on Populism in the Dakotas, but this critically important part of the story has not yet received book-length treatment. In contrast, farm organizations in Kansas have been thoroughly studied. Among the leading works are Gene Clanton, *Kansas Populism: Ideas and Men* (Lawrence, Kans., 1969); and McNall, *Road to Rebellion*. For Nebraska, see Robert W. Cherny, *Populism, Progressivism, and the Transformation of Nebraska Politics, 1885–1915* (Lincoln, Nebr., 1981); and Stanley B. Parsons, Jr., *The Populist Context: Rural Versus Urban Power on a Great Plains Frontier* (Westport, Conn., 1973).

Most of the works just cited provide evidence that cooperatives played a substantial role in the spread of the Alliance, in the West as well as in the South. For a contrary view, see Parsons et al., "The Role of the Cooperatives in the Development of the Movement Culture of Populism."

4. Farmers, Laborers, and Politics: Interest Groups and Insurgency, 1890

The intellectual structure of farmer-labor social criticism is treated in Chester McArthur Destler, *American Radicalism,*

1865–1901 (Chicago, 1966); Bruce Palmer, *"Man Over Money":* *The Southern Populist Critique of American Capitalism* (Chapel Hill, 1980); Laurie, *Artisans into Workers*; and Pollack, *The Just Polity*. My thinking on Henry George and Edward Bellamy is very much influenced by John L. Thomas, *Alternative America: Henry George, Edward Bellamy, Henry Demarest Lloyd and the Adversary Tradition* (Cambridge, Mass., 1983).

The standard biography of Leonidas Polk is Stuart Noblin, *Leonidas Polk, Agrarian Crusader* (Chapel Hill, 1949). Polk's work of sectional reconciliation is depicted in most general treatments of the movement, including Clanton, *Populism*, from which his Kansas speech is quoted.

In *Populism in the Mountain West*, Robert W. Larson argues convincingly that the agrarian movement in the Rocky Mountain region was much more than a front for silver interests. His state-by-state account demonstrates clearly that the movement resembled in many respects the Alliance and labor movements in the South and the Great Plains. A particularly strong study of the movement in a single Mountain state is James Edward Wright, *The Politics of Populism: Dissent in Colorado* (New Haven, 1974), from which Alfred King's poem and Joseph Buchanan's slogan are quoted. A good introduction to the tradition of radical unionism among western miners is found in Melvyn Dubofsky, *We Shall Be All: A History of the Industrial Workers of the World* (Chicago, 1969).

My assessment of the Alliance in California rests primarily on John T. McGreevy, "Farmers, Nationalists, and the Origins of California Populism," *Pacific Historical Review*, 58 (1989): 471–95 (from which the speech on the business agency is quoted); and Michael Magliari, "Populism, Steamboats, and the Octopus: Transportation Rates and Monopoly in California's Wheat Regions, 1890–1896," *Pacific Historical Review*, 58 (1989): 449–69. The work of Carlos A. Schwantes is crucial for understanding farmer-labor movements and Sinophobia in the Pacific Northwest. See especially *Radical Heritage: Labor, Socialism, and*

Reform in Washington and British Columbia, 1885–1917 (Seattle, 1979); and "Protest in a Promised Land: Unemployment, Disinheritance, and the Origin of Labor Militancy in the Pacific Northwest, 1885–1886," *Western Historical Quarterly*, 13 (1982): 373–87.

The Alliance as community is discussed in McMath, *Populist Vanguard*, McNall, *Road to Rebellion*, and other standard sources. The role of women in the Alliance and kindred organizations has now begun to attract the serious scholarly attention it deserves. See especially Julie Roy Jeffrey, "Women in the Farmers' Alliance: A Reconsideration of the Role and Status of Women in the Late Nineteenth Century South," *Feminist Studies*, 3 (1975): 72–91; Marilyn Dell Brady, "Populism and Feminism in a Newspaper by and for Women of the Kansas Farmers' Alliance," *Kansas History*, 7 (1985): 280–90; Donna Wagner, "Farms, Families, and Reform: Women in the Farmers' Alliance and Populist Party" (Ph.D. dissertation, University of Oregon, 1986); and Ostler, *The Fate of Populism*.

Three works particularly useful for placing the story of women in the Alliance in its larger context are Mari Jo Buhle, *Women and American Socialism, 1870–1920* (Urbana, 1981); Ruth Bordin, *Women and Temperance: The Quest for Power and Liberty, 1873–1900* (Philadelphia, 1981); and Sara M. Evans, *Born for Liberty: A History of Women in America* (New York, 1989).

The politics of the "Alliance yardstick" is described in the general works already cited and in a number of fine southern state studies that are enumerated in the bibliographies mentioned above. See also William F. Holmes, "The Georgia Alliance Legislature," *Georgia Historical Quarterly*, 68 (1984): 479–514; and Ford, "Rednecks and Merchants," from which I have taken the quotation on the Alliance in South Carolina politics.

The politics of the "Alliance ticket" in the Great Plains is described in the works cited by Clanton, Ostler, and Cherny. (From the last of these I have quoted the frightened Nebraska Republican.) Also important for understanding Kansas Populism is the work of Peter H. Argersinger, including *Populism and Politics: William Alfred Peffer and the People's Party* (Madison, Wisc., 1970), and Peffer's memoir, which Argersinger edited. Still valuable for understanding the reform background of Kansas Populists and the vagaries of the movement in that state is James C. Malin, *A Concern About Humanity: Notes on Reform, 1872–1912, at the National and Kansas Levels of Thought* (Lawrence, Kans., 1964).

5. Creating a Political Culture: The People's Party, 1891–92

The series of national and regional conferences that created the People's Party are described in all of the general histories of the movement. Clanton's account of the Cincinnati conference is particularly useful, as is Goodwyn's description of the Waco meeting. Hicks's description of these events is still valuable. George Tindall provides a concise narrative of the party's history and a useful compilation of its platforms in "The People's Party," in Arthur M. Schlesinger, Jr., ed., *History of U.S. Political Parties*, Vol. 2: *1860–1910: The Gilded Age of Politics* (New York, 1973). Similar accounts of the origins of the name "Populist" are given in Clanton, *Populism*, and in George B. Tindall, "Populism: A Semantic Identity Crisis," *Virginia Quarterly Review*, 48 (1972): 501–18.

The failure of the Alliance yardstick campaign is illuminated in William F. Holmes's previously cited article on the Georgia legislature and in various state histories. The idea that the elite status of farm organization leaders contributed to that failure is advanced in two articles: Dwight Billings, "Class and Class Politics in the Southern Populist Movement of the 1890s," *Sociological Spectrum*, 1 (1981): 259–92; and Michael Schwartz et al., "Leader-Member Conflict in Protest Organizations: The Case of the Southern Farmers' Alliance," *Social Problems*, 29 (1981): 22–36.

The campaign of political education and the ideology that undergirded it are the subject of Theodore Mitchell, *Political Education in the Southern Farmers' Alliance, 1887–1900* (Madison, Wisc., 1987). Mitchell makes useful comparisons with class-based political education in Latin America, as depicted in Paolo Freiri, *Pedagogy of the Oppressed* (New York, 1970). Goodwyn provides the most thorough treatment of the National Reform Press Association and its role in the formation of the People's Party. The description of farmers' camp meetings is drawn from Robert C. McMath, Jr., "Populist Base Communities: The Evangelical Roots of Farm Protest in Texas," *Locus*, 1 (1988): 53–64.

The importance of political "wars of maneuver" in the formation of state People's parties is demonstrated in the sociological studies of Barnes and McNall previously cited and more fully by Jeffrey Ostler in *The Fate of Populism*. Ostler not only provides the first full account of Populism's failure in Iowa, but by comparing the Iowa experience with successful movements in Kansas and Nebraska he demonstrates the significance of major-party response to agrarian protest for local success or failure. The war of maneuver in Kentucky is depicted in Argersinger, *Populism and Politics*, and in Hambleton Tapp and James C. Klotter, *Kentucky: Decades of Discord, 1865–1900* (Frankfort, 1977), from which the quote about appeasing the Alliance is taken. The agrarian movement in Kentucky still awaits modern monographic treatment. That is not the case with Georgia, for which Barton Shaw, *The Wool-Hat Boys: Georgia's Populist Party* (Baton Rouge, 1984), is a model study. In addition to his perceptive analysis of the machinations of Georgia politics, Shaw's depiction of Tom Watson challenges the portrait drawn in Woodward's classic biography.

Gene Clanton has provided good accounts of the formation of a congressional Populist Party, both in *Populism* (from which I drew the exchange between Livingston and Watson) and in " 'Hayseed Socialism' on the Hill: Congressional Populism, 1891–1895," *Western Historical Quarterly*, 15 (1984): 139–62. Equally valuable for an assessment of Populists in state legislatures is

Peter H. Argersinger, "Ideology and Behavior: Legislative Politics and Western Populism," *Agricultural History*, 58 (1984): 43–69.

My description of third-party mobilization in the West is drawn largely from Larson, *Populism in the Mountain West* (including the depiction of the Johnson County war), and Wright, *The Politics of Populism*. Previously cited state studies provide detailed accounts of the same event in the South. The quotation from Alabama's Milford Howard is taken from Tindall, "The People's Party." For an excellent analysis of third-party formation at the boundary between West and South, see Worth Robert Miller, *Oklahoma Populism: A History of the People's Party in the Oklahoma Territory* (Norman, Okla., 1987).

The relationship of the Populist movement to African-Americans in the South has been the subject of ongoing research and debate since the publication of Woodward's biography of Watson over fifty years ago. A classic study that traces the complexities of this relationship is Helen G. Edmonds, *The Negro and Fusion Politics in North Carolina, 1894–1901* (Chapel Hill, 1951). Examples can be found of closely knit and courageous alliances of black and white Southerners under the People's Party banner. The most dramatic example in the literature is Lawrence Goodwyn, "Populist Dreams and Negro Rights: East Texas as a Case Study," *American Historical Review*, 78 (1971): 1435–56, which reconstructs from oral sources the story of Populism in Grimes County and its violent suppression by Democrats. Ongoing research into the Agricultural Wheel and other descendants of the radical Republican tradition in the South will no doubt produce similar examples.

But the idea that southern Populism did in fact represent a biracial coalition has been challenged from many quarters. See, among others, Gerald H. Gaither, *Blacks and the Populist Revolt: Ballots and Bigotry in the New South* (University, Ala., 1977); William F. Holmes, "The Demise of the Colored Farmers' Alliance," *Journal of Southern History*, 41 (1975): 187–200; Robert

Saunders, "Southern Populists and the Negro, 1893–1895," *Journal of Negro History*, 45 (1960): 38–44; and Shaw, *Wool-Hat Boys*. Black community and political leaders who joined the Populist movement typically left few historical traces or were represented in caricature by the Democratic press. A useful corrective to this gap in our knowledge will be provided by Gregg Cantrell's forthcoming biography of Texas Populist leader John B. Rayner.

The Populist campaign of 1892 is placed in context by R. Hal Williams, *Years of Decision: American Politics in the 1890s* (New York, 1978); and by H. Wayne Morgan, "Election of 1892," in Arthur M. Schlesinger, Jr., ed., *History of American Presidential Elections, 1789–1968*, Vol. 2 (New York, 1971), from which I drew the quotation from Rutherford B. Hayes. For an account of national politics that places more emphasis on ethnocultural conflict than this present work, see Paul Kleppner, *The Third American Electoral System, 1853–1892: Parties, Voters, and Political Cultures* (Chapel Hill, 1979).

6. The Crisis of Populism, 1893–98

The Columbian Exposition has been much written about. My account, including quotations from Debs and Lloyd, draws on the treatment of the Exposition in Alan Trachtenberg, *The Incorporation of America: Culture and Society in the Gilded Age* (New York, 1982). A vivid introduction to the depression that began in 1893 is found in Painter, *Standing at Armageddon* and in Williams, *Years of Decision*. The moving letter to Governor Lewelling is quoted in Fite, *The Farmers' Frontier*, and the fiery speech of Colorado's Davis Waite is taken from Wright, *The Politics of Populism*.

The antecedents of the free-silver campaign of the 1890s are outlined in Allen Weinstein, *Prelude to Populism: Origins of the Silver Issue, 1867–1878* (New Haven, 1970); and Walter T. K. Nugent, "Money, Politics, and Society: The Currency Question," in H. Wayne Morgan, ed., *The Gilded Age*, revised and enlarged edition (Syracuse, 1970). The standard history of the industrial armies is Carlos Schwantes, *Coxey's Army: An American Odyssey* (Lincoln, Nebr., 1985), but Painter adds significant detail in *Standing at Armageddon*. The Pullman strike and its implications for labor organizing and politics are addressed in Nick Salvatore, *Eugene V. Debs: Citizen and Socialist* (Urbana, 1982); and Shelton Stromquist, *A Generation of Boomers: The Patterns of Labor Conflict in Nineteenth-Century America* (Urbana, 1987). My account of the labor-Populist coalition in Illinois relies heavily on Destler, *American Radicalism* (the editorial on the triumph of Republicanism is from that source), and on the treatment of Henry Demarest Lloyd in Thomas, *Alternative America*. Roy V. Scott, *The Agrarian Movement in Illinois, 1880–1896* (1962), emphasizes the relative prosperity of Illinois farmers in explaining the failure of Populism in that state.

The general histories of Populism present varied interpretations of the movement after 1892. Goodwyn emphasizes the power of the silver interests to promote a "shadow movement" that took institutional form in the American Bimetallic League and found a candidate in William Jennings Bryan. Clanton places more emphasis on the impact of the depression and the unintended effect of Populism on the two-party system. Similar variations are found in the regional and state studies previously cited. Peter Argersinger's conclusion most nearly parallels the view put forth in this study, that, as a movement, Populism had lost its vitality by the end of 1894.

The twists and turns of Populism and fusion in the South are succinctly summarized in Woodward, *Origins of the New South*, and Palmer, *"Man Over Money."* In addition to the southern state studies previously mentioned, see Sheldon Hackney, *Populism to Progressivism in Alabama* (Princeton, 1969); and Dwight Billings, *Planters and the Making of a "New South": Class, Politics, and Development in North Carolina, 1865–1900* (Chapel Hill, 1979). Edmonds, *The Negro and Fusion Politics in*

North Carolina, is still the necessary beginning point for an understanding of that complicated subject.

William Jennings Bryan has not wanted for biographers. The most thorough is Paolo E. Coletta, *William Jennings Bryan*, 3 vols. (Lincoln, Nebr., 1964–69), but Robert W. Cherny provides an accessible brief treatment in *A Righteous Cause: The Life of William Jennings Bryan* (Boston, 1985), from which I quoted two of Bryan's statements. Williams, *Years of Decision*, has a crisp summary of the rise of the silver campaign and Bryan's role in it, as well as a good account of the 1896 campaign.

The fullest and most dramatic description of the Populists' 1896 convention is found in Goodwyn, *Democratic Promise*. For a well-written account of the Populist campaign of 1896 that puts Marion Butler and the fusionists in a more favorable light than I do, see Robert F. Durden, *The Climax of Populism: The Election of 1896* (Lexington, Ky., 1965). Most general histories of Populism, quite naturally, put the People's Party at the center of things in describing the election of 1896. For a broader perspective, see H. Wayne Morgan, *William McKinley and His America* (Syracuse, 1963); and Richard McCormick, *The Party Period and Public Policy: American Politics from the Age of Jackson to the Progressive Era* (New York, 1986).

The question of whether Populists were victimized by or collaborated in the disfranchisement of southern blacks is still a matter of considerable debate. In a thorough quantitative analysis, J. Morgan Kousser finds that disfranchisement was largely the work of conservative Democrats intent on rooting out Populism as well as black voting: Kousser, *The Shaping of Southern Politics: Suffrage Restriction and the Establishment of the One-Party South* (New Haven, 1974). However, several state and community studies have challenged Kousser's findings and suggested that Populists were willing participants in the process of disfranchising blacks.

In 1972 George Tindall catalogued the various uses to which journalists of that era had put the term "Populist." ("Populism:

A Semantic Identity Crisis," previously cited.) Such usage has not abated, but there is as yet no satisfactory study of the twentieth-century legacy of Populism in America. Dan T. Carter's forthcoming biography of George C. Wallace will shed light on what can be described, in an oversimplified way, as "conservative" Populism. This subject is treated in two recently published works, the first by an architect of the Republican strategy of absorbing "Populist" anger into the GOP: Kevin Phillips, *The Politics of Rich and Poor: Wealth and the American Electorate in the Reagan Aftermath* (New York, 1990); and Thomas Byrne Edsall with Mary D. Edsall, *Chain Reaction: The Impact of Race, Rights, and Taxes on American Politics* (New York, 1991).

Populism in the United States needs very much to be compared with similar movements elsewhere, especially with twentieth-century movements in this hemisphere. The literature on both is voluminous. Useful beginning points are Michael L. Conniff, ed., *Latin American Populism in Comparative Perspective* (Albuquerque, 1982); and J. F. Conway, "Populism in the U.S., Russia, and Canada: Exploring the Roots of Canada's Third Parties," *Canadian Journal of Political Science*, 11 (1984): 139–62. Comparison would be particularly fruitful between Populism in the United States and in the Prairie provinces of Canada, especially Saskatchewan and Manitoba, where in the twentieth century Populist-like parties won power and put into practice some of the programs advocated by Great Plains Populists in the 1880s and 1890s.

Index